GLOSCAT LIBRARIES
00020914

STUDIES IN ECONOMIC AND SOCIAL HISTORY

This series, specially commissioned by the Economic History Society, provides a guide to the current interpretations of the key themes of economic and social history in which advances have recently been made or in which there has been significant debate.

Originally entitled 'Studies in Economic History', in 1974 the series had its scope extended to include topics in social history, and the new series title, 'Studies in Economic and Social History', signalises this development.

The series gives readers access to the best work done, helps them to draw their own conclusions in major fields of study, and by means of the critical bibliography in each book guides them in the selection of further reading. The aim is to provide a springboard to further work rather than a set of pre-packaged conclusions or short-cuts.

ECONOMIC HISTORY SOCIETY

The Economic History Society, which numbers around 3000 members, publishes the *Economic History Review* four times a year (free to members) and holds an annual conference. Enquiries about membership should be addressed to the Assistant Secretary, Economic History Society, P.O. Box 190, 1 Greville Road, Cambridge, CB1 3QG. Full-time students may join at special rates.

STUDIES IN ECONOMIC AND SOCIAL HISTORY

Edited for the Economic History Society by L. A. Clarkson

PUBLISHED

Bill Albert Latin America and the World Economy from Independence to 1930
B. W. E. Alford Depression and Recovery? British Economic Growth, 1918–1939
B. W. E. Alford British Economic Performance, 1945–1975
Michael Anderson Approaches to the History of the Western Family, 1500–1914
Michael Anderson Population Change in North-Western Europe, 1750–1850
P. J. Cain Economic Foundations of British Overseas Expansion, 1815–1914
S. D. Chapman The Cotton Industry in the Industrial Revolution
Neil Charlesworth British Rule and the Indian Economy, 1800–1914
J. A. Chartres Internal Trade in England, 1500–1700
R. A. Church The Great Victorian Boom, 1850–1873
L. A. Clarkson Proto-Industrialization: The First Phase of Industrialization?
D. C. Coleman Industry in Tudor and Stuart England
P. L. Cottrell British Overseas Investment in the Nineteenth Century
M. A. Crowther Social Policy in Britain, 1914–1939
Ralph Davis English Overseas Trade, 1500–1700
M. E. Falkus The Industrialisation of Russia, 1700–1914
Peter Fearon The Origins and Nature of the Great Slump, 1929–1932
T. R. Gourvish Railways and the British Economy, 1830–1914
Robert Gray The Aristocracy of Labour in Nineteenth-century Britain, c. 1850–1900
J. R. Harris The British Iron Industry, 1700–1850
John Hatcher Plague, Population and the English Economy, 1348–1530
J. R. Hay The Origins of the Liberal Welfare Reforms, 1906–1914
R. H. Hilton The Decline of Serfdom in Medieval England
E. L. Jones The Development of English Agriculture, 1815–1873
John Lovell British Trade Unions, 1875–1933
Donald N. McCloskey Econometric History
Hugh McLeod Religion and the Working Class in Nineteenth-Century Britain
W. J. Macpherson The Economic Development of Japan c. 1868–1941
J. D. Marshall The Old Poor Law, 1795–1834
Alan S. Milward The Economic Effects of the Two World Wars on Britain
G. E. Mingay Enclosure and the Small Farmer in the Age of the Industrial Revolution
Rosalind Mitchison British Population Change Since 1860
R. J. Morris Class and Class Consciousness in the Industrial Revolution, 1780–1850
J. Forbes Munro Britain in Tropical Africa, 1880–1960
A. E. Musson British Trade Unions, 1800–1875
Patrick K. O'Brien The Economic Effects of the American Civil War
Cormac Ó Gráda The Great Irish Famine
R. B. Outhwaite Inflation in Tudor and Early Stuart England
R. J. Overy The Nazi Economic Recovery, 1932–1938
P. L. Payne British Entrepreneurship in the Nineteenth Century
G. C. Peden Keynes, The Treasury and British Economic Policy
Roy Porter Disease, Medicine and Society in England, 1550–1860
G. D. Ramsay The English Woollen Industry, 1500–1750
Elizabeth Roberts Women's Work 1840–1940
Richard Rodger Housing in Urban Britain 1780–1914
Michael E. Rose The Relief of Poverty, 1834–1914
Michael Sanderson Education, Economic Change and Society in England, 1780–1870
S. B. Saul The Myth of the Great Depression, 1873–1896
Arthur J. Taylor Laissez-faire and State Intervention in Nineteenth-century Britain
Peter Temin Causal Factors in American Economic Growth in the Nineteenth Century
Joan Thirsk England's Agricultural Regions and Agrarian History, 1500–1750
Michael Turner Enclosures in Britain, 1750–1830
Margaret Walsh The American Frontier Revisited
J. R. Ward Poverty and Progress in the Caribbean 1800–1960

OTHER TITLES IN PREPARATION

The Industrial Revolution
A Compendium

Edited for
The Economic History Society by
L. A. CLARKSON
Professor of Social History,
The Queen's University, Belfast

MACMILLAN

The Cotton Industry in the Industrial Revolution, 2nd edition by
S. D. Chapman © The Economic History Society, 1972, 1987:

British Entrepreneurship in the Nineteenth Century, 2nd edition
by P. L. Payne © The Economic History Society 1974, 1988.

Proto-Industrialization: The First Phase of Industrialization?
by L. A. Clarkson © The Economic History Society 1985. Selection
and Introduction © The Economic History Society 1989.

Enclosures in Britain, 1715–1830 by Michael Turner © The Economic
History Society 1984.

All rights reserved. No reproduction, copy or transmission
of this publication may be made without written permission.

No paragraph of this publication may be reproduced, copied
or transmitted save with written permission or in accordance
with the provisions of the Copyright Act 1956 (as amended),
or under the terms of any licence permitting limited copying
issued by the Copyright Licensing Agency, 33–4 Alfred Place,
London WC1E 7DP.

Any person who does any unauthorised act in relation to
this publication may be liable to criminal prosecution and
civil claims for damages.

First published 1990

Published by
MACMILLAN EDUCATION LTD
Houndmills, Basingstoke, Hampshire RG21 2XS
and London
Companies and representatives
throughout the world

Printed in Hongkong

British Library Cataloguing in Publication Data
The Industrial Revolution: a compendium
1. Great Britain. Industrialisation, ca.
1750–1880
I. Clarkson, L.A. (Leslie Albert), *1933–*
II. Economic History Society
338.0941
ISBN 0–333–49459–8

Contents

Editor's Preface	vi
Introduction *L. A. Clarkson*	vii
The Cotton Industry and the Industrial Revolution Second edition *S. D. Chapman*	1
British Entrepreneurship in the Nineteenth Century Second edition *P. L. Payne*	65
Proto-Industrialization: The First Phase of Industrialization? *L. A. Clarkson*	149
Enclosures in Britain 1750–1830 *Michael Turner*	211
Index	297

Editor's Preface

WHEN this series was established in 1968 the first editor, the late Professor M. W. Flinn, laid down three guiding principles. The books should be concerned with important fields of economic history; they should be surveys of the current state of scholarship rather than a vehicle for the specialist views of the authors, and above all, they were to be introductions to their subject and not 'a set of pre-packaged conclusions'. These aims were admirably fulfilled by Professor Flinn and by his successor, Professor T. C. Smout, who took over the series in 1977. As it passes to its third editor and approaches its third decade, the principles remain the same.

Nevertheless, times change, even though principles do not. The series was launched when the study of economic history was burgeoning and new findings and fresh interpretations were threatening to overwhelm students – and sometimes their teachers. The series has expanded its scope, particularly in the area of social history – although the distinction between 'economic' and 'social' is sometimes hard to recognise and even more difficult to sustain. It has also extended geographically; its roots remain firmly British, but an increasing number of titles is concerned with the economic and social history of the wider world. However, some of the early titles can no longer claim to be introductions to the current state of scholarship; and the discipline as a whole lacks the heady growth of the 1960s and early 1970s. To overcome the first problem a number of new editions, or entirely new works, have been commissioned – some have already appeared. To deal with the second, the aim remains to publish up-to-date introductions to important areas of debate. If the series can demonstrate to students and their teachers the importance of the discipline of economic and social history and excite its further study, it will continue the task so ably begun by its first two editors.

The Queen's University of Belfast   L. A. CLARKSON
General Editor

Introduction

The industrial revolution remains, rightly, *the* great event in economic history. This is not an interpretation derived from a narrow study of English economic history but because the industrial revolution has affected the history of all countries. It is, in the words of Professor Hartwell, 'the Great Discontinuity', the dividing line between the old world of slow economic change and enduring social orders and the new world of rapid growth and rising personal incomes [6, *42–59*]. The countries of the modern world, indeed, can be divided almost into two groups: those that have experienced industrialization and those that are still striving to do so.

Several pamphlets in this series touch on the industrial revolution and there are other studies of banking, the woollen and iron industries, and social consequences of industrialization in progress. The four essays contained in this volume all deal with issues central to the history of the industrial revolution and reflect the changing historiography of the subject.

The first considers the archetypal industry of the industrial revolution. The cotton industry illustrates several vital aspects of the process. Historians give it crucial importance because, as Dr Chapman notes, 'the mechanisation of the cotton industry . . . is seen as a starting point of the modern technique of production that we call the factory system' [Chapman, *17*]. The earliest historian of the industrial revolution, Arnold Toynbee, identified the early textile inventions as the fundamental cause of the end of the domestic system [12]. Much later the American economist, David Landes, generalized the point. 'The heart of the Industrial Revolution', he wrote, 'was an interrelated succession of technological changes' principally in textiles, steam power and the metallurgical and chemical industries [10, *1*].

Chapman's essay also draws attention to questions of capital supply and industrial structures, markets and labour relations.

These themes are also the subject of Professor Payne's pamphlet which considers them in the context of the performance of Britain's entrepreneurs during the nineteenth century. When the essay was first published, in 1974, it was in part a contribution to the debate about the allegedly declining quality of entrepreneurship from the halcyon days of the industrial revolution. The belief that British entrepreneurs have failed has since breached the banks of academic discussion and flooded into popular history [see 13]. An assessment of the role of entrepreneurs is vital, for as innovators, organizers, risk-bearers, managers, and market-seekers they were responsible for applying new techniques to production, producing new goods for new markets, and creating new forms of organization. In 1974 the study of entrepreneurial functions still owed more to theoretical speculation than to empirical research. In the new edition of the pamphlet [1988] the author can still write of the need for more information, but a glance at the revised bibliography reveals how much economic historians have contributed to our understanding of this aspect of economic life.

An important element in Professor Payne's discussion concerns the social origins of entrepreneurs: were they the products of society or were they men apart? The verdict seems to be that entrepreneurial skills were those current throughout society although it took men of ability and resource to exploit market opportunities. The point has more general relevance. The industrial revolution has long been understood as a social process and not merely as a sequence of mechanical changes in a few industries. This perspective has been most elegantly presented by Ashton in 1948 [3]; and more recently the wider social setting of industrial change has appeared in the literature in the guise of the somewhat clumsy concept of proto-industrialization, the subject of the third essay in this volume.

In its original formulation proto-industrialization was concerned with the transition from earlier forms of cottage industry to factory-based production, but the ramifications of the thesis go much wider. The concept has a strong demographic dimension, directing attention to the links between population growth and industrial change, and to the effects of industrialization on the structure and functions of the family.

Thus it explores themes that have been part of the industrial revolution debate since the nineteenth century and which are treated by other pamphlets in this series, notably those by Anderson [1, 2]. Proto-industrialization also focuses on the changing nature of work and the relationship between the owners of capital and the workers they employed, and particularly on the metamorphosis of formerly self-employed artizans into an industrial proletariat. Never absent from the industrial revolution literature in the past, such issues have become more prominent in the recent general surveys of Berg [4] and the specialized monograph of Hudson on the West Riding woollen industry [7].

According to the former 'historians of proto-industrialization have looked to the countryside for the most significant manufacturing development of the eighteenth century' [4, *92*]. In fact the importance of agricultural changes for industrialization has always been appreciated by historians of the industrial revolution and was the subject of two of the original studies in this series [9, 11]. The more recent essay by Turner included here concentrates on just one aspect of agricultural development, but a most important one. Enclosures provided the organizational framework for a myriad of agricultural practices – many of them known for generations – designed to increase productivity. Productivity gains in agriculture during the later seventeenth and eighteenth centuries led to a growth in output which enabled industry and commerce to absorb growing shares of the labour force. There have, however, been interesting suggestions since Turner's essay was written that, notwithstanding enclosure, the growth of agricultural productivity slowed down after 1740 [8].

Significant differences exist between the treatment of the relationship between agriculture and industrial change in the proto-industrialization literature reviewed by Clarkson and the enclosure writings discussed by Turner. Proto-industrialization emphasizes the agricultural origins of industry and offers two (contradictory) explanations of how cottage industry evolved into factory industry. One sees rural labour as becoming too expensive to sustain industries in the countryside, thus compelling manufacturers to set up centralized workshops and instal labour-saving machinery. The other argues that persistently cheap rural labour permitted the accumulation of profits which financed new machinery and plant [see Clarkson, *30*]. Historians of enclosure, on the other hand, treat agriculture and industry as separate sectors, and one strand of discussion argues that in the later eighteenth century land prices were rising faster than labour costs thus encouraging enclosure as a way of using land more efficiently and generating a greater demand for labour during the enclosure process. Enclosure was thus holding labour within agriculture rather than releasing it for industry [see Turner, *79*]. Such tensions in interpretations are commonplace in history and it is the purpose of this series to bring them to the attention of readers rather than to resolve them.

What areas of industrial revolution history are not covered in this volume? An international dimension is largely missing although a projected monograph on French industrialization will provide a comparative perspective. There is little on the intellectual origins of technical change, although there are hints in Chapman's essay and bibliography. The standard of living debate appears only fleetingly but will be treated fully in a forthcoming contribution to the series. Chapman and Payne touch more substantially on the wider issues of economic growth but for a fuller discussion students need to turn to the specialist works of Crafts [5] and others. But then it is the purpose of the whole series to introduce students to a wider literature and to encourage them to explore it for themselves.

References

[1] Michael Anderson, *Approaches to the History of the Western Family, 1500–1914* (London, 1980).

[2] Michael Anderson, *Population Growth in Western Europe, 1750–1850* (London, 1988).

[3] T. S. Ashton, *The Industrial Revolution, 1760–1830* (London, 1948).

[4] Maxine Berg, *The Age of Manufactures, 1700–1820* (London, 1985).
[5] N. F. R. Crafts, *British Economic Growth During the Industrial Revolution* (Oxford, 1985).
[6] R. M. Hartwell, *The Industrial Revolution and Economic Growth* (London, 1971).
[7] Pat Hudson, *The Genesis of Industrial Capital: A Study of the West Riding Wool Textile Industry, c. 1750–1850* (Cambridge, 1986).
[8] R. V. Jackson, 'Growth and Deceleration in English Agriculture, 1660–1790', *Economic History Review*, 2nd ser., XXXVIII (1985).
[9] E. L. Jones, *The Development of English Agriculture, 1815–1873* (London, 1968).
[10] David S. Landes, *The Unbound Prometheus: Technological Change and Industrial Development in Western Europe from 1750 to the Present* (Cambridge, 1969).
[11] G. E. Mingay, *Enclosure and the Small Farmer in the Age of the Industrial Revolution* (London, 1968).
[12] Arnold Toynbee, *Lectures on the Industrial Revolution in England* (Oxford, 1884).
[13] Martin J. Weiner, *English Culture and the Decline of the Industrial Spirit, 1950–1980* (Cambridge, 1981).

The Cotton Industry in the Industrial Revolution

Prepared for
The Economic History Society by

S. D. CHAPMAN
Pasold Reader in Business History
University of Nottingham

Second Edition

Note on References

References in the text within square brackets refer to the numbered items in the bibliography. Colons separate italicised page numbers from their appropriate references and semicolons separate different references.

1 The Early Development of the Cotton Industry, 1600–1760

MOST of what is known about the early development of the cotton industry in Britain can be found in Wadsworth and Mann's *The Cotton Trade and Industrial Lancashire, 1600–1780*. It appears that the manufacture of cotton came to Britain from the Low Countries in the sixteenth century, one of the range of 'new draperies' that was transforming the textile industry in the later Tudor period. It was brought to East Anglia by Walloon and Dutch immigrants who settled in Norwich and other towns and established the manufacture of fustian, a mixture of linen with cotton imported from the Levant. Towards the end of the sixteenth century fustian reached Lancashire and began to oust the woollen industry from the western side of the county.

The developments that took place from this introduction to the middle of the eighteenth century cannot concern us in any detail. It is only possible to pick out the characteristics of the trade that emerged in this period and which help to explain its phenomenal success after that time. Three closely related subjects traced by Wadsworth and Mann require attention: the influence of London as a market and a supplier of raw materials and capital; the emergence of the domestic system of industrial organisation in Lancashire; and the part played by oriental influences on fashion and overseas trade generally.

Economic historians of the early period have rightly emphasised the important role of London in the national economy, calling on centres of regional specialisation both for the basic needs of its growing population and for the wealthy classes who were coming to regard it as proper to buy town houses and gather in the metropolis for the season. It was this growing market, fed, so far as textiles were concerned, through Blackwell Hall, that provided the major encouragement to the emergent manufacture in the seventeenth century. London dealers, often of Lancashire extraction, might employ an agent in Manchester to buy up cloth from the scattered manufacturers, or Manchester fustian dealers might forward goods to Blackwell Hall, the London cloth market, on their own account. Most of the raw cotton was imported through London and forwarded to Manchester on credit terms that encouraged the northern manufacturer. By the late seventeenth century the bill of exchange drawn on London had become the predominant means of payment for Lancashire dealers, and this financial support was crucial to the development of the trade.

London also played an important role in technical innovation in the cotton industry, acting as a nursery for techniques brought from the Continent or from India until they were ready for transplanting to the provinces, where there was less competition for land, labour and capital. Thus the 'Dutch engine loom', a complicated machine that made several linen or cotton tapes at once, found its way to Manchester via London. It was introduced by alien (probably Dutch) settlers early in the seventeenth century and was in use in Manchester by the Restoration. By 1750 there were at least 1500 Dutch looms in use in the parish of Manchester, concentrated in enlarged workshops distinct from the weavers' cottages, and Wadsworth and Mann recognise the Dutch loom workshops as a first step in the transition to the factory system.

The technique of printing fustians with bright-coloured designs was also a London industry before it migrated to the North-west to become the foundation of the Lancashire calico-printing industry. Most dyes available in the seventeenth century had a weak affinity for cotton, and the fundamental technique, copied from Indian craftsmen on the Malabar coast, was the application of mordants to fix the dye in the cloth so that it could be washed without losing its character. Calico printing was established in London by 1675 and soon began to achieve success in imitating the popular oriental designs; by 1712 'the East India Company was informing its agents that printing could be done in England at half the price charged for Indian goods and in better colours and patterns'. Unhappily this success aroused the enmity of the established woollen and silk industries, and during a prolonged agitation coinciding with the depression in trade caused by the outbreak of war with Spain in 1718, they succeeded in persuading Parliament to prohibit the sale, use and wear of English calicoes. However, the Act left two loopholes from which Lancashire was to benefit: it allowed calico printing for the export trade, and exempted the printing of fustians. In practice, English fustian was increasingly difficult to distinguish from Indian calico, and manufacturers took advantage of this similarity not only in the domestic market, but also in selling on the Continent, particularly in France, where calico printing had been banned in 1686.

The original role of Lancashire was to weave the fustian cloth which was sent to London for bleaching, printing and marketing. The fustian manufacturing process in the seventeenth and eighteenth centuries was organised on what is often called the domestic system. The entrepreneur was a merchant resident in Manchester, Bolton or Blackburn, and having trade connections with London. He distributed raw cotton and linen to a dispersed army of domestic spinners and weavers through local agents (or middlemen) called fustian manufacturers. The domestic workers were wage-earners, but they might own their own wheels and looms, and some drew support from farming activities [5: *72–91, 314–23*]. By the middle of the eighteenth century a large proportion of the population of Lancashire and the adjacent parts of the West Riding and Cheshire were dependent on the textile industry. Analysis of the baptismal registers shows that in the neighbourhood of Manchester from 50 to 70 per cent of the fathers recorded worked in some branch of the textile industries, while in Saddleworth (an area of some 40 square miles of gritstone Pennines between Oldham and Huddersfield) there were as many as 85 per cent.[1] The important point is that the Lancashire region saw the evolution of a capitalist class and an experienced workforce for nearly two centuries before the first water-powered cotton mills were built in the area. William Radcliffe of Mellor (near Stockport) recounted how a child brought up in a home where the cotton manufacture was carried on acquired 'a practical knowledge of every process from the cotton bag to the piece of cloth', and how such training laid the foundation for an independent career in the industry during the rapid growth of the trade in the 1780s and 1790s.[2]

There was a third innovation which was nourished in London for most of the seventeenth century before migrating to the provinces. The stocking frame was invented by the Revd William Lee, an obscure Renaissance genius who came from Calverton, a village just to the north of Nottingham, and took his complex mechanism to London in the hope of obtaining royal support in 1589. He was disappointed, but his workmen settled in the capital and succeeded well enough to obtain a charter from Cromwell in 1657. Lee's frame was originally used to make silk and worsted stockings, but in 1732 a Nottingham workman succeeded in his attempts to knit cotton on the machine. By this time the East Midlands, which had retained some residual interest in the stocking frame after Lee left for London, were rapidly reasserting their right to the invention, offering cheaper labour and living costs, and freedom from the restricting ordinances of the chartered company. At the middle of the eighteenth century the merchant hosiers of Nottingham, Leicester, Derby and the satellite towns were employing large numbers of domestic framework knitters and, from small origins, were becoming a wealthy trading elite. Like the Lancashire merchants, they were still dependent on London for their market, but were becoming sufficiently independent to take the initiative in seeking both new techniques and new markets.[3]

London enterprise and capital also played the pioneer role in the early development of the factory system in the provinces. The earliest water-powered silk mill in Britain was built at Derby by Thomas Cotchett, a London silk reeler, following a lease of water rights on the Derwent in 1704. By 1707 Cotchett had installed '16 double Dutch mills', so it is possible that he was trying to apply power to the Dutch engine loom as well as to reeling silk. Cotchett's works proved expensive and were probably not successful technically; at any rate he became bankrupt in 1713 and the mill was released to Cotchett's friend John Lombe, who already had some silk-reeling machinery at work in London. Lombe and his half-brother Thomas Lombe, a wealthy London silk merchant, extended the works with the benefit of additional technical knowledge from Leghorn, where silk-reeling mills were already an important part of industrial structure. The Lombes succeeded in making the Derby silk mill pay its way, not only because John was well informed on the most up-to-date Italian technology, but also because, as manager, he succeeded in establishing a regimen of order and discipline for the 300 workers employed at the mill.[4] The buildings and organisation at Derby were copied in six mills at Stockport between 1732 and 1768, and in others at Congleton (1754), Macclesfield (1756), Sheffield (1768) and Watford (1769), and they exercised an influence over the development of the early factory system in the cotton industry, partly because Arkwright's Derby partner, Jedediah Strutt, consciously copied the organisation of the Derby mill, and partly because the mills at Stockport and Sheffield were converted to cotton in the early and still experimental period of Arkwright's success. The history of Stockport shows that the organising ability, inventive capacity and upward social mobility that came to be regarded as characteristic of cotton were found in the town's silk industry a generation earlier [48: *23–9*].

Up to this point the growth of the cotton industry has been analysed mainly from the supply side; it is now time to examine the problem of the increase in demand. Some reference has been made to the influence of oriental technique and design, and this can be examined first. Since Wadsworth and Mann completed their book, the historians of design have become keenly interested in the origins of printed textiles and their expertise has radically improved our understanding of the subject. In their *Origins of Chintz*, John Irwin and Katharine Brett show that the East India Company at first imported Indian fabrics only as novelties or curiosities, mainly using them as exchange in the spice trade with Malaya. However, by 1643 the Company's directors were beginning to realise the possibilities of the home market, and instructed their agents that the design of imported chintzes should respond to taste in the London market. By 1669 the directors were sending out patterns to be copied, and ordering 2000 pieces at a time. To keep pace with the accelerating demand, English and Dutch traders settled Indian cotton painters within the protected area of their own trading stations. British governments' attempts to restrict the calico trade in 1700 and 1720 never achieved total prohibition, and the competition of the East India Company's factories continued to present a challenge to English manufacturers to improve their craftsmanship until the end of the eighteenth century [63].

Some reference has already been made to the large export of printed cottons at the middle of the eighteenth century. For the first three-quarters of the century, until the new technology began to undermine the competitive position of Continental producers, most of the overseas demand came from Africa (where brightly printed cottons were exchanged for cargoes of slaves for the West Indian or Virginian plantations) and from the American and West

Indian colonists. As Wadsworth and Mann explain, this highly successful trade 'was prophetic of Lancashire's later pre-eminence in providing for warm climates and coloured races'. It was the carefully cultivated domestic and overseas market, rather than superior technology, that was the key to British achievement in the cotton industry until after the middle of the eighteenth century [5: *Ch. 8*].

In the second half of the eighteenth century a major shift in fashion, always a potent factor in the fortunes of the textile industry, gave new impetus to the rise of cotton. Down to the 1760s European fashions largely followed those of the French court at Versailles, featuring elaborate garments, with a profusion of ornate silks and ribbons. In the last 40 years of the century English fashions overtook the French, sober country simplicity conquering the expensive and impractical creations of the French court, with linens and cottons becoming increasingly popular for women's dresses and plain woollen cloths for men's wear. In this period ladies' magazines and pocket books already circulated widely, keeping the provinces in step with London fashions. Homogeneity of taste created a single national market for British textile manufacturers, while London fashion leadership extended that market to the Continent, the United States and the Colonies. As *The Magazine à la Mode* insisted in 1777, 'every variation of the fashions gives new life to trade, both in town and country' [62: *221*]. Fashions reached all classes of society as the upper classes distributed their cast-offs in the servants' hall and a large market in second-hand clothing developed. This fashion-conscious society was a major factor in the mechanisation of the cotton industry, for it was clear that every reduction in price of plain and printed cotton fabrics would find ever more eager buyers in the lower classes [57: *204–10*].

2 Technology

A GREAT deal of interest has attached to the mechanisation of the cotton industry because it is seen as a starting point of the modern technique of production that we call the factory system. Spinning was traditionally a simple handicraft consisting of only two motions, stretching then twisting the clean combed cotton fibres, and it proved relatively easy to imitate this activity with a machine. The earliest invention in economic use, James Hargreaves' spinning jenny, simply replicated the work of a number of spinners, and it was sufficiently small to be located in the workers' homes or in adjacent workshops [6: *42–4*]. The vital economic advance took place when this machine, and rivals invented or patented by Richard Arkwright and Samuel Crompton, had grown to a size that made manual operation too laborious. Power had to be introduced and the workers became machine minders rather than machine operatives [*11: 114–26; 16: 176–9*].

The father of modern economics, Adam Smith, showed in his *Wealth of Nations* (1776) how the greatest economies in manufacturing came from the 'division of labour', illustrating his idea with a factory that employed 16 different processes and workers to make pins. This form of manufacturing organisation, which has been called a proto-factory, also occurred in the early cotton industry, especially in calico printing [*25: 451–78*]. When various forms of power – horses, water wheels, windmills and steam engines – were harnessed to the new spinning machines, along with their complementary cleaning, carding, roving and other processes, a new form of organisation was born, the fully-evolved factory. During the course of the nineteenth century, the power-driven (fully-evolved) factory gradually superseded the proto-factory in weaving, printing, knitting and other textile processes, and presently in a range of other industries. But before surveying the diffusion of cotton industry techniques to complementary and competing industries, we must examine the late eighteenth-century changes rather more closely.

Richard Arkwright and his partners had to instal a horse capstan in their first factory (a converted house in Nottingham) in 1769, and many of those who copied the technique at first used the same source of power. Horse capstans were cheap to instal (insurance records show that they were seldom valued at more than £50) and particularly suited to the stage at which small fustian manufacturers or hosiers were adapting existing premises to factory production, either for warp spinning (Arkwright's technique) or, a little later, for the carding engine and power-assisted mule. Horse capstans were indeed so common that few contemporaries thought them worthy of note, but scattered references suggest that they were possibly the most common kind of power installation until the end of the century, and formed an important stepping-stone from domestic to factory production [14: 47–9].

However this may be, there can be little doubt that water wheels provided most of the power for the cotton industry until after 1820. Early in the eighteenth century the traditional paddle (or 'undershot') water wheels began to be replaced by the more efficient breast and overshot wheels, particularly after John Smeaton, the most famous engineer of the age, demonstrated the increased power of the latter with experimental models in some lectures to the Royal Society in London in 1751.[5] The power requirements of the cotton industry were at first quite modest (it has been estimated that in 1795 the whole of the year's import of cotton could have been spun with 5000 h.p.) and, in the Pennines, where a typical minor stream draining into the Manchester embayment could generate more than 400 h.p., increased power demands appear to have been met without an immediate shortage of water power. Again, the importance of this factor is that costs were kept low during the crucial pioneer years, enabling entrepreneurs of limited resources to enter or retain a place in the industry.

By the middle of the eighteenth century the Newcomen steam engine was employed in most mining districts for drainage, and was soon at work replenishing reservoirs in locations of the textile industry where coal was plentiful and cheap. Local shortages of water power, especially on the Midland plain and the urban centres of the cotton industry, compelled factory owners who wanted to remain on the same site to consider the possibility of using James Watt's rotary steam engine in direct transmission to carding and spinning machinery. Several of the leaders of the industry, notably Arkwright, the Peels and Major Cartwright (brother of the inventor Edmund Cartwright), were involved in some costly failures with pioneer steam mills, and those who persevered complained of high maintenance costs, slow after-sales service and, above all, capital and running costs, much in excess of a water wheel on a good stream. The cost of power is very difficult to calculate for this period as data are scarce, and every water-power site involved the buyer or lessee in a different outlay and presented its own individual return to the investment; but such evidence as is available points to the conclusion that those occupying sites yielding more than 10 to 20 h.p. found them competitive until the late 1830s, when the efficiency of steam engines began to increase [8: *1–24*; 16, *204–24*].

Unfortunately, there are no general surveys of the comparative importance of water and steam power until 1835, when the steam engine, after more than half a century of continuous improvement, had become the predominant form of power in every cotton town in the North of England except a few Pennine centres like Glossop, Mottram and Halifax. By that time, as the figures in Table I show, steam was responsible for three-quarters of the power used in the industry. The table draws particular attention to the dominance of the Northern region (i.e. Lancashire and the adjacent parts of Cheshire, Derbyshire and the West Riding), which was clearly secured by steam power. At the end of the eighteenth century this region had contributed something like 70 per cent of the cotton manufacture; but in 1835 it had reached 90 per cent. Steam power was still as expensive as water power, but its

Table I Water and Steam Power in 1835

	No. of mills	Steam h.p.	Water h.p.
Northern region	934	26,513	6,094
Scotland	125	3,200	2,480
Midlands	54	438	*c.* 1,200
Total	1,113	30,151	*c.* 9,774

Source: [1: *386–92*].

use was economised, partly by specialisation on manually operated power-*assisted* mules, partly by the increasing concentration of the cotton industry on the Lancashire coalfield. In the peripheral areas the older roller spinning technique of Arkwright, extravagant with the more abundant water-power resources of the Peak district and Scotland, continued to specialise on coarse spinning [36: 135–53]. However, these distinctions demand some basic appreciation of the nature of the two principal methods of production, and warrant closer examination.

The most important features of the introduction of mechanised carding and spinning are the spectacular increase in output, the fundamental improvement in quality of yarns, and the continuous trend of falling prices. The easiest way of illustrating the quantitive change is to reproduce the data on labour productivity in Catling's study of *The Spinning Mule*, where the modern concept of O.H.P. (i.e. the number of Operative Hours to Process 100 lb. of cotton) is applied to historical situations (see Table II). The only qualification that must be made to this table is that there was frequently a time-lag between the introduction of improved machinery and its widespread adoption. Catling's estimates do not cover the older (Arkwright) technique of roller spinning, but it is possible to make calculations from contemporary descriptions of mills. Specifications of the most efficient mills suggest that they fell within the 250–370 O.H.P. range in the 1780s and 1790s, i.e. that productivity was as high as in mule spinning during the pioneer years.[6] The labour force at Arkwright-type mills was mostly unskilled females and juveniles on low wages, while mules were operated by men whose skill was scarce and expensive, so that as long as the two systems could compete in quality, entrepreneurs with capital pursued the Arkwright system.

Table II   Labour Productivity in Cotton Spinning

Indian hand spinners (18th cent.)	50,000 + O.H.P.
Crompton's mule (1780)	2,000 ,,
100-spindle mule (*c.* 1790)	1,000 ,,
Power-assisted mules (*c.* 1795)	300 ,,
Roberts's automatic mules (*c.* 1825)	135 ,,
Most efficient machinery today (1972)	40 ,,

Source: [7: 54].

The quality of yarn was the decisive factor in the competition between the rival systems. The traditional one-thread hand wheel spun 'little or no thread finer than 16 to 20 hanks in the pound, each hank measuring 840 yards', and evenness depended on the delicacy of touch of the spinner. (This degree of fineness – the count of the yarn – was expressed, by trade convention, as 16s to 20s, and other achievements *pro rata*.) Hargreaves's jenny, duplicating the motions of the hand spinner, reached the low 20s, while Arkwright, at the pinnacle of his achievement, attained 60s [6: *44*]. Apart from calico printing, the competition was principally focused on quantity rather than quality up to this time. The manufacture of fine articles still depended on highly skilled workers, and the Swiss towns of Zürich, Wädenswil, Horgen, Stäfa and St Gall had practically the European monopoly; the only competition attempted was from the cambric manufacturers at St Quentin and Tarare, towards 1756, and Glasgow in 1769. Crompton's mule, which was soon spinning 80s, and reached 300s by the end of the century, transformed the situation almost overnight. Thomas Ainsworth at Bolton (1780) and Samuel Oldknow at Anderton and Stockport (1782–4) began making muslins, and three years later, in 1787, Britain already produced 500,000 pieces.

Lancashire success in the mechanisation of fine spinning not only absorbed the enterprise and capital of the region in the 1780s and 1790s, but also began to divert capital from Arkwright's system. By 1795, when M'Connel & Kennedy of Manchester succeeded in applying a Boulton & Watt steam engine to the two 'heavy' motions of the four-movement cycle of the mule, many of the pioneers of the Arkwright system, like the Peels and Douglases, began to direct their investment into the new and rapidly developing technique, though the older system (as Strutt's experience illustrates) continued to provide prosperity for a number of efficient firms. Consequently, mule spinning quickly superseded warp spinning in importance, and was the predominant system for the remainder of the period covered by this study. The only exception to this generalisation was the early 1830s, when investment in power looms, which were at first only suitable for the coarser yarns, led to a temporary revival of interest in warp spinning [18: *235–56*].

Spinning by power commands more attention than any other

technique because it set in motion a sequence of technical and organisational changes in connected branches of the industry. Success at the spinning stage of the production process immediately created the need for an increase of output at the earlier stages, and all the important inventors of spinning machines were compelled to divert their minds to preparation machinery. The cotton from the bale had to be picked and cleaned, 'batted' (or beaten, to open the fibres), carded into a continuous sliver, 'drawn' (to lay the fibres parallel) and 'roved' (to attenuate the sliver) before it reached the spinning frames, and in the lifetime of Arkwright and Crompton a community of fertile minds in the Lancashire cotton towns succeeded in mechanising these processes. The outcome was the perfection of a system of continuous (or flow) production in which the cotton was mechanically handled from the moment the bales were hoisted from the drays to the top floor of the mill to that at which it was dispatched, in carefully graded yarns, from the ground-floor warehouse. Rapid dispersion of these ideas was the work of a corps of specialised millwrights and machine builders, who erected the mill buildings and machinery on uniform lines, originally imitating the achievements of Arkwright, Peel and other pioneers [14: *99*; 9: *16*].

The Hargreaves and Arkwright techniques of spinning superseded the old hand spinning wheels with a speed that, in retrospect, appeared almost dramatic. In 1768–9 there were some angry demonstrations in the Blackburn area by people who feared unemployment, but the general experience was probably reflected by William Radcliffe's comment on the change at Mellor (Stockport). 'The hands, turned adrift from hand cards and the spinning wheel, soon found full employ in the loom on machine yarn, with three to four fold more wages than they had been able to earn in their own trade', he recalled. Some families with no reserves of capital, Radcliffe infers, were forced out of the industry, but for those with initiative there was a golden opportunity to earn unprecedented wages and establish themselves as independent manufacturers.[7]

The rising costs that led to the era of inventions in the spinning section of the industry found a parallel in some other sections, particularly weaving, knitting, bleaching, dyeing and calico printing. Wadsworth and Mann wrote of a 'rapid transition to industrial capitalism' in these later stages of production between

1750 and 1780, and though they were evidently reviewing a variety of precocious enterprises rather than the typical firm, there can be no doubt that the period saw considerable growth in the size of workshops. Weaving looms and knitting frames were beginning to be concentrated in workshops employing supervised wage-earners, either to reduce the time wasted in distributing raw materials and collecting goods from domestic workers, or to improve the quality of the finished product. By the early nineteenth century, according to Bythell, there were isolated weaving sheds 'with as many as 150 or 200 handlooms, quite a few with between 50 and 100, and a considerable number with 20 or more. Such sheds were to be found in town and country throughout the weaving area.' This development, Bythell maintains, 'represented a half-way stage between true domestic industry and the modern power-driven weaving shed'. In the printing section of the industry there is also evidence of concentrations of labour and capital. The leviathan of the industry, Livesey, Hargreaves & Co. of Blackburn, employed about 900 workers shortly before their bankruptcy in 1788 [65: *33*; 43: *29*].

The traditional bleaching technique involved repeated immersions of the cloth in sour milk (lactic acid), followed by weeks of tentering in the open fields to allow the sun to complete the process. The whole process lasted seven or eight months in all. Dr John Roebuck's sulphuric acid plants in Birmingham (1746) and Prestonpans, Scotland (1749), inaugurated a sharp decline in the price of this industrial chemical, and it was soon replacing sour milk in bleaching, reducing the process to about four months. However, the most drastic economy of time, as a result of which bleaching lasted little more than a day, was not made until the end of the century. Charles Tennant of Glasgow, exploiting the discoveries of Berthollet, Scheele and pioneer plants in Manchester, Nottingham, Aberdeen and other centres of the cotton industry, successfully launched the commercial manufacture of bleaching powder. The new techniques called for specialised knowledge of chemistry, and bleaching powder manufacturers seldom had interests in spinning or weaving, though a few of them were also active as dyers and printers. Both bleachworks and dyeworks used water wheels through the period covered by this study, the former to power 'wash wheels' and 'dash wheels' (hammers to wash and pound the cloth free of acid), the latter to grind down dyewoods. Steam power was introduced to calico printing from about 1760, when Asterleys of Wandsworth installed 'a fire engine' at their printworks [12: *Ch. 8*; 25: *459*].

Weaving and knitting were technically more difficult to subject to the water wheel and steam engine, and when efficient machines were finally developed (in weaving in the 1830s, in knitting in the 1850s), their adoption was inhibited by the poor wages of handloom weavers and framework knitters. The earliest patents for a power loom were taken out by the Revd Edmund Cartwright in 1786–8, and he and his brother (Major John Cartwright) tried to develop the invention in factories at Doncaster and Retford (Notts.), but neither succeeded. Cartwright's loom was brought to commercial success by Radcliffe, Horrocks, Marsland and other Stockport manufacturers in the first years of the nineteenth century, but the general adoption of their looms was deferred until the investment booms of 1823–5 and 1832–4. In 1833 there were estimated to be 100,000 power looms in Britain, a number which can be compared with 250,000 handloom weavers [1: *228–40*]. Meanwhile a major new advance was taking place in mechanised spinning, and it was this and the power looms that dictated a multiplication of the scale of the most efficient factories.

The change in scale began in the middle 1830s with the widespread adoption of Roberts's automatic mule. In 1832 an expert wrote that 'self-acting mules have long been a desideratum in the trade and have occupied the attention of intelligent managers and mechanics for some years past; [but] although several have been invented and secured by patent yet none seem to be possessed of sufficient merit to cause any excitement in the trade; in fact they seem so unimportant as to be seldom spoken of'. Eight years later he was producing detailed calculations to show that automatic mules were 15 per cent cheaper to operate than hand mules. Meanwhile, Dr Andrew Ure was publicising a new type of mill designed specifically for automatic mules by William Fairbairn, who was reaching the peak of his career as a Manchester millwright.[8] In 1822 the representative size of the Manchester cotton mill was still 100 to 200 hands, and in the satellite towns it was probably even smaller. This impression was confirmed in another technical work, where a representative factory unit whose costs were 'all calculated from the cost and expense of establishments that have been lately erected' was only a little larger than the

Arkwright prototype, though it contained 4500 spindles and 128 power looms and cost just over £8000. The new mills, by contrast, contained 40,000 spindles and cost over £80,000 – an increase of ten times the capacity of the familiar scale of production. For over fifty years mules had been operated by highly skilled and semi-independent artisans on standard piece-rates, and there was no particular economy in concentration of their numbers; experience showed that the optimum production was reached with 264–288 spindles. But the perfection of Roberts's work enabled one man, with the help of two or three boys, to work 1600 spindles as easily as he had previously worked 300, and mills were doubled in width to accommodate the much enlarged machines [186, *76–81*]. These details may try the patience of those who lack interest in technical problems, but a basic appreciation of the scale and timing of technical change is essential for adequate understanding of such problems as the structure of enterprise and of industry, of capital formation and of labour relations, that follow.

According to the research of von Tunzelmann, there was no perceptible fall in the cost of power used by cotton manufacturers from the 1790s to the mid 1830s, and possibly for another decade after that. Meanwhile, the prices of cotton yarns and fabrics continued to decline, by the 1830s producing unacceptably thin profit margins in the industry. Mill owners looked for ways of reducing costs, economising wherever possible, running machinery and engines faster, integrating spinning and weaving plants, and finally adopting the more efficient type of steam engine whose use had been pioneered in the Cornwall mining industry. Tunzelmann believes that the high cost of power delayed the diffusion of more automated machinery, and there was unquestionably a hiatus in the growth of scale in the 1830s and 1840s. In later chapters it will be seen that there were other factors, notably finance, markets and skilled labour, restraining further evolution of scale until after mid-century [16: *212–24*; 2: 313–18].

3 Capital and Structure of the Industry

A GLANCE at the bibliography will confirm that there has been more academic interest in the amount of capital invested in firms in the cotton industry than in any other aspect of its long history. There are two reasons for this. The original one is that historians have for long been fascinated by the notion most clearly formulated in Samuel Smiles' *Self-Help* (1860), that enterprise was open to men of limited capital who had the character to exploit the opportunities open to them. More recent interest derives from strong interest in development economics, that is, in the conditions necessary for industrialisation, including the initial investment costs. Both topics are evidently much wider than the cotton industry but have focused on it because of the major role played by cotton in the first Industrial Revolution, i.e. in the Industrial Revolution in Britain.

Modern studies have featured growing scepticism about the ability of men of 'humble birth' to become entrepreneurs. Harold Perkin's *Origins of Modern English Society* (1969) scorns the idea as a myth, 'one of the most powerful instruments of propaganda ever developed by any class to justify itself and seduce others to its own ideal' (p. 225), while Katrina Honeyman's *Origins of Enterprise* (1982), which includes an analysis of the origins of Arkwright-type mills and of Bolton and Oldham mule spinning workshops, concludes that restrictions on upward mobility remained as insuperable as they always had been (p. 170). However, a more recent analysis by the French Professor François Crouzet entitled *The First Industrialists* (1985) discerns that while neither the upper class nor the lower orders made a large contribution to the recruitment of industrialists, there was a good deal of upward social mobility in the middle ranks of society (p. 141). To explain this mobility we shall need to look at the capital needs of the entrepreneurs in the cotton industry, while the total capital invested in the industry will aid our understanding of the take-off process.

In the last chapter it was explained that the early technology of the British cotton industry was essentially simple, and most of the mills were on a very small scale compared with developments later in the nineteenth century. Now we must look at the problem of costs, examining the fixed and working capital needs of the early mills and printworks. A few firms owned more than one works, and were sometimes involved in a variety of related activities (merchanting, banking, machine building, etc.) and we shall survey what is known of these forms of capitalism.

Practically all studies of the early factory system in the cotton industry begin with Patrick Colquhoun's pioneer census of Arkwright-type mills in 1788. Colquhoun noted 143 mills dispersed over 27 counties in England, Scotland and Wales, but his figures were assembled in a great hurry for a parliamentary pressure group and have recently been shown to have been a serious underestimate of the total and distortion of the geographical spread. There were at least 208 mills, with many more in Yorkshire, Cheshire and Derbyshire than was previously realised. The building of mills had nearly all taken place since 1781, when Arkwright's patents were first successfully challenged in the courts. The proliferation of plants was largely due to the fact that most of them were built on a simple pattern which closely followed Arkwright's mills at Cromford, three- or four-storey mills measuring about 30 x 10 yards and intended to drive 1000 spindles with a 10-horse-power water wheel [9: *10–15*]. At first sight surviving examples may appear like a gaunt terrace of eight or ten working-class houses.

The early mills were highly vulnerable to destruction by fire so most of them were insured. Consequently we have a measure of their cost (or at any rate, replacement cost), which was around £3000 for the basic 1000 spindles mill, and £5000 for a unit about twice the size that had already made its appearance in 1788. Synthesising these details, and adding estimates made by Hugh Watts of the Sun Fire Office in 1797 and for the Samuel Crompton census of mule spinning machinery in 1812, it is possible to assemble some estimates of the total amount of capital invested in the spinning sector of the cotton industry in its early years (Table III). The spinning mule, which incorporated some of the best technical features of Hargreaves' and Arkwright's machines, was at first manually operated in small workshops in

Bolton, Stockport, and other centres, and again required little fixed capital [29: *107–10*; 52: *186–96*]. The accumulation of fixed capital was not impressive until after the French Wars (Table IV).

The figures assembled here take on more meaning when compared with some earlier developments. In Britain's traditional woollen industry, fulling mills were typically worth £100 to £200 and collections of workshops for various processes seldom rose above £500. In the silk industry, two or three reeling mills built on the Italian model earlier in the century cost over £5000, but these were clearly quite exceptional, and most silkworks evidently cost much less. In any case the total numbers of silk mills were quite small, just 20 or so built over a 50-year period (1720–70). Similarly, a handful of calico-printing works cost over £5000, but much more commonly cost under £2000, and there were probably not more than 50 before 1775. It was the dramatic growth and dispersion of Arkwright-type mills, as much as the size, that marked them out from earlier developments in the textile industry (25: *451–78*; 27: *475–9*].

The number of firms in the industry was always significantly less than the number of factories, for several leading firms had two or more factories. Peels, the biggest firm in 1795, had twenty-three mills centred on Blackburn, Bury, Bolton, Burton upon Trent and Tamworth; William Douglas and his partners had nine, divided between Pendleton (Manchester), Holywell (North Wales coast), Carlisle and Scotland; and Robinsons of Nottingham, who are regularly mentioned in the textbooks as the first firm to buy a Watt steam engine for a cotton mill, had five mills strung along a stream just to the north of the town. David Dale, lately Arkwright's partner in Scotland, had two large mills with two others being built. The great majority of entrepreneurs in the industry were, however, men of much more limited means, dragging themselves up the economic ladder by their bootstraps.

Although the stresses of the French Wars persuaded some moneyed entrepreneurs to withdraw from the industry, and weeded out many of the struggling small men, the structure of the industry continued to be polarised, that is, characterised by a few giants and many small men dependent on the credit of merchants or merchant-manufacturers. By 1812, when the next survey of the industry was taken, mule spinning had easily overtaken roller

Table III Estimates of the Number of and Fixed Capital Invested in British Cotton-spinning Mills, 1787–1812

Estimate	Date	Number of Arkwright-type factories	Number of mule factories and workshops	Value of an Arkwright mill	Adjustment for mule factories	Total fixed capital (£m)	Revised total (£m)
Colquhoun	1787	208	n.d.	£5,000	+£285,000	1.0	1.3
Chapman	1795	c.300	n.d.	£3–5,000	+£500,000	2.0	2.0
Watts	1797	—900—		£3,000	−£200,000	2.7	2.5
Crompton	1812	n.d.	673	n.d.	(none)	3.0–4.0	5.0–6.0

Sources: [18: 235–66; 9: 5–27].

Table IV Estimates of Fixed and Working Capital in the British Cotton Industry, 1834–56

		Spinning and Weaving				
Estimate	Date	Fixed capital (£m)	Working capital (£m)	Total (£m)	Finishing trades (£m)	Total capital (£m)
McCulloch	1834	14.8	7.4	22.2	11.8	34.0
Baynes	1856	31.0	14.5	45.5	30.0	75.5

Source: [17: 358–81].

spinning in importance, but this did not terminate the business careers of all the old leaders. When M'Connel & Kennedy showed the successful application of Watt's steam engine to the 'heavy' motions of the mule, the giants of the industry began to switch their capital to the new system. In 1812, 70 per cent (or 472 out of 673) of the firms in mule spinning had fewer than 10,000 spindles, but a few firms had many times this number: Samuel Horrocks of Preston had 107,000 in eight mills, while Peter Marsland of Stockport, M'Connel and Kennedy, and A and G Murray of Manchester, each had over 80,000, to mention only the leaders. The first two were second-generation firms that had pioneered the industry, the second two machine builders who had begun in the early 1790s with very little capital [29: *107–10*]. The leaders of 1795 had disappeared from the top of the table, but this is partly explained by the limitations of the 1812 census, which did not count the Arkwright-type mills unless they were also used for mule spinning, and extended to only sixty miles around Manchester. Big firms like the Strutts, Arkwrights, Oldknow and Peels at Tamworth and Burton upon Trent, the Douglasses at Holywell, were thus excluded by definition. Evidence to a Parliamentary Committee in 1815–16 adds some details on the size of the workforce in some of the best-known concerns. Robert Owen, the successor to David Dale at New Lanark, was employing 1600–1700, James Finlay and Co 1529 at three mills in Scotland, the Strutts, 1494 at Belper (near Derby), A and G Murray 1215 and M'Connel and Kennedy 1020 [27: *475–9*]. Nevertheless, small entrepreneurs continued to make their way into the industry, especially in the early 1820s.[9]

Useful data on the changing structure of the cotton industry for the period 1815–41 exist in the Manchester rate books and a Factory Inspector's survey of the latter year. The different sources are identified here because they may help to explain differences in the conclusions of scholars who have extracted and analysed the figures. R. Lloyd-Jones, concentrating on the Manchester material, emphasises the high mortality of small firms, and particularly *new* small firms. He maintains that the more successful firms were generally those launched as middle-sized enterprises [33: *72–82*]. V. A. C. Gatrell, concentrating on the 1841 material, prefers to speak of the industry as consisting predominantly of 'small-to-middling sized' firms, and after considering a larger group of firms than that available to Lloyds-Jones for study, concluded that 'the difference between the vulnerability of small firms as against mixed, was surprisingly slight' [20: *121*].

The common ground between these two writers is that, even by the more modest standards of the early nineteenth century, the cotton industry was never dominated by the handful of big capitalists, and it is wrong to write (as Engels did in 1844) of 'ever-increasing concentration of capital in fewer and fewer hands'. The interesting question is to ask the reasons for the apparent failure of big capitalists to dominate the second- and third-generation leadership as Arkwright, Peel, Horrocks, Oldknow and others had the first. Several answers have been offered. D. A. Farnie, taking the long view (1815–96), notices that the combined spinning and weaving firm first appeared in numbers in the 1830s but failed to proliferate due to geographical separation and specialisation, spinning in south Lancashire and the Stockport area, weaving in the north of the county [2: *313–18*]. Gatrell, after querying the existence of substantial economies of scale in the early cotton mills, finds an answer in 'social constraints', a sense of 'moderation in enterprise' among contemporary entrepreneurs (20: *117*]. This obtains some support from the most recent research on cotton mill technology, that referred to at the end of last chapter, which suggests that a further leap forward in the optimum scale of production was delayed until the mid 1840s. However, that would not have dissuaded ambitious entrepreneurs from acquiring several mills.

A further answer is suggested by various authors who have drawn attention to the financial restraints in the growth of firms in the early cotton industry. For most of the period covered by the present study, the provincial money market was evolving from very elementary beginnings, and entrepreneurs in need of capital drew on very diverse sources. The favourite source of capital was retained profits, and during the restricted growth period of Arkwright's patents (1769–85) profit rates are known to have been very high; Robinsons of Nottingham, to take just one example, were earning 100 per cent on their investment in mills and plant in 1784.[10] Even so, working capital requirements were so much larger than fixed capital, and the time-lag between decisions to build and profits so long, that financial difficulties could be experienced. 'I have been with Mr Robinson and he says . . .

building etc. hath swallowed so much money that at present he sells [only] for ready cash', Thomas Oldknow wrote to his brother Samuel at Stockport in 1783 [48: *13*]. Similarly, the first Sir Robert Peel said that in the early part of his career 'the greatest difficulty which he had to surmount was the want of capital to keep pace with his schemes of extension. The profits of the business were exceedingly great, and it admitted of great extension, but for some time the firm were hampered by the limited amount of their capital and credit' [43: *70*]. The correspondence of M'Connel & Kennedy, the Manchester leaders of the fine cotton-spinning industry, makes constant reference in the critical periods of the war years to the difficulties of raising money and to the reluctance of bankers to discount bills [52: *221*]. If the leaders of the industry suffered from intermittent financial strain, it cannot be expected that those who entered the industry after the years of abnormal profits, or who began with fewer connections, were insulated from such difficulties, and several other studies illustrate the financial problems of a variety of firms [40: *171–87*; 39, *32ff*].

Small firms that could not feed their own growth usually turned to their own families, and then to local business and social contracts for help, but of course not all had such connections. The law did not recognise shareholding in the modern sense until the Limited Liability Acts of 1855–6, but from the early part of the eighteenth century it became common for small businesses to borrow money on bond, and widows, clergymen, trustees, executors, retired tradesmen and other people with small savings were often glad to take advantage of this security. Small manufacturers might draw on the resources of a handful of local people who knew and trusted them, but this source of capital was not unfamiliar to much larger concerns. Cardwell, Birley & Hornby, the Blackburn cotton spinners, had ninety-seven small investors on their books in 1812, with a total investment of £36,000. In this instance, nearly all the loans were secured by a simple promise to pay, probably because the lenders were local people known personally to the partners [52: *255–7*]. In Scotland the legal framework was different; six, eight or ten partners in manufacturing concerns was already an established practice at the middle of the eighteenth century, and there was not the same need to draw on external sources.

However, sleeping partners were not uncommon in the English cotton industry, despite the risk of unlimited liability for the debts of the firm. Merchants were sometimes willing to enter into partnership with cotton manufacturers. A good example is provided by Gardom, Pares & Co. of Calver Bridge, near Sheffield, the partners in which consisted of representatives of the Heygate family, London hosiers and bankers, the Pares family, Leicester merchant hosiers, and the Gardoms, a line of Derbyshire hosiers that had become licensees of Arkwright in 1778 [64: *26–8*]. Retired manufacturers would sometimes offer partnerships to promising young men, and a range of speculators entered the trade on similar terms, not infrequently to their loss. Improving landlords were often willing to provide or improve buildings for their tenantry, so that the cotton industry in Manchester and other parts of Lancashire owes something to the self-interest of the Earls of Derby, that of Glossop to the Duke of Norfolk, the Colne valley to Lord Dartmouth, and the Mansfield area (Notts.) to the Duke of Portland. In Glasgow the trading elite were intermarrying with the leading landowning families in Scotland in the second half of the eighteenth century, and partnerships to develop and exploit the best water-power sites in the country areas were common. Manufacturers fortunate enough to own land or buildings could readily mortgage them to raise capital or convert them to new uses [52: *195–8*].

Other channels might be open to entrepreneurs who were seeking working capital. A variety of historical business records show that widespread encouragement was given to small manufacturers by the supplier merchants' habit of allowing four to eight months' credit, a sufficient period to work up the raw material and sell the product to wholesalers who, in some cases, might make payments in cash or bills of exchange [52: *225–30*]. The difficulty with such records is that they may not be representative; certainly they are likely to neglect the kind of small entrepreneur whose pocket-book records have seldom survived. The early development of mercantile credit was certainly a factor in the growth of the cotton industry, but many of those who became manufacturers were men of little education and few connections, and lived from hand to mouth. Authentic spokesmen from their ranks are difficult to find, but there is an occasional voice. Thus John Dugdale of the Lowerhouse Print Works, near Burnley, made some remarks in 1847 which, when translated from the vernacular, read: 'If you'll look back for the last six years, you'll find half of the printers are broken [bankrupt], and half of those that are left cannot break, for nobody will trust them; and the rest get on as well as they can.' A firm-by-firm survey of the Lancashire calico printers in 1846 confirms the impression of a preponderance of small and struggling entrepreneurs, with a high turnover of firms [4: *70–3*].

London merchants and wholesale dealers also provided credit for northern manufacturers, but experience taught them to be highly selective. The spectacular bankruptcy in 1788 of Livesey, Hargreaves & Co. of Blackburn, the leading calico printers in the trade, was a severe setback to a number of London bankers. Samuel Oldknow, the early leader of the English muslin industry, was refused £5000 credit by Saltes, his main London customers, in 1790 [48: *148*; 43: *28–33*]. John Watson & Sons, the leading Preston cotton manufacturers, were more persuasive with their London customers, and at the time of their failure in 1809 had over £10,000 in credit from them[11]. These examples, and others which can be extracted from the records of the court of bankruptcy, show that the granting of credit was a risky business, even with the leading firms.

However, it seems that the most significant cause of stunted growth was the immaturity of the capital markets in the textile regions of the north of England. The early country banks were small family enterprises whose partners were characteristically inexperienced in banking and unprepared to meet the unprecedented developments in industry and overseas markets. Bank failures were frequent and prudent manufacturers often felt it wisest to avoid all banks. After 1826 the Bank of England lost its monopoly of joint-stock banking in the industrial districts, and the capital held by the private banks was quickly superseded by that of new local joint-stock banks. However, the new banks, governed by part-time directors, often proved even more erratic in their business than the older private banks, and after the financial crisis of 1836–7 the survivors were forced to resort to the most conservative policies, granting credit on only the strongest security and avoiding risk wherever possible. The period following the French Wars also saw the rise of what are now known as merchant banks, originally leading merchants of London, Glasgow and Liverpool who accepted (i.e. guaranteed payment of) bills of exchange, usually for foreign trade, but financial crises also compelled these firms to pursue conservative policies [19; 22]. The problem of recruiting adequate working capital continued as a serious restraint on the growth of cotton manufacturers until incorporation of firms became common towards the end of the century.

4 Commercial Organisation and Markets

ALL the raw material used in the cotton industry was imported, and an organisation had to be evolved to supply the manufacturers with increasing quantities of raw cotton (or cotton wool, as it was generally known). From the early 1780s merchants and manufacturers recognised that further growth depended on increased supplies of cotton at low prices, particularly the finer qualities, and they were not slow to press their views with the Board of Trade and the planters. However, projects to increase the cotton crop in the West Indies (especially the Bahamas) and introduce the commodity into Sierra Leone met with only a limited response. The East India Company was reluctant to export the finer Indian staples as it was anxious to maintain its trade in Indian muslins, which depended on a restricted supply. The most encouraging response at first came from Brazil, where the crop was encouraged by the Portuguese government, but this source was quickly superseded in the 1790s by the rapid expansion of cotton in the southern plantations of the recently established United States of America. In the early 1790s the profits on the cotton crop were high, and quickly displaced other cash crops, such as rice, indigo and tobacco. The supply of land seemed almost unlimited, particularly after the Louisiana purchase of 1801, and the United States cotton crop rose from 2 million lb in 1791 to 182 million lb in 1821, becoming the major source of Lancashire's supply at the turn of the century. The high elasticity of supply of cotton, due primarily to the responsiveness of the American planters and the adoption of Whitney's cotton gin, was clearly a crucial factor in the phenomenal growth of the British cotton industry in these years [52: Ch. 5].

The American planters were so successful in increasing the productivity of the cotton plantations, and the marketing machinery improved to such an extent, that after 1800 prices embarked on a course of more or less continuous decline. The

United States Government's attempts to impose restrictions on exports in the period from December 1807 to May 1810 caused erratic fluctuations in prices at Liverpool, but did not affect the long-term trend. The elements of cost in the price of yarn can be illustrated from the data shown in Table V. During the period of the French Wars, when it became more difficult to import wool from the Continent to supply the West Riding and other English manufacturers, the price of wool rose steeply, bringing an unexpected bonus to the cotton industry, and offering a further incentive to woollen and worsted manufacturers and merchants to turn over to cotton. The best price data available can give little conception of the lament of England's old staple industry. As early as 1802 Robert Davison, a Nottingham hosier and spinner, complained that 'the high price of wool has produced a very great and alarming rivalry in cotton fabrics . . . the substitution of the latter for the former is immense . . . large mills and factories originally destined to the working of woollens have been compelled to devote their works to cotton' [26: *215*]. In the West Riding, the displacement of worsteds by calicoes was at first amply compensated for by the rise of carpet making, upholstery, coach linings and other new branches, but by 1808 the Manchester trade dominated the Halifax and Colne areas and the upper Calder valley. The outcome was that the woollen and worsted

Table V   Elements of Cost in the Price of Yarn, 1779–1812

	Yarn 40 hanks to the lb (roller spun)			
	1779	1784	1799	1812
Selling price	16s. 0d.	10s. 11d.	7s. 6d.	2s. 6d.
Cost of cotton	2s. 0d.	2s. 0d.	3s. 4d.	1s. 6d.
Labour and capital	14s. 0d.	8s. 11d.	4s. 2d.	1s. 0d.
	Yarn 100 hanks to the lb (mule spun)			
	1786	1796	1806	1812
Selling price	38s. 0d.	19s. 0d.	7s. 2d.	5s. 2d.
Cost of cotton	4s. 0d.	3s. 6d.	3s. 0d.	2s. 4d.
Labour and capital	34s. 0d.	15s. 6d.	4s. 2d.	2s. 10d.

Source: T. Ellison, *The Cotton Trade of Great Britain* (1886) p. 55; see [53: *75–83*].

industry, and not least the older centres in the West Country and East Anglia, suffered more reverses during the French Wars than did cotton.[12]

The organisation that evolved to market the cotton wool, the spun cotton yarns and cotton cloth was a complex one, and we can deal only with its salient features here. The need for numerous specialised functions can be readily appreciated from features of the industry that have already been noticed: the preponderance of small manufacturers, rapidly changing technology, considerable day-by-day fluctuations in market prices (sometimes due to war or commercial crisis, sometimes to capricious movements in fashion, and occasionally to unfounded rumour), and fairly widespread and regular shortages of capital. To these factors must be added slow and expensive communications, especially to the American, Indian and other distant markets, and the fact that the structure of commerce was slowly evolving for most of our period, certainly from 1780 to 1830. Much of what follows in the remainder of this section illustrates these features.

London was the principal port for cotton until at least 1795, and after that time London merchants and their agents were active in Liverpool, Manchester and other northern centres. Towards the end of the century Liverpool rivalled London because most of the mills and workshops in the cotton industry were situated within sixty or eighty miles of the port, and had good canal and river connections with it. The rise of the United States as the major supplier of raw cotton was also an important factor. The cotton planter was separated from the mill owner by a range of specialised intermediaries; some big manufacturers tried to by-pass the system and deal directly with the growers, but commitment to any one source was found to be an unwise policy. The cotton wool was imported by ship-owning merchants or commission agents acting for the planter or exporter, often a British merchant resident in the United States. In the late eighteenth century the bags of imported cotton were brought up and distributed by Manchester cotton dealers, but these men were gradually superseded by the Liverpool cotton brokers, particularly after the opening of the Liverpool and Manchester railway (1830). Some of the brokers were offshoots of Liverpool merchant houses, but most of them migrated to the port from Manchester and the manufacturing districts. The successful broker combined knowledge of the needs of the industry (derived from his early experience in the mills and regular contacts with buyers) with daily intimacy with the cotton market and a reputation for 'strict probity and honour'. He needed capital, though many began their careers at Liverpool with slender financial resources. The fifty Manchester cotton dealers mentioned in a local directory of 1804 had been replaced by some ninety firms of Liverpool brokers in 1841, the year the Cotton Brokers' Association was formed. The cotton market at Liverpool was a highly competitive one, approximating to the economist's definition of a 'perfect market'. By constant circulation of samples and information bulletins (known as 'cotton circulars'), the brokers provided the 'perfect knowledge' necessary for the maintenance of this market [52: *Ch. 6*; 53: *75–83*].

As the cotton trade expanded and became more sophisticated in its organisation and finance, the Liverpool family firms who had provided the enterprise for the eighteenth-century development of the port were augmented by branches of merchant houses from the United States, London and Glasgow. The number of merchants importing cotton into Liverpool in any one year ran into hundreds, but a large proportion of the trade was handled by a small group of some thirty operators who specialised in the import of cotton, mostly from the United States alone [56: *182–211*].

In discussing the structure of the industry, we have already examined the trend towards disintegration that set in at an early stage of expansion. Vertically integrated firms like Peels, Arkwrights and Douglases were exceptional even in their day, and their relative importance appears to have declined. The existence of a large number of small firms specialising in carding and spinning gave rise to another specialised market, that for yarns. The larger spinners, like Strutts of Belper and M'Connel & Kennedy of Manchester, had selling agents in all the markets – Glasgow, Belfast, Nottingham and other centres – constantly instructing them on prices for the different yarn counts. The smaller spinners were usually dependent on yarn merchants or brokers, who allowed them cotton wool on credit and bought up their small consignments. Here, as elsewhere, the market was a highly competitive one, and those with little capital depended on the favour of merchants and were most vulnerable to sudden changes in demand [46: *Ch. 5*; 44: *Ch. 11*; 52: *Ch. 7*].

Between 1780 and 1815 the market for cotton cloth continued to be centred on London, but that period saw a decisive shift of the focus of trade towards Manchester. Though a few outstanding northern firms like the Peels of Manchester and I. & R. Morley, the Nottingham hosiers, opened their own warehouses in London before the end of the century, the London tradesmen's more ready access to capital and their close contact with fashion movements contrived to tie provincial merchants and manufacturers to them. There appear to have been three common types of connection between the centre of trade and the centres of manufacturing. Some firms in the provinces had a partner in London or a working agreement with a London merchant, and this close personal connection was particularly important in fashion lines like calico printing and hosiery. Other goods from the provinces were handled by commission agents who sold by private contract or at weekly public sales, or by warehousemen who bought goods outright from the provincial manufacturers. Unwin's *Samuel Oldknow and the Arkwrights* provides some fascinating insights into the ways a London buyer could advise a manufacturer on market requirements and encourage him to improve his product, take up new lines and drop more traditional ones.

The emergence of Manchester as the international emporium for cotton goods can be traced to a number of developments around the turn of the century. The necessity for keeping a warehouse or stockroom in Manchester soon spread beyond the Lancashire manufacturing region. In the 1790s Midlands and West Riding cotton spinners were maintaining stocks for sale in the town, and the Scots soon learned that it saved time to meet drapers there rather than travel the country towns for small orders. London warehousemen found it an advantage to keep an agent posted at the centre of manufacturing. A growing concourse of country drapers was drawn to the street markets and inns to scramble for bargains, or to jostle at the counters of the ever-increasing numbers of warehouses. Some idea of the rapidity of growth of trade is indicated by the number of warehouses in the town, which leaped from 120 in 1772 to 729 in 1815 and 955 in 1829, though many of these would be converted tenements in the original warehouse district in and around Cannon Street and High Street [52: *172–4*; 35: *80*].

In the train of provincial manufacturers and London warehousemen came overseas merchants. The technical advances of the later eighteenth century were quickly sought out by the French government, who soon had English artisans working in their country. 'You can keep a secret in a German factory, because the workers are obedient, prudent, and satisfied with a little; but the English workers are insolent, quarrelsome, adventurous and greedy for money. It is never difficult to seduce them from their employment', the French minister Calonne declared in 1788. Scattered accounts of the careers of English artisans who went abroad suggest that several showed similar personality traits in their dealings with European firms and governments and not infrequently cost their hosts much expense and trouble with little benefit. The French Revolution and the French Wars dislocated trade severely, and hampered the illegal migration of men and machinery across the Channel, so that it was not until the 1830s that French and Belgian textile technology showed signs of catching up with the British, while the Germans and other Continental countries were even further behind. One consequence was that increasing numbers of German, Dutch, Swiss, French and Italian merchants were drawn to Manchester, and after 1835 they were followed by Greeks, Spaniards, Portuguese, Russians and other traders [3: *25*; 49: *99–115*; 50: *10–48*].

The presence of this large colony of Continental merchants in Manchester must not be taken as indicative of British merchants' lack of interest in the export market. We have already noticed the existence of a vigorous export trade to Africa, America and France at the middle of the eighteenth century. There is, however, evidence to suggest that the dramatic growth of industrial production in the Industrial Revolution period severely strained the existing commercial organisation and led, after an interval, to new organisation of overseas marketing.

For most of the eighteenth century, London merchant enterprise maintained its traditional leadership, reinforced by the immigration of branches of wealthy houses from the Continent and from the English provinces. The period from about 1770 to the end of the French Wars saw the first vigorous generation of provincial manufacturers taking initiatives in marketing, often beginning with connections in the US and sometimes backed by the financial resources of well-established mercantile houses in London, Amsterdam, or one of the other Continental centres. This can be seen as part of a wider process of the extension of entrepreneurs' functions on the 'new frontiers' of British industrial expansion. However, a large turnover of firms (especially during the difficult trading conditions of the French Wars), heavy losses in some new markets (especially Latin America), and the emergence of specialisation within the industrialising regions, soon reduced this bold initiative to small proportions. The business of exporting was taken over, in the first quarter of the century, by a new three-tier structure consisting of provincial manufacturers, overseas commission merchants, and leading London merchants (soon to be called merchant banks or accepting houses). The latter took the financial strain by lending their names to ('accepting') the bills of exchange that were general means of payment in international trade.[13]

The system worked tolerably well during the periods of growth but was liable to grind to a halt during the recurrent periods of commercial crisis (1788, 1797, 1808, 1825, 1836–7, 1847–8 . . .) that hit the British and international economies. At these times, a train of bankruptcies at home and abroad evaporated confidence so quickly that it became nearly impossible for the most creditworthy manufacturers and commission houses to obtain the credit they needed, while similar firms and those with their profits invested in unsalable land or property often went to the wall. Manufacturers and merchants selling in the more distant markets, such as India, China and South America, were particularly vulnerable to sudden shifts in confidence in the financial markets. They were moreover unusually exposed to risks from ignorance of varying fashions in such distant places due to the long months in which letters and cargoes were in transit. The struggles of firms that tried to make their living in these markets make fascinating reading; a handful made fortunes and established dynasties, but most did not last a generation.

Nevertheless the overseas demand for British cottons grew dramatically. The figures recalculated by the late Ralph Davis (Tables VI and VII) make earlier estimates obsolete. From the mid 1780s to the mid 1840s, cottons came to account for something approaching half of all British exports (Table VI). Until the end of the eighteenth century, practically all the exports went to Continental Europe, North America and the West Indies, though some of the gains were at the expense of Britain's traditional export of woollen cloth. Exports to these 'old' markets continued to

Table VI Total British Exports and Exports of British Cottons 1784–1856 (£m)

	1784–6	1794–6	1804–6	1814–16	1824–6	1834–6	1844–6	1854–6
Total	12.7	21.8	37.5	44.4	35.3	46.2	58.4	102.5
Cotton	0.8	3.4	15.9	18.7	16.9	22.4	25.8	34.9
(%)	6.0	15.6	42.3	42.1	47.8	48.5	44.2	34.1

Source: adapted from [51: *15*].

Table VII Export of Cotton Goods to 'Old' and 'New' Markets 1784–1856 (£m)

	'Old markets'	'New markets'	Total	New as % of total
1784–6	0.8	0	0.8	0
1794–6	3.4	0	3.4	0
1804–6	15.2	0.7	15.9	4.4
1814–16	17.0	1.7	18.7	9.1
1824–6	12.3	4.5	16.9	26.6
1834–6	15.0	7.4	22.4	33.0
1844–6	13.2	12.6	25.8	48.8
1854–6	16.0	19.0	34.9	54.4

Source: calculated from [51: *21*].

increase in the first half of the century, but as a proportion of total exports they fell quite sharply. The introduction of the American tariff in 1815 and the removal of British restrictions on the export of machinery in 1843 are well-known bench marks in this shift, but industrialisation of the more advanced countries was the underlying cause. By contrast, the share of new markets in Latin America and the Orient showed astonishing growth, with British India taking the largest share (Table VII). This trend was accompanied by an overall deterioration in the quality of cotton fabrics produced so as to meet the needs of consumers in poorer countries.

5 Labour and Industrial Relations

IN approaching the problems of recruitment of labour and of industrial relations, it is convenient to make an initial distinction between factory and domestic labour. Increasing quantities of cotton goods at falling prices were responsible for increases in the numbers of men, women and juveniles employed in both categories for most of the period covered by this study, but in almost all other respects the characteristics of the labour force in the two sectors were quite different. They must therefore be considered separately, while recognising the important links between them.

The main problem in recruiting a factory labour force was the reluctance of workers to enter the mills, particularly in the country areas where even large workshops were unfamiliar. Arkwright had no difficulty in filling his Manchester mill in 1783 – indeed he had so many applications that he had to turn good families away – but eight miles away, at Styal, the Gregs had to scrape together a labour force from the country round about and from more distant workhouses [66: *14*]. Similar contrasts can be drawn between the experience of mill owners in Nottingham and Glasgow and those in the respective country areas [26: *164–8*; 40: *188–95*], with the proviso that the first major factory enterprise in the smaller towns might soak up the entire available labour supply. When Charles Hulbert opened a cotton mill at Shrewsbury in 1803, he found that his main difficulty was to recruit a labour force, because 'the great linen mills of Messrs Marshall, Benyon and Bage had taken the lead and the great portion of young people willing to be employed in manufactories were engaged'. Moreover, Hulbert explained, young people in agricultural areas (where the mill owners were forced to resort for water power) were slower to learn, and 'many of our instructed workpeople, notwithstanding all were engaged at regular wages for three years, left us for Manchester, Stockport, etc. . . . We soon found that if business must be carried on to any great extent where hand labour was required, it must be in the neighbourhood of like manufactories, where an advance of wages would speedily obtain the number of hands required.'[14]

The mill owners' problem can only be understood by examining the recruitment of skilled workers (machine builders, millwrights and mule spinners) separately from that of the unskilled machine minders who formed the majority of the labour force in Arkwright-type mills. The fundamental difficulty in obtaining skilled men was simply the consequence of the rapid growth of the cotton industry, which made artisans with relevant skills very much at a premium. Local newspaper advertisements, memoirs, private correspondence and high wage rates all bear testimony to the acute shortage of craftsmen whose skills could be applied to textile machine building or to the installation of water wheels and transmission systems.

The aversion of unskilled labour to employment in cotton mills largely stemmed from dislike of long, uninterrupted shifts in the mill (agricultural and domestic labour was generally more intermittent), and from the similarity of the early factories to the parish workhouses. The comparison often made between the two was not so much a question of architecture, or of the stigma attached to workhouse labour, so much as the insistence in both on close and continuous supervision of work by overseers. The consequence of this popular repugnance to factory life was that employment in the mills often represented casual labour for those who, for the time being, could find nothing better, and as late as the 1830s Samuel Greg regarded the 'restless and migratory spirit' of his mill workers as one of the main problems which troubled him as an employer.[15]

The literature on labour in the early factory system is very largely an examination of the techniques that were used to recruit and retain a workforce, and the varying responses to them. The obvious solution, as Hulbert concluded, was to offer better wage rates than one's competitors, and factory wages quickly rose above those offered to agricultural labourers and to workers in domestic industry; by 1834 it was claimed (without contradiction) that 'The wages in the cotton factories of Lancashire are the best in England', while 'the poor's rate is lower than in any other manufacturing district' [66: 47, n. 3]. However, experience soon showed that big wage packets were not the only solution, particularly where it was necessary to attract workers to isolated mill sites. At Cromford, Arkwright found it necessary to offer employment to whole families, and to build houses before they could be induced to move from Nottingham, Derby or Manchester. By 1790 he was providing a public house, a weekly market and garden allotments to retain his workforce [44: *246–60*]. The Strutts at Belper, David Dale at New Lanark, the Evanses at Darley Abbey, the Gregs at Styal, and other factory colony builders had to offer comparable incentives, but, like Arkwright, they found that the establishment of a new community was an expensive and often frustrating experience, and labour turnover continued at a very high rate [40: *188–95*; 69: *277–301*; 66: *39–43*].

The remoter mills were unable to collect a labour force even by advertising, and had to have recourse to the workhouse for their unskilled workers. The late eighteenth century was a period of rapid population growth, and many of the workhouses of London and the southern counties were glad to send consignments of pauper children to the northern mills for an apprenticeship of anything from a year to eight years, depending on their age. The pauper apprenticeship system has often been discussed in terms of exploitation of juvenile labour, and there can be no doubt that the children worked long hours for abysmal wages. But the few records of the system that have survived show that the apprenticeship system was not as cheap as free labour. It was in any case short-lived, partly because as the first generation of apprentices grew to adulthood the colony became self-perpetuating, but more especially because after the turn of the century the Arkwright-type mills were giving way to mule spinning factories, for which the availability of water power was a less important factor in location [26: *169–71*; 66: *45*].

Having collected and housed his labour force, the factory master's problems were by no means over. He had to train his machine operatives and, what was much more difficult, to induce them to become willing, obedient, regular, punctual and sober servants of his company. The most successful entrepreneurs of the Industrial Revolution were those who succeeded in imposing their system of work discipline on their labour force, and the cotton industry nurtured two or three of the outstanding figures in this small group of men of iron determination. Arkwright, according to the earliest informed account of his activities, introduced into every department of the cotton manufacture 'a system of industry, order and cleanliness, till then unknown in any manufactory where great numbers were employed together, but which he so effectually accomplished that his example may be regarded as the origin of almost all similar improvement'.[16] Like Arkwright, the first Sir Robert Peel 'introduced among his operatives that order, arrangement and sub-division of employment which form the marked characteristics of the factory system . . . he insisted on a system of punctuality and regularity which approached the discipline of military drill' [43: 56].

Pollard has analysed the methods that were used to institute and maintain this new regimen.[17] The most common deterrents were corporal punishment (for juveniles), fines for breaking the factory rules, and the threat of dismissal. However, the history of industrial relations in the industry shows that workers were not always easily intimidated, and James Montgomery's *Carding and Spinning Master's Assistant* (1832) advised that 'operatives are generally unwilling to submit to fines either for bad work or improper conduct; it seems to be a general feeling amongst them that they would much rather have the master turn them away than fine them'. Incentives, notably some system of payment by results, were also widely used. The third method, comprehensible only in the light of the employers' need to establish a novel pattern of work on a large scale, was the attempt to inculcate in the workers the mill owners' own set of values and priorities. The ultimate aspiration of the mill owner for his workpeople can be seen in the Strutts' boast of their success in bringing sober and industrious habits to Belper. The manufacturing squires at factory colonies like Belper had virtual control of the whole of the local population, but their authority must not be exaggerated. Boyson's recent study of the Ashworths of Turton (a factory colony near Bolton) portrays two brothers with a messianic sense of the cotton manufacturers' destiny as the nation's spirit of enterprise and social conscience, but adds that their employees 'accepted the social and moral standards set by the Ashworths, but politically their views were their own' [39: 135].

The early nineteenth-century literature on the cotton industry has distorted our view of the industry by giving undue prominence to the factory colonies; influential work like J. P. Kay's *Condition of the Working Classes employed in the Cotton Manufacture in Manchester*

(1832) and W. Cooke Taylor's *Notes of a Tour in the Manufacturing Districts of Lancashire* (1841) saw the model factory colony as the ideal arrangement of industrial society. But, as we have already noted, the factory colony had reached its meridian by the turn of the century, and at the end of the French Wars the urban mule spinning mills had become the predominant form of enterprise; Bolton was much more typical of the industry than Belper. Mule spinners have already been mentioned as one of the grades of artisans whose skills were very much at a premium, and their position in the structure of industrial relations must now be examined more closely. Mule spinning, as we saw in Section 2, was only mechanised slowly, and even when the automatic mule became widely adopted (after about 1835), the spinner retained his quasi-independent status. A generation after the period covered by this book, the finest spinning still depended on the sensitive touch of the mule spinner, while spinners of the medium and coarser yarns successfully contrived to introduce individuality to their machines. Catling explains that 'every operative spinner was firmly of the opinion that no two mules could ever be made alike. As a consequence he proceeded to tune and adjust each of his own particular pair of mules with little respect for the intentions of the maker or the principles of engineering. Before very long, no two mules ever were alike . . . [and] it was usually unwise to move a spinner about other than in exceptional circumstances' [7:*118, 149*].

All the available wage statistics confirm that the mule spinner was the best-paid artisan in the cotton industry (apart from overlookers) throughout the period covered by this study [e.g 1: *436, 438, 442–3*]. In the mill, he enjoyed semi-independent status, was paid on piece-rates, employed his own assistants (one or two 'piecers' for each mule) and owed responsibility only to the spinning room overlooker, who was (with the engineer, the carder and the warehouseman) answerable to the general manager. The accounts of a typical small warp and mule spinning mill of the mid 1830s, employing forty people, show that the four mule spinners and their piecers took half of the weekly wage bill of £24. Outside the mill, his status in the community was recognised by the best rooms in some public houses being marked 'Mule Spinners Only'. The mule spinners maintained their own trade unions, the Manchester one well established in 1795, and those in other centres apparently close to its heels. By 1815 the mule spinners' unions, together with those of the equally elite calico printers, impressed the employers as a 'most formidable' group of militant organisations which they had to reckon with [7: *Chs 9–10*; 43: 95–6].

In Section 2 we saw that carding and spinning became factory processes some thirty or forty years before weaving, and the consequence was an ever-increasing demand for handloom weavers, many of whom had to be recruited further and further afield from the old centres of the cotton industry. Cardwell, Birley & Hornby, the Blackburn merchants and spinners, increased their weavers from 132 in 1777 to 770 in 1788; at the other extremity of the Lancashire region, William Radcliffe was distributing warps to weavers up to thirty miles from Mellor, on the Pennine side of Stockport. By the end of the century Sir Robert Peel had fifteen depots as far apart as Blackburn in the north, Stockport in the south, Chapel-en-le-Frith (Derbyshire) to the east, and Walton (Liverpool) to the west. Very often the growth points were no more than a mile or two out of town, as surviving loomhouses on the Pennine scarp above Oldham and Rochdale show, but in other instances villages at a distance from the established urban centres were suddenly brought to new prosperity by migrating capital. Burnley, for instance, because a major centre of the cotton industry when several Bolton merchant-manufacturers 'began to employ a great number of weavers and spinners in the cotton branch'. Similarly, the skills of the muslin weavers of Paisley induced Peels, Arkwrights and other Lancashire cotton firms to invest capital in developments there, and so successful was this partnership that when John Marshall (the Leeds flex spinner) visited Scotland in 1803, he maintained that Manchester fine spinning and Paisley production of fine fabrics were the two complementary branches of the cotton industry.[18]

Bythell's important study of *The Handloom Weavers* shows the difficulties of acquiring reliable estimates of the total number of cotton weavers before 1833, but it is possible to calculate the order of magnitude (see Table VIII). In 1811, G. A. Lee and Thomas Ainsworth conducted a census of mule spinning and concluded that it employed 150,000 weavers and was responsible for two-thirds of the output of the industry. The other third obviously came from the sector operating Arkwright's technique and, *pro*

*Table VIII   Estimates of the Numbers of Domestic Workers in the Cotton Industry,
1795–1833*

	Handloom weavers (cotton only)	Auxiliaries		Framework knitters
1795	75,000[a]	15,000[b]	1782	20,000[c]
1811	225,000[a]	45,000[b]	1812	29,600[c]
1833	250,000[b]	50,000[b]	1844	48,500[c]

Sources: [a] G. J. French, *The Life and Times of Samuel Crompton* (1859; new edn 1970) pp. 275–8.
  [b] D. Bythell, *The Handloom Weavers* (1969) pp. 54–7, 86.
  [c] Hosiery statistics most conveniently summarised in D. M. Smith, 'The British Hosiery Industry at the Middle of the Ninteeenth Century', *Transactions of the Institute of British Geographers*, XXXI (1963) 129.

rata, must have found employment for 75,000 weavers, making 225,000 in all. Until the mid 1790s the mule sector was still very small, and after that time the Arkwright sector ceased to grow, so that 75,000 cotton weavers would approach a fair estimate for 1795. These figures are consistent with abundant literary evidence of the rapid growth of handloom weaving from around 1780 to the end of the French Wars. The number of domestic framework knitters also multiplied, but unfortunately there are no statistics to distinguish cotton frames from those engaged on knitting wool, silk and linen. The number of workers in the domestic sector of the cotton industry may be compared with 220,000 employed in nearly 1200 mills in Great Britain and Ireland in 1833 [*1*: *394*]. Clearly, the number of domestic workers exceeded the number of factory workers until at least the mid 1830s, when the power loom won the confidence of the mill owners.

The dispersion of the handloom weavers over a large part of Lancashire and the adjacent parts of Cheshire, Derbyshire and the West Riding, as well as the Glasgow–Paisley area, prevented them from uniting to defend their living standards, and their protracted capitulation to the power loom constitutes one of the most miserable chapters of social history. Inevitably, such pathos has attracted a great deal of writing and a variety of interpretations, often flavoured by the political presuppositions of the contributors to the debate. Most recently, Bythell, and Thompson's *The*

Making of the English Working Class, have offered sharply contrasting explanations of the significance of the downward trend of weavers' incomes after the French Wars. Thompson sees self-employed weavers, yeoman weavers and journeyman weavers all thrust down into the same debased proletariat, while Bythell maintains that by 1815 cotton handloom weaving had largely become an unskilled and casual occupation which provided part-time work for women and children, a reservoir of labour that was accustomed to flow into varying channels with the changing seasons and state of trade. While admitting that 'there was terrible suffering in some districts in the 1820s, 1830s, and early 1840s' (particularly in fringe areas like Burnley, Colne and Padiham, where few new mills were being built or equipped with power looms), Bythell thinks that 'most of the handloom weavers in the cotton industry were absorbed into alternative employment with remarkable speed and ease' [65: *271*]. This divergence of views, both depending on incomplete evidence, can only be evaluated when we have the benefit of more local studies, particularly those founded on parish registers and the census enumerators' returns of 1841, 1851 and 1861. In the meantime, the only safe comment that can be made is that the standards of living of workers in the cotton industry, like those in the economy at large, show a bewildering variety of contrasts, not only between occupations, but over periods of time and between different localities.

6 The Role of Cotton in the Growth of the Economy

THE period between about 1450 and 1750 saw relatively few mechanical inventions introduced into the European textile industries; the stocking frame at the end of the sixteenth century and the Dutch loom in the seventeenth appear to be the only conspicuous exceptions to this generalisation. The great burst of invention that began with Arkwright and Crompton has some roots reaching down earlier in the century, but the desultory reception of Kay's flying shuttle and Lewis Paul's roller spinning in the 1730s and 1740s occurred in a different economic climate from the last thirty years of the century. Most of the explanations that are offered on the causes of this unprecedented period of technical development have been familiar to historians for a long time: a chronic shortage of yarn and steeply rising costs as weavers adopting the flying shuttle had to draw their yarn supplies from domestic spinners further and further away; the physical qualities of cotton, which make it peculiarly amenable to mechanical handling; and the high elasticity of supply of raw cotton from the rapidly growing United States.

The growing consumption of cotton must have been initiated by an increase in demand and on this point Eversley provides some help. He postulated that between 1750 and 1780 the number of households in the middle income range (£50 to £400 p.a.) rose from 15 per cent of the population of England to 20 or even 25 per cent. In Eversley's model the foundation of the Industrial Revolution was laid by the sale of articles of everyday life to this 'middle class' of consumers.[19] Cotton fits well into this thesis in the middle decades of the eighteenth century in so far as the widespread and growing sale of linen mixtures and printed goods largely issued from this sector of the population, and formed the basis from which sales of cheaper machine-spun and printed cottons accelerated after about 1780, aided by a shift in fashion.

The role of cotton in the British economy in the last two decades of the eighteenth century has been the subject of lively debate following the publication of Rostow's 'take-off' theory of economic growth. Searching for a framework in which to set the evolution of modern industrial societies, he suggested that there were five stages of economic growth: the traditional society, the satisfaction of preconditions for 'take-off', the 'take-off', the drive to maturity, and the age of high mass consumption. In Rostow's words, 'the "take-off" consists, in essence, of the achievement of rapid growth in a limited group of sectors, where modern industrial techniques are applied'. He identified cotton textiles as the leading sector in 'take-off' in Britain, and defined the take-off period as 1783–1802, citing the spectacular increase in the import of raw cotton in the decades 1781–91 (319 per cent) and 1791–1801 (67 per cent) as his empirical support [74, *4–12, 53–4*].

The idea of cotton making the decisive advance that impelled the whole economy forward into rapid industrial growth is evidently a bold one, and provoked critical examinations by a number of economists and historians, particularly by Phyllis Deane and W. A. Cole. They calculated that it is unlikely that cotton contributed more than 5 per cent of the British national income by the end of Rostow's take-off (see Table IX). The figure (assuming for a moment that it is correct) demonstrates that cotton was already making an impressive contribution to the economy. But Habakkuk and Deane also calculated that iron was making an equivalent contribution to the economy at the period, and if their figures are accepted it is difficult to understand how cotton alone can be labelled *the* leading sector [72: *71*].

However, Deane and Cole's estimates of the value of the output of the cotton industry are admitted to be 'highly tentative', and any calculation of its contribution to British national income must be even more hazardous. These calculations depend on a sequence of estimates extracted from the controversial pamphlet literature of the period (see Table IX col. (2)). The best that can be said for them is that they appear to have been synthesised from statistics of the value of retained imports (i.e imports minus re-exports), but (Table IX col. (3)), shows that the different estimators multiplied these figures by anything from 2.0 to 5.3, an inconsistency that hints strongly at the possibility of error. The

Table IX Estimates of the Output of the Cotton Industry and its Contribution to National Income, 1760–1817

Years	(1) Retained imports (£m)	(2) Gross value of output (£m)	(3) Multiplier (2) ÷ (1)	(4) Value added (£m) (2)−(1)	(5) National income (£m)	(6) Value added as % of national income
1760	0.2	0.6	3.0	0.4		
1772–4	0.2	0.9	4.5	0.6		
1781–3	1.0	4.0	4.0	2.0	c. 160	c. 1%
1784–6	1.6	5.4	3.4	3.8		
1787–9	2.3	7.0	3.0	4.7		
1795–7	2.6	10.0	4.0	7.4		
1798–1800	5.7	11.1	2.0	5.4		
1801–3	4.0	15.0	3.7	11.0	230	4–5%
1805–7	4.5	18.9	4.2	14.4		
1811–13	5.3	28.3	5.3	23.0	301	7–8%
1815–17	8.3	30.0	3.7	21.7		

Source: [71: *185, 188*]. Table 42 has been simplified and col. (3) inserted by present author (see text).

value of the imported raw material was more than doubled at the spinning stage (see Table V), and one suspects that the estimates used by Deane and Cole neglect value added at the bleaching, dyeing and (above all) printing stages. Peels, the leading printers at the end of the eighteenth century, sold their rolls at £4 to £5 each, but it seems they were worth only £1.30 as white calico [43: 79].

The possible errors in Table IX can be illustrated in another way. Their estimate for 1798–1800 may appear to be an exception to my remarks about the limitations of Deane and Cole's figures for gross output, as it was made by Eden for the Globe Insurance Company. Eden's original figure was £10 million, but the previous year the secretaries of the Sun Fire Office, Royal Exchange and Phoenix insurance companies procured information 'from cotton spinners and from an engineer who has built many mills' and calculated that the value of the output of the industry 'amounts to about £20 million'. The difference between the two estimates can be explained by the London insurance companies' determination to take note of bleach and printing works.[20] In 1834 capital invested in the finishing trades was equal to half that in spinning and weaving (see Table IV), and though there is no direct relationship between capital invested and value of output, it is reasonable to recognise this as a further indication of the importance of bleaching, dyeing and printing. Until more is known about the finishing trades it is not possible to be too emphatic, but it seems that Deane and Cole's figures may underestimate the contribution of the industry to the gross national product. If £20m is a realistic estimate of the gross value of output in 1797, value added was £17m, and cotton was already contributing over 7 per cent of the national income.

The importance of the subject and the doubts about the validity of Deane and Cole's figures have induced other econometric historians to enter the field. C. K. Harley has recalculated the size of the various sectors of the British economy from 1700 to 1841 by working back from the occupational data of the 1841 census of population, the earliest to provide comprehensive information. His new indices imply that eighteenth-century industry was nearly twice as large as previous estimates indicated so that its subsequent transformation was less dramatic than the phase 'Industrial Revolution' or Rostow's concept of it would suggest [73: 267–89].

The literary evidence surveyed in the earlier part of this book could offer some support for this interpretation in so far as there is ample evidence of a strong domestic industry and vigorous growth of the proto-factory in the eighteenth century, while the early cotton mills were on a more modest scale than the first generation of economic historians surmised. N. F. R. Crafts, in a difficult book on *British Economic Growth during the Industrial Revolution* (Oxford, 1985) has taken up Harley's work and incorporated it with a range of other econometric work to offer another interpretation of the process of economic growth. He agrees with Harley that earlier estimates 'exaggerate growth' and that some of Deane and Cole's estimates are 'implausible', but believes that 'It is the experience of the revolutionised cotton industry that stands apart' [70: 30–3]. In other words, we are back to an interpretation of British economic growth that assigns a unique role to cotton, albeit within a more gradual overall growth of the economy.

However, before rushing to embrace the latest thesis on offer, we should pause once again to check the supporting material. At the outset of his book, Crafts recognises that estimates of economic growth prior to the mid nineteenth century can never be more than 'controlled conjectures' [70: 9], though this does not restrain him and other econometricians from reaching some very firm conclusions from them. This is not the place to embark on any systematic assessment of this research, but so far as the cotton industry is concerned, it is worth noticing that Crafts simply adopts Deane and Cole's estimates, despite the criticism made in the first edition of this book in 1972 and despite his own trenchant criticism of other haphazard calculations. If Harley's estimates are combined with a much more realistic view of the growth of cotton than that offered by Deane and Cole and by Crafts, we should presumably conclude identifying an industry whose contribution to the economy appeared quite outstanding, or at any rate more than that so far recognised by any of them.

Fortunately the literary evidence is less confusing and offers some undisputed evidence of the wide-ranging contribution of cotton to the growth of the British economy between 1770 and mid nineteenth century. Arkwright's techniques were not difficult to apply to worsted spinning, and worsted mills modelled on his cotton mills were soon being built in the hosiery districts of the Midlands and in parts of Lancashire, the West Riding and Scotland

[9: *25*–*7*; 32: *75*–*95*]. Cotton displaced some fabrics formerly made in worsted, but the overall effect was to stimulate it, particularly for new lines such as carpets.[21] In the linen industry, John Marshall of Leeds inaugurated the factory system by adopting Arkwright's techniques and factory organisation.[22] Wool was unsuitable for roller spinning, but easily succumbed to the mule.[23] The hosiery and lace industries were still organised under a species of the domestic system, but benefited from cheaper and finer yarns. When the power loom won acceptance in cotton, it was soon being modified for wool, worsted, linen and silk yarns. If the cotton industry did not lead the national economy, it certainly led the British and (until the early 1830s) the European and American textile industry in its technology, in the development of the factory system, and in standardised production for the popular market.

It is also possible to demonstrate some direct connections between the cotton industry and the birth of new activities in other sectors of the economy. The first multi-storey cotton mills built in the 1790s introduced the idea of iron-framed buildings, a technical innovation with far-reaching consequences for architecture and the building industry. Early in the next decade these mills were among the first public buildings to be lit by gas, and the excitement with which contemporaries gazed at the illuminated mills guaranteed the spread of the technique [14: *Ch. 8*]. The early factory colonies introduced new standards of working-class housing which were widely copied in the surrounding areas and helped to effect a general improvement of housing standards in the Midlands and North of England.[24] The pioneers of factory production, Arkwright, Strutt, Peel and others, had to build most of their own plant, and in so doing established the practice of using specialised machinery for mass production of components such as spindles, rollers, gear wheels and bolts [43: *39*]. The idea of *standardised* production of cotton machinery was introduced in the 1830s by Richard Roberts, the Manchester inventor of the automatic mule, and was quickly carried over into other branches of engineering, such as the building of railway locomotives [12: *478*]. The earliest railway line built for regular passenger and goods services linked Liverpool and Manchester, and the first major phase of railway construction in the 1840s Lancashire investors contributed most of the capital.[25] Many of the ironfounding, engineering and chemical firms in Lancashire, the Glasgow region, the West Riding and the Vale of Trent (Nottingham region) owed their birth or growth to the enormous stimulus given to the regional economies during Rostow's 'take-off' period [12: Ch. 13; 26: 147–53]. These connections between cotton and other developments in the economy are clearly very important, but their development took place after the 'take-off' period, and they are not the same as the direct multiplier effect involved in the argument of Deane and Cole. However, they could reasonably be included in Rostow's definition of the 'forward effects' of the growth of the leading sector, a dimension that is practically impossible to measure.

The controversy that followed the publication of the Rostow thesis focused particular attention on the period between 1780 and 1880. One of the merits of Deane and Cole's work is that it identifies other periods of expansion, and draws attention to the 'peak period of growth' in cotton in the quarter-century after 1815, when raw cotton imports multiplied four and a half times. Data from Ellison, a well-informed nineteenth-century writer, have been reproduced by Deane and Cole to indicate that payments to labour (wages, salaries, etc.) took a falling percentage of the gross receipts of the cotton industry in the 1820s, 1830s and 1840s, and consequently they advance the suggestion that the spectacular growth of the quarter-century was financed by 'a marked increase in the share of profit in net output' [71: 189]. The point, if it can be substantiated, has important implications for the hotly debated issue of the standard of living, as well as for investment trends. However, business histories offer no support for this thesis. They show that Ashworth Brothers, M'Connel & Kennedy, and Kirkman Finlay, respectively leading cotton firms in Bolton, Manchester and Glasgow, were all experiencing falling profit margins in these decades. Lee concludes his study of M'Connel & Kennedy with the view that 'productivity did not increase quick enough in this period to offset the declining [raw] cotton/yarn price margin's effects' [39: 27–33; 46: 138–43]. Of course it might be argued that these three big firms were not representative of the whole industry. In the first half of the nineteenth century the average capacity of cotton mills increased thirteen times (see Table X) as the numerous small entrepreneurs struggled to assimilate the achievements of the pioneers of factory production, and it seems reasonable to suppose that rapid strides in efficiency were

Table X   Number and Average Size of Cotton Mills in Britain, 1797–1850

	No. of spinning factories	Approx. annual UK import of cotton (million lb)	Average annual input per factory (lb)
1797	c.900	30	33,000
1833–4	c.1,125	300	270,000
1850	1,407	600	430,000

Sources: Table III, and E. Baines, *History of the Cotton Manufacture* (1835) p. 394; B. R. Mitchell and P. Deane, *Abstract of British Historical Statistics* (1962) pp. 178–9.

accompanied by thin but improving profit margins. However, we must wait for some more business histories before this problem can be decided.

Turning from investment and production (the supply side) to domestic and overseas markets (the demand side), it is necessary first of all to emphasise that British superiority in quality production had secured a firm foothold in consumer tastes before the era of the great inventors. Until recently, the superiority of eighteenth-century French copperplate cotton prints was taken for granted, but the discovery of English pattern books with a wide variety of floral and pictorial designs of high quality has convinced art historians that London and Dublin, rather than Paris, perfected the techniques of designing, engraving and colouring of printed textiles in the third quarter of the eighteenth century. The history of the ceramic and fine metal industries in the English provinces is dominated by the names of Wedgwood and Boulton, entrepreneurs whose reputation and commercial success were based on the exploitation of a large variety of tastefully designed goods, and it is at least plausible that Lancashire's great achievement was based on comparable flair. However Lévy-Leboyer, a leading French economic historian, has won support for a theory suggesting that in the Industrial Revolution British cotton manufacturers concentrated on mass production, compelling the French producers to concentrate on quality [58: *175*]. Kusamitsu, a Japanese scholar, believes that the new type of British entrepreneur who rose to power in the period subverted the traditional craftsman-designer [61: *77–95*]. Most recently, the question has been taken up by British art historians who, concentrating on surviving fabrics rather than contentious literature of the period, have been impressed by the ingenuity of Lancashire textile printers and commended many of the designs which are far removed from the popular conception of Victorian drabness [59: *102–15*; 60: *181–9*]. Comparison of the careers of two leading Lancashire printers of the first half of the nineteenth century, James Thompson who concentrated on high-quality designed goods and John Brooks who produced large quantities of cheap imitations for the domestic and Indian markets, reveals the existence of high profits and catastrophic losses in both [58: *183–92*]. Between them lay a whole range of printers specialising in particular markets, techniques or fashions, all more or less vulnerable to sudden shifts in demand from the fickleness of fashion or taste at home or abroad. In this period British textile producers were out to win the world market for both cheap mass-produced *and* quality fabrics, and to a remarkable degree they succeeded.

In practice the two aspects of consumer demand cannot be separated for, as the work on Wedgwood and Boulton illustrates, capturing the quality market is the key to large popular sales. A recent book on *The Birth of a Consumer Society* is a fresh reminder of the passion for novelty and buying that seized all classes in eighteenth-century England, and of the fluidity of a society in which constant changes in dress like all other material possessions, affected all ranks of society with remarkable speed.[26] Overseas trade was important to the modest industrial growth that was going on before the Industrial Revolution, but was not essential to the 'take-off' [51: *63*]. The foundations of the success of cotton in the Industrial Revolution lay in a consumer society with seemingly unsatiable appetite for new fashion, and a corps of entrepreneurs with the ingenuity, versatility and resource to feed that demand and then to sustain the growth of the industry by increasing overseas sales, first in traditional markets and then in distant parts of the world.

References

1. M. T. Wild, 'The Saddleworth Parish Registers', *Textile History*, I (1969).
2. W. Radcliffe, *Origins of Power Loom Weaving* (Stockport, 1828), pp. 10, 65–6.
3. J. D. Chambers, *Nottinghamshire in the Eighteenth Century* (1932), Ch. 5.
4. W. H. Chaloner, *People and Industries* (1963), Ch. 1.
5. D. S. L. Cardwell, 'Power Technologies and the Advance of Science 1700–1825', *Technology and Culture*, VI (1965).
6. Calculations based on data in Notts CRO, Portland Mss DD4P 79/63, and Public Record Office (PRO) Chatham Mss 30/8/187.
7. Radcliffe, op. cit., p. 62.
8. James Montgomery, *Carding and Spinning Master's Assistant* (Glasgow, 1832), p. 170, and *A Practical Detail of the Cotton Manufacture in the USA ... compared with that of Great Britain* (Glasgow, 1840) pp. 75–81; A. Ure, *The Cotton Manufacture of Great Britain* (1836), pp. 297–313.
9. E. Butterworth, *Historical Sketches of Oldham* (1856) pp. 140, 153, 183, shows that from 1821 to 1825 the number of cotton manufacturers rose from 60 to 139.
10. Notts CRO, DD4P 79/63.
11. PRO, B1/124, p. 21.
12. Abraham Rees, *Cyclopaedia*, article on 'Cotton' (*c*. 1808). S. D. Chapman, *The Devon Cloth Industry in the 18th C.* (Torquay, 1978), pp. xx–xxiii.
13. S. D. Chapman, *The Rise of Merchant Banking* (1984), Ch. 1.
14. C. Hulbert, *Memoirs of Seventy Years of an Eventful Life* (1852), p. 195.
15. A. Redford, *Labour Migration in England 1800–1850* (1926), Ch. 2.
16. Rees, *Cyclopaedia*, article on 'Cotton'.
17. S. Pollard, *The Genesis of Modern Management* (1965), Ch. 5.

18. S. D. Chapman, Introduction to G. J. French, *The Life and Times of Samuel Crompton* (1859; new edn, 1970), p. vi.
19. D. E. C. Eversley, 'The Home Market and Economic Growth in England, 1750–80', in E. L. Jones and G. E. Mingay (eds), *Land, Labour and Population in the Industrial Revolution* (1967).
20. PRO, Chatham Mss., 30/8/187.
21. Rees, *Cyclopaedia*, article on 'Worsted Manufacture' (c. 1818).
22. W. G. Rimmer, *Marshalls of Leeds, Flax Spinners* (1960).
23. D. T. Jenkins and K. G. Ponting, *The British Wool Textile Industry 1770–1914* (1982) pp. 110, 264–5.
24. S. D. Chapman, 'Workers' Housing in the Cotton Factory Colonies 1770–1850', *Textile History*, VII (1976).
25. S. Broadbridge, 'The Early Capital Market: the Lancashire and Yorkshire Railway', *Economic History Review*, VIII (1955–6).
26. N. McKendrick, J. Brewer and J. H. Plumb, *The Birth of a Consumer Society* (1982).

Select Bibliography

GENERAL WORKS
[1] E. Baines, *History of the Cotton Manufacture in Great Britain* (1835), 2nd edn (Cass, 1966). Now used only as a reference work, though quite readable.
[2] D. A. Farnie, *The English Cotton Industry and the World Market 1815–96* (Oxford, 1979). Concentrates on the structure of the industry and its world market; as the title implies, much of this book covers the period after the Industrial Revolution.
[3] M. Lévy-Leboyer, *Les Banques européenes et l'industrialisation internationale* (Paris, 1964). Includes valuable insights into British economic development, especially in textiles.
[4] G. Turnbull, *A History of the Calico Printing Industry in Great Britain* (Altrincham, 1951). Useful outline but parts of the book now superseded (see [43], [57]–[63]).
[5] A. P. Wadsworth and J. de L. Mann, *The Cotton Trade and Industrial Lancashire 1600–1780* (Manchester, 1931). Remains the standard work on the early period.

TECHNOLOGY
[6] C. Aspin, *James Hargreaves and the Spinning Jenny* (Helmshore, 1964). The best account of the inventor and his invention.
[7] H. Catling, *The Spinning Mule* (Newton Abbot, 1970). Historical perspective by a textile technologist; for an economist's view see [67].
[8] S. D. Chapman, 'The Cost of Power in the Industrial Revolution', *Midland History*, I (1970) 1–23. A study of Robinsons, the earliest firm to buy a steam engine for direct transmission to cotton-spinning machinery.
[9] S. D. Chapman 'The Arkwright Mills', *Industrial Archaeology Review*, VI (1981), 5–27. Describes the Arkwright prototype mill and revises the widely-quoted estimate of the number built by 1788 from 150 to over 200.

[10] H. J. Habakkuk, *American and British Technology in the Nineteenth Century. The Search for Labour-saving Inventions* (Cambridge, 1962). Classic study with valuable insights on the cotton industry.
[11] R. L. Hills, 'Hargreaves, Arkwright and Crompton. Why Three Inventors?' *Textile History*, X (1979), 114–26. Analyses the merits of the key inventions in layman's language.
[12] A. E. Musson and E. Robinson, *Science and Technology in the Industrial Revolution* (Manchester, 1969). Includes useful essays on the Lancashire chemical and engineering industries, showing how they grew out of the cotton industry.
[13] M. E. Rose, 'Samuel Crompton (1735–1827) Inventor of the Spinning Mule', *Transactions of the Lancashire and Cheshire Antiquarian Society*, LXXV (1965–6), 11–32. Brings G. J. French's biography, *Life and Times of Samuel Crompton* (1859), up to date.
[14] Jennifer Tann, *The Development of the Factory* (1970). Based on the valuable records of Boulton and Watt, the steam engine patentees who supplied many early cotton mills. Well illustrated.
[15] Jennifer Tann, 'Richard Arkwright and Technology', *History*, LVIII (1973) 29–44. Suggests that Arkwright's most original contribution was in production engineering, rather than spinning or mechanical power.
[16] G. N. Tunzelmann, *Steam Power and British Industrialisation to 1860* (Oxford, 1978). An econometric analysis of the adoption of steam power showing why water power was more widely favoured until so late as the 1840s.

CAPITAL

[17] M. Blaug, 'The Productivity of Capital in the Lancashire Cotton Industry during the Nineteenth Century', *Economic History Review*, 2nd ser., XIII (1961), 358–81. Assembles and analyses contemporary estimates for the period 1833 to 1886.
[18] S. D. Chapman, 'Fixed Capital Formation in the British Cotton Industry 1770–1815', *Economic History Review*, 2nd ser., XXIII (1970), 235–66. Synthesises new estimates of capital formation from fire insurance registers, explaining why fixed capital needs were lower than had been supposed.

An extended version of this essay, taking the analysis down to 1835, is in J. P. P. Higgins and S. Pollard (eds), *Aspects of Capital Investment in Great Britain 1750–1850* (1971), pp. 51–107.

[19] S. D. Chapman, 'Financial Restraints on the Growth of Firms in the Cotton Industry, 1790–1850', *Economic History Review*, XXXII (1979), 50–69. Argues that the numerous small firms and high mortality of firms typical of Lancashire cotton were consequence of long-term shortages of working capital.

[20] V. A. C. Gattrell, 'Labour, Power and the Size of Firms in Lancashire Cotton in the Second Quarter of the Nineteenth Century', *Economic History Review*, XXX (1977), 95–125. Assembles data to show the 'small to middling' size of most firms in Lancashire cotton at the period and considers some explanations.

[21] F. Stuart Jones, 'The Financial Needs of the Cotton Industry during the Industrial Revolution: A Survey of Recent Research', *Textile History*, XVI (1985), 45–68. A helpful guide to and summary of the debate.

[22] F. Stuart Jones, 'The Cotton Industry and Joint-Stock Banking in Manchester', *Business History*, XX (1978), 165–85. Chronicles the formation of Manchester banks.

[23] M. B. Rose, 'The Role of the Family in Providing Capital and Managerial Talent in Samuel Greg and Co 1784–1840', *Business History*, XIX (1977). A useful case-study illustrating some familiar features of the cotton industry at the period. See also [45].

[24] S. Shapiro, *Capital and the Cotton Industry* (Cornell, New York, 1967). Written before scholarly debate on the subject took off, this book is now mainly interesting for case-studies.

THE STRUCTURE OF THE INDUSTRY

(A) Interpretations

[25] S. D. Chapman, 'The Textile Factory before Arkwright: A Typology of Factory Development', *Business History Review*, XLVIII (1974), 451–78. Distinguishes the workshop, factory, and proto-factory, and compares their various fixed costs in the eighteenth century.

[26] S. D. Chapman, *The Early Factory Masters* (Newton Abbot, 1967). An analysis of the origins of enterprise and problems faced by cotton mill owners in the midland counties in the eighteenth century.

[27] J. H. Clapham, 'Some Factory Statistics of 1815–16', *Economic Journal*, XXV (1915), 475–9. Useful reference article.

[28] F. Crouzet, *The First Industrialists. The Problem of Origins* (Cambridge, 1985). The best contribution to the self-help debate; digests numerous studies of the cotton industry to demonstrate upward social mobility.

[29] G. W. Daniels, 'Samuel Crompton's Census of the Cotton Industry in 1811', *Economic History*, II (1930–3), 107–110. Useful reference article.

[30] K. Honeyman, *Origins of Enterprise, Business Leadership in the Industrial Revolution* (Manchester, 1982). Examines the origins of Arkwright-type mill owners and Bolton and Oldham mule spinners.

[31] A. Howe, *The Cotton Masters 1830–1860* (Oxford, 1984). The main focus of this work is political, but the first two chapters provide a valuable reconstruction of the second-generation 'millocracy'.

[32] D. T. Jenkins, 'The Cotton Industry in Yorkshire, 1789–1900', *Textile History*, X (1979), 75–95. Surveys a neglected area of the cotton industry.

[33] R. Lloyd-Jones and A. A. Le Roux, 'The Size of Firms in the Cotton Industry 1815–41', *Economic History Review*, XXXIII (1980), 72–82. Draws on Manchester rate books to emphasise the importance of middle- rather than small-sized firms; see also [19] and [20] for the debate on the size of firms.

[34] R. Lloyd-Jones and A. A. Le Roux, 'Marshall and the Birth and Death of Firms: the Growth and Size Distribution of Firms in the Early 19th Century Cotton Industry', *Business History* XXIV (1982), 140–55. Rejects Marshall's 'trees in the forest' concept of industrial growth as a model for understanding the early cotton industry.

[35] R. Lloyd-Jones and M. J. Lewis, 'The Economic Structure of "Cottonopolis" in 1815', *Textile History*, XVII (1986), 71–89. Examines Manchester warehouses in 1815 to make comparison with the scale of investment in mills.

[36] H. B. Rodgers, 'The Lancashire Cotton Industry in 1840',

Transactions of the Institute of British Geographers, XXVIII (1960), 135–53. Concentrates on the spatial distribution of the industry, complementing [37] and [38].
[37] A. J. Taylor, 'Concentration and Specialisation in the Lancashire Cotton Industry, 1825–50', *Economic History Review*, 2nd ser., I (1948–9), 114–22. Should be read in conjunction with [36] and [38].
[38] K. L. Wallwork, 'The Calico Printing Industry of Lancastria in the 1840s', *Transactions of the Institute of British Geographers*, XLV (1968), 143–56. Complements H. B. Rodger's analysis of the distribution of the cotton industry, focusing on the most important of the finishing branches.

(B) Case-studies of firms
[39] R. Boyson, *The Ashworth Cotton Enterprise* (Oxford, 1970). A valuable study of one of the best known second-generation firms.
[40] John Butt (ed.), *Robert Owen, Prince of Cotton Spinners* (Newton Abbot, 1971). A collection of essays on Owen and his famous community at New Lanark.
[41] W. H. Chaloner, 'Robert Owen, Peter Drinkwater and the Early Factory System in Manchester 1788–1800', *Bulletin of the John Rylands Library*, XXXVII (1954), 78–102. Provides the Manchester context of R. Owen, *Life of Robert Owen* (1854).
[42] S. D. Chapman, 'James Longsdon (1745–1821), Farmer and Fustian Manufacturer: the Small Firm in the Early English Cotton Industry', *Textile History*, I (1970), 265–92. Examines the problems of a typical small first-generation enterprise.
[43] S. D. Chapman and S. Chassagne, *European Textile Printers in the Eighteenth Century: A Study of Peel and Oberkampf* (1981). A comparative study of the most successful first-generation British and French factory owners in this branch of the cotton industry.
[44] R. S. Fitton and A. P. Wadsworth, *The Strutts and the Arkwrights* (Manchester, 1958). An outstanding business history, but now in need of some updating with more recent research.
[45] Mary B. Rose, *The Gregs of Quarry Bank Mill. The Rise and Decline of a Family Firm 1750–1914* (Cambridge, 1986). The

only history of a cotton dynasty, a nice introduction to the famous National Trust cotton mill village near Manchester.
[46] C. H. Lee, *A Cotton Enterprise 1795–1840: A History of M'Connel and Kennedy, Fine Cotton Spinners* (Manchester, 1972). Examines the valuable records of this important Manchester firm of mule spinners.
[47] Robert Owen, *Life of Robert Owen* (1857). The most illuminating autobiography covering the early years of the factory system in Lancashire and Scotland, but see also [40; 41].
[48] G. Unwin *et al.*, *Samuel Oldknow and the Arkwrights* (Manchester, 1924). A pioneer business history that is still important.

MARKETING

(A) Supply of cotton and selling organisation
[49] S. D. Chapman, 'The Foundations of the English Rothschilds: N. M. Rothschild as a Textile Merchant 1799–1811', *Textile History*, VIII (1977), 99–115. Case-study of Anglo-Continental trade.
[50] S. D. Chapman, 'The International Houses: the Continental Contribution to British Commerce 1800–1860', *Journal of European Economic History*, VI (1977), 5–48. Explains how and why textiles were marketed in Europe by firms of Continental origin.
[51] Ralph Davis, *The Industrial Revolution and British Overseas Trade* (Leicester, 1979). Recalculation of the volumes and values of British imports and exports in the period; indispensable.
[52] M. M. Edwards, *The Growth of the British Cotton Trade 1780–1815* (Manchester, 1969). Closely examines the commercial development of the industry during its most rapid period of growth.
[53] F. E. Hyde, B. B. Parkinson and S. Mariner, 'The Cotton Broker and the Rise of the Liverpool Cotton Market', *Economic History Review*, VIII (1955–6), 75–83. Revision of an early classic, T. Ellison's *Cotton Trade of Great Britain* (1886).
[54] J. R. Killick, 'Bolton, Ogden and Co: A Case Study in Anglo-American Trade 1790–1850', *Business History Review*, XLVIII (1974), 501–19. An American firm exporting cotton to Europe.

[55] A. Slaven, 'A Glasgow Firm in the Indian Market: John Lean and Sons, Muslin Weavers', *Business History Review*, XLIII (1969), 496–522. Informative case-study of the problems of supplying Britain's principal export market last century.

[56] D. M. Williams, 'Liverpool Merchants and the Cotton Trade 1820–1850' in J. R. Harris (ed.), *Liverpool and Merseyside* (1969), pp. 182–211. Measures the structure of the Liverpool mercantile community in its heyday.

(B) Consumerism and fashion

[57] Aileen Ribeiro, *Dress in Eighteenth Century Europe 1715–89* (1985). The best-informed of a range of costume histories.

[58] S. D. Chapman, 'Quality versus Quantity in the Industrial Revolution: the Case of Textile Printing', *Northern History*, XXI (1985), 175–92. Argues that the French by no means dominated the production of 'up-market' cotton prints [cf. 3: *60*].

[59] H. Clark, 'The Design and Designing of Lancashire Printed Calicoes during the first half of the 19th Century', *Textile History*, XV (1984), 101–18. A fashion historian's view.

[60] D. Greysmith, 'Patterns, Piracy and Protection in the Textile Printing Industry', *Textile History*, XIV (1983), 163–94. The role of fashion design and plagiarism in cotton printing.

[61] T. Kusamitsu, 'British Industrialisation and Design before the Great Exhibition', *Textile History*, XII (1981), 77–95. Argues for deterioration in standards of British design in calico printing and other industries as a consequence of the factory system; for another view see [58] and [63].

[62] B. Lemire, 'Developing Consumerism and the Readymade Clothing Trade in Britain 1750–1800', *Textile History*, XV (1984), 21–44. Considers various factors in the demand side of the growth of the cotton industry.

[63] F. M. Montgomery, *Printed Textiles: English and American Cottons and Linens 1700–1850* (1970). An attractive survey of the early history of calico printing by an art historian.

LABOUR AND INDUSTRIAL RELATIONS

[64] M. H. Mackenzie, 'Calver Mill and its Owners', *Derbyshire Archaeological Journal*, LXXXIII (1963) 24–34. Arkwright-type factory colony with London connections.

[65] D. Bythell, *The Handloom Weaver* (Cambridge, 1969). Should be read in conjunction with E. P. Thompson, *The Making of the English Working Class* (1963), as explained in Section 5 of the text.

[66] Frances Collier, *The Family Economy of the Working Classes in the Cotton Industry* (Manchester, 1965). Analyses family income of employees in some early cotton mills.

[67] M. Cruickshank, *Children and Industry: Child Health and Welfare in North-West Textile Towns during the Nineteenth Century* (Manchester, 1981). Useful study of a large literature.

[68] William Lazonick, 'Industrial Relations and Technical Change: The Case of the Self-Acting Mule', *Cambridge Journal of Economics*, III (1979) 231–62. Shows that mule spinners were an elite of skilled workmen, rather than an exploited proletariat; see also [7].

[69] Jean Lindsay, 'An Early Industrial Community. The Evans' Cotton Mill at Darley Abbey, Derbyshire 1783–1810', *Business History Review*, XXXIV (1960), 277–301. Useful case-study.

COTTON IN THE ECONOMY

[70] N. F. R. Crafts, *British Economic Growth during the Industrial Revolution* (Oxford, 1985). Contains a synthesis of recent econometric work on the industrial revolution, including [71] and [73], as well as the author's own research.

[71] P. Deane and W. A. Cole, *British Economic Growth 1688–1959* (Cambridge, 1967). Pioneer econometric work containing influential interpretations of the role of cotton at variance with those of Rostow [74].

[72] H. J. Habakkuk and P. Deane, 'The Take-off in Britain' in W. W. Rostow (ed.), *The Economics of Take-off into Sustained Growth* (1965). Criticises Rostow's assessment of the fundamental role of cotton in the industrial revolution [see 74].

[73] C. K. Harley, 'British Industrialisation before 1841: evidence of slower growth during the Industrial Revolution', *Journal of Economic History*, XLII (1982) 267–89. Econometric analysis suggesting that the transformation of the industrial sector in eighteenth-century Britain was less dramatic than Rostow supposed [see 74].

[74] W. W. Rostow, *The Stages of Economic Growth* (Cambridge, 1960). An economist's concept of the process of industrialisation which assigns a central role to cotton in the case of Britain.

British Entrepreneurship in the Nineteenth Century

Prepared for
The Economic History Society by
P. L. PAYNE
Professor of Economic History
in the University of Aberdeen

Second Edition

Acknowledgements

I wish to thank the Cambridge University Press and Professor Peter Mathias, editor of *The Cambridge Economic History of Europe*, vol. 7, for kindly permitting me to reproduce several passages from my contribution to that volume entitled 'Industrial Entrepreneurship and Management in Britain, *c.* 1760–1970'.

Note on References

References in the text within square brackets refer to the numbered items in the Select Bibliography, followed, where necessary, by the page number, e.g. [155: *129*]. Other references in the text, numbered consecutively, relate to sources, not in the Select Bibliography, itemised in the Notes and References section.

1 Introduction

The quality of British entrepreneurship in the nineteenth century is continually being reassessed. Until the mid 1960s a major *leitmotiv* in accounts of British economic development from the heroic days of the Industrial Revolution to the eve of the First World War was the steady dissipation of a fund of entrepreneurship which, it has been implied, reached its greatest abundance during and immediately after the Napoleonic Wars. From being organisers of change who were 'instrumental in delivering society from the fate predicted for it by Malthus' [254: *129*] by having the 'wit and resource to devise new instruments of production and new methods of administering industry' [172: *161*], British entrepreneurs had, by the latter decades of the nineteenth century, come to be responsible for Britain's failure to retain its role as workshop of the world. Britain's international economic dominance, once so obvious, had been yielded to indefatigable and enterprising American manufacturers and their 'drummers' (commercial travellers), and to persevering, multi-lingual, scientifically-trained Germans.

The fundamental cause of this relative decline, the subject of so much controversy, seemed incontrovertible: there was a weakness in entrepreneurship. The conclusion of Burnham and Hoskins, following a careful study of the iron and steel industry, seemed to have a general applicability: 'If a business deteriorates it is of no use blaming anyone except those at the top, and if an industry declines relatively faster than unfavourable external and uncontrollable factors lead one to expect, the weakness can only be attributable to those who are in control of its activities' [79: *271*]. And these, it was widely believed, had 'grown slack, [had] let . . . business take care of itself, while . . . shooting grouse or yachting in the Mediterranean'.[1] This argument seemed attractively persuasive to many students of economic history. Nobody except examination candidates desperately short of facts, understanding or time, expressed it in quite such simple terms, but even those who entertained grave misgivings about the general condemnation of the British entrepreneur gave it some credence, and those for whom the entrepreneur and his shortcomings represented a major element in any explanation of Britain's loss of industrial leadership were greatly encouraged by David Landes's masterly contribution to the *Cambridge Economic History of Europe* in 1965 [241], perhaps the most eloquent expression of the hypothesis of entrepreneurial failure.

Thereafter a reaction took place. Detailed case-studies and the application of econometric methods resulted in a more sympathetic understanding of the problems of confronting the British entrepreneur. Indeed, in 1971, McCloskey and Sandberg, leading advocates of quantitative assessment, came to the conclusion that 'It is fair to say . . . that the late Victorian entrepreneur . . . is well on his way to redemption' [247: *108*]. Nevertheless, some economic historians continued to entertain doubts about the validity of some of the assumptions underlying the statistical manipulations involved in the quantitative approach, and case-studies sufficiently detailed for quantitative judgements were still all too rare.

In the last few years, much new material has appeared, some of which permits the employment of new methods of analysis, and new criteria for judging entrepreneurial performance have been suggested. Yet there remains much to be discovered about the nineteenth-century entrepreneur and his influence on British economic performance. This brief essay can do little more than attempt to indicate the course of the debate so far and to speculate upon some of the relevant themes. The sheer inconclusiveness of the discussion is challenging, so many questions are as yet unanswered, so much new material – in the form of business archives – is becoming available for research. It may well be that explorations in this most difficult territory will never result in completely satisfying conclusions, but there is no denying the fascination attached to the study of this facet of British economic history.

2 The Entrepreneur: Role and Function

Ideally, one should begin with a universally acceptable definition of the concept of entrepreneurship, but it is a peculiarity of this branch of economic history that it has been plagued with almost as many essays discussing the function of the entrepreneur as with detailed case-studies of his actual role at different periods of time.

Now one and now another prime characteristic has been emphasised. Economists have stressed innovation, risk-bearing, organisation and leadership, sometimes arguing that many other functions performed by entrepreneurs are more strictly managerial; but definition in these terms involves further problems. Exactly what is meant, for example, by innovation? Must it mean doing something that has never been done anywhere before (Schumpeter's concept), or can it mean bringing into an industry something which has been done before but not in that region or in that sphere of economic activity (Fritz Redlich's 'derivative innovation' [212])? This is an important question because, as many of those who have discussed the entrepreneur have to some extent been influenced by Joseph Schumpeter's concept of innovation, there exists a tacit belief that 'entrepreneurship is confined to the big, spectacular, and comparatively infrequent' [234: *112*]. But, as Coleman has observed, 'much activity with an equal right to be called entrepreneurial is carried on in short- or medium-term situations'; and is involved in 'the continuous adaptation of the technical and/or organisational structure of an *existing* business to small changes in the market both for factors and for final products' [*ibid*, emphasis supplied]. Indeed, empirical studies, which reveal the vast majority of entrepreneurs to have been imitative, enhance the correctness of this judgement. They also suggest the abandonment of innovation as a necessary criterion of entrepreneurship and the essential accuracy of G. H. Evans's definition of the entrepreneur as 'the person, or a group of persons, in a firm whose function is to determine *the kind of business* that is to be conducted'. Three core decisions are involved: 'the kinds of goods and services to be offered, the value of these goods and services, and the clientele to be served'. Once these decisions have been made, 'other top-level' decisions have become essentially management decisions – that is, decisions designed to achieve the goals set by the entrepreneurial determination of the kind of business to be operated [184: 25, 252].

Whatever the merits of these, and innumerable other interpretations,[2] few students of economic history would fail to recognise the picture of the entrepreneur provided by Flinn in his provocative essay on the *Origins of the Industrial Revolution*: '[He] organised production. He it was who brought together the capital (his own or somebody else's) and the labour force, selected the most appropriate site for operations, chose the particular technologies of production to be employed, bargained for raw materials and found outlets for the finished product' [186: 79].

Although Flinn's definition contains elements which Evans might regard as subordinate management functions, any confusion may be resolved if it is understood that the concepts of entrepreneurship and management alter with the changing structure of industry and enterprise. During the Industrial Revolution it *is* true to say that the entrepreneurs often 'fulfilled in one person the function of capitalist, financier, works manager, merchant and salesman' [254: *132*], but a consequence of the slow supercession of the one-man business or the small partnership by the joint-stock limited liability company during the course of the nineteenth century was not only that the entrepreneurial role became more specialised – a whole range of functions appropriate to the days of the 'complete businessman' being shed – but that the association, rather than the individual, came to perform this role [170: 5].

Developments in the capital market – including, for example, the financial activities of the legal fraternity, the evolution of country banking and the rise of the provincial stock exchanges [180] – coupled with changes in company law, permitted entrepreneurs to finance their undertakings with funds other than their own (for a magnificent regional example, see [115]). The function of the capitalist became a separate one. Furthermore, whereas the sheer novelty of many of the inter-related problems exercising the pioneers had, in the absence of technical and commercial expertise within the firm, the locality or even the economy, to be solved personally, with growing experience, and the evolution of specialised intermediaries in many branches of industrial and commercial activity – factory architects, consulting engineers, accountants, selling agents, and the like – the solution to questions that once had necessitated the master's decision were capable of being handled by the managerial staff, or partially determined by specialists employed either within the organisation or as consultants. Hence, in the larger concerns, a second functional split occurred between those who made strategic decisions, the senior partners on the board of directors acting as a team (albeit one sometimes drawn entirely from a single family or from a small group of related families), and those who kept the firm going from day to day, the managers or the administrators.

Thus, as the century progressed, the entrepreneur, acting either as an individual or jointly with others in an organised association, having set up his business or taken over an existing one, could confine his activities to determining major policy decisions involving, *inter alia*, the exploitation of technical and/or organisation innovations and the continuous adaptation of the firm so as most profitably to exploit his chosen markets. The problems associated with the entrepreneurial function may not have been significantly reduced, but the necessity of personally mastering the details of a host of technological and commercial activities certainly had. In the biggest firms, such as the reconstituted Calico Printers' Association, decisions by the executive directors came to be based on the reports of advisory committees [51: 528–9]; smaller firms commissioned reports from consultants; and even newcomers to many branches of economic activity, indistinguishable in many ways from their classic forebears, could usually obtain, for example, accurate performance specifications from those who supplied their machinery and plant, information sadly lacking to the pioneers. In some ways it was all made easier, and in so far as the decision-makers were no longer operating solely with capital provided by themselves, less risky. But was the response to less difficult conditions a growing laxity, a diminution of entrepreneurial energy and application?

This brief discussion is intended not merely to introduce what is to many an interesting problem in semantics, but to draw attention to the implications of the dynamic nature of entrepreneurship, and to indicate the necessity of an excursion into the evolution of the structure of the business firm in nineteenth-century Britain.

3 The Structure of the Firm in the Nineteenth Century

As late as 1919 Marshall – with an unrivalled knowledge of institutional arrangements – could write that until 'not very long ago the representative firm in most industries and trades was a private partnership . . . [45: *314*]. Indeed, throughout most of the nineteenth century, the *fundamental* business unit was the individual proprietorship or partnership [33: *111*; 8: *10*]. This was not *simply* a consequence of the Bubble Act of 1720, whereby the creation of a joint-stock company with transferable shares and corporate status was possible only with the consent of the State, but because there appears to have been no pressing necessity to depart from the traditional organisational framework [26: *27*].

There are several reasons for this. The common law partnership – based as it was on professional and commercial skill and personal knowledge – possessed many advantages as a form of business organisation. To some extent it may legitimately be regarded as the product of risk-avoidance. By the unification of ownership and control, the entrepreneur was able to reduce the real or imagined dangers inherent in trusting his business – or even part of his business – to a manager, when the growing size of his firm or his own increasing infirmities necessitated some delegation of authority. Instead, the more capable and conscientious employee who had risen to a position of some managerial authority within the concern would be offered a partnership, thus ensuring that his own fortunes were intimately bound up with the more wealthy, if not the original, partners [209: *150–1*].

This, moreover, represents but one illustration of the inherent adaptability of the partnership form. What is remarkable about those associations that are well documented is their kaleidoscopic nature. Partnerships were created, supplemented, and frequently terminated when conditions called for change. The principal entrepreneurs associated with others in the same or in related branches of activity, both to enlarge the scale or scope of their original enterprises, and to acquire the co-operation of those who possessed some area of expertise in which they themselves were relatively deficient. Examples of the former motive are legion. Extremely elaborate partnership systems were built up by Richard Arkwright [204: *232*; 284: *78*], David Dale [111: *171–2*], James and Kirkman Finlay [258: *4–30*] and the Peel family [269: *80–4*]; but no less interesting are those partnerships which brought together persons possessing complementary skills and talents. Boulton and Watt [330] and Wedgwood and Bentley [305] are perhaps the best-known cases.

The fact that the common law partnership was sufficiently elastic to accommodate the introduction of new partners possessing either capital or expertise, and was so employed, cannot but shed some doubt on the notion of the entrepreneur as typically the owner-manager, which historians have perhaps too readily taken over from the classical economists. Undoubtedly, many early entrepreneurs did conform to this 'ideal' and did perform the entire range of roles suggested by Wilson [254], but probably more common were small, often family-linked, partnerships, reliant in varying degrees on capital provided by sleeping partners, whose active members concentrated on different entrepreneurial functions. Indeed it would be surprising had this not been so, for there is some evidence that the successful performance of different tasks calls for individuals with different personality traits [173: *107–12*].

But, leaving aside internal questions, what was remarkable was the ability of manufacturing and trading partnerships to grow without recourse to the corporate form of organisation. The practice of self-financing, coupled with a growing reliance on an increasingly sensitive network of monetary intermediaries [115], was able to meet the capital requirements of most firms. The essential simplicity of so many of the productive processes, characterised as they were by a growth pattern involving simply the multiplication of units, rather than by radical reorganisation, *permitted* continued direction by the single entrepreneur, or by the small group of enterprises far bigger than had once been thought feasible. The word 'permitted' has been emphasised because Gatrell has demonstrated the apparent absence of any overwhelming benefits of scale in the very industry, cotton textiles, which might have been expected most fully to have experienced such benefits

[18]. But when the capital requirements of some enterprises necessitated a very large partnership, to which the descriptive term 'society' or 'company' was frequently applied, the prohibition on claims to corporate status and on the free transferability of shares became more and more irksome, and those growth-inhibiting technicalities stemming from the Bubble Act, which could not be circumvented by the ingenuities of the legal profession, were increasingly ignored. DuBois's study makes it clear that the unincorporated joint-stock company became of significant importance in the decades preceding the repeal of the Bubble Act in 1825, particularly in insurance, the mineral industries and the brass and copper trades (13: *220ff*; 26: *21ff*].

Whatever success such unincorporated companies enjoyed, and however well legal disabilities were repaired in the opening decades of the nineteenth century, the liability of all partners remained unlimited. The inevitable consequence was that 'no prudent man [could] . . . invest his surplus in any business that he [could not] himself practically superintend' [26: *29*]. The principle of limited liability was finally adopted in 1855 only after heated debate, but it is significant that the initial impetus to change was provided by 'a group of middle class philanthropists, most of whom accepted the title of Christian Socialists', who wished to create 'facilities to safe investments for the savings of the middle and working class' [56: *419–20*], and by London financial interests which sought profitable industrial outlets for potential investors [29: *10*], not by those who argued in terms of freedom of contract or by the industrialists themselves, whose voices were seldom heard in the discussions that preceded the Joint Stock Companies Act of 1856 and 1862 (56: *432*].

The response of the industrialists to this legislation confirms their muted interest.[3] Although by the mid 1870s the limited company had secured a foothold in almost every branch of economic activity, in 1885 such companies account for, at most, between 5 and 10 per cent of the total number of important business organisations, and only in shipping, iron and steel, and cotton could their influence be said to have been considerable [29: *105*; 52: *56ff*]. Although the firms that were limited were by far the most important in their spheres of activity, judged by size of unit and amount of fixed capital, the vast majority of the manufacturing firms of the country continued to be unincorporated family businesses in the mid 1880s

[8, vol. III: *203*; 53: *171–3*]. Nevertheless, by the mid 1860s a legal structure existed in Great Britain which made fundamental changes in the structure of the individual enterprise possible. The way was open for the emergence of the corporate economy, even though few trod the path. In contrast with the expectations, even intentions, of the statesmen responsible for the early Company Acts, there developed the private company (legally unrecognised until 1907) [27]. Since many of the concerns adopting this form of organisation had previously existed as partnerships or joint-stock companies, the object of private registration was to obtain limited liability while retaining the original management and maintaining the privacy of the past. Further growth was made possible, but only to the extent of the capital of the shareholders named in the Articles of Association, and the introduction of new entrepreneurial talent to the board was inhibited [51: *520*; 58: *408*]. Thus entrepreneurs operated within organisations which show little alteration from those of their pioneering forebears. Certainly there was little movement towards the differentiation of management from ownership, towards the elongation of organisational hierarchies.

It would appear that the experience of Thomas Vickers was not untypical. Giving evidence to the 1886 Commission on the Depression in Trade and Industry, he said that 'it has been an advantage to my company to be a Limited Liability Company – because I have always had as much power as a director of this company as I had as a partner and the resources of the company are greater than the resources of the old partnership.' Indeed, the witnesses from the northern industries constantly reiterated that the direction and management of their concerns were usually identical with those of the former partnerships. The adoption of corporate status with limited liability frequently meant that the technical ownership of many businesses, while sometimes in more hands, had not yet changed the groups of leading entrepreneurs [29: *116*, *118*, *403*]. This was especially so when 'outsider' investors were allowed to purchase only non-voting securities, such as preference shares and debentures [10: *164*; see also W. J. Reader's 'Reflections on the History and Nature of the Limited Liability Company' in 50: *192*, *197*].

Alongside these superficially transformed enterprises were 'the vast majority' of manufacturing concerns, which as late as the mid 1880s preferred the old ways, whatever legal provision for growth and change may have been open to them. Clapham has indicated the branches of industry which remained dominated by family businesses in 1886–7:

> all, or nearly all, the wool firms; outside Oldham, nearly all the cotton firms; and the same in linen, silk, jute, lace and hosiery. Most of the smaller, and some of the largest, engineering firms, and nearly all the cutlery and pottery firms, were still private. Brewing was a family affair. So, with certain outstanding exceptions, were the Birmingham trades and the great, perhaps the major, part of the shipbuilding industry. In housebuilding and the associated trades there were very few limited companies; few in the clothing trades; few in the food trades . . . Merchants of all kinds had rarely 'limited' their existing firms, and the flotation of a brand new mercantile company was not easy. Add the many scores of thousands of retail businesses, 'unlimited' almost to a shop. [8, vol. III: *203*]

There is, then, little evidence of any significant divorce of control from ownership before the end of the century. Substantial growth in the size of the average firm – difficult though it is to measure [51: *519*] – appears to have taken place without any appreciable dilution of proprietorial control. This may be explained partly by the nature of the growth pattern, characterised as it frequently was by the multiplication of existing plants and processes producing a fairly limited range of related products, rather than by bold diversification (which might have necessitated the recruitment of executive talent from outside), and partly by the evolution of a network of trade associations, in the absence of which many shaky firms may have been absorbed by their more enterprising competitors into amalgamations of sufficient scale to have made a more bureaucratic internal structure imperative.

But even this latter development was not inevitable. At the close of the nineteenth century there took place a burst of very large mergers in branches of the textile industry and in brewing, iron and steel, cement, wallpaper and tobacco [21; 43; 63], and if there was one common characteristic of the giant businesses which resulted, it was the great extent to which the vendors retained their hold over their businesses when mergers took place [51, section 2]. Thus, even in the relatively efficient and integrated Associated Portland Cement Manufacturers Ltd, there were, in addition to the managing directors, no less than forty ordinary directors who were appointed because 'there were so many individual interests that had to be considered since it was most important to retain the services of all those who had been most instrumental in conducting the business' [43: *114*]. And when the Imperial Tobacco Company was formed in 1901 the attitude of the heads of the original family businesses was, Sir Wilfred Anson said, 'not unlike that of the thirteen States of America, who, when the federal constitution was first adopted by the United States, gave the central government as little authority as possible and retained as much as they could in their own hands' [14: *65–6*].

Similar sentiments were expressed about the Calico Printers' Association, formed in 1899 by the amalgamation of fifty-nine firms controlling about 85 per cent of the British calico-printing industry and having an original capital of £9,200,000. This giant concern was to be described in 1907 as 'a study of disorganisation' [43: *xi*]. In addition to the heavy burden of over-capitalisation, the Association handicapped itself still further by creating a board of directors of eighty-four members, of whom eight were managing directors. In fact, the 'administration resembled the crude democratic expedient of government by mass meeting'. 'The Directors were but imperfectly acquainted with each other or, what was of great importance, with each other's views' [51: *528*]. It remained for the vice-chairman of English Sewing Cotton Ltd – another great concern suffering similar initial difficulties – explicitly to draw the obvious conclusion, applicable to a large proportion of the giant British combines, that 'it was an awful mistake to put into control of the various businesses purchased by the company the men from whom the businesses were purchased, because these men have got into one groove and could not get out of it' [43: *133–4*]. The consequence was unwieldy boards of directors, frequent breakdowns of internal communications, and an unwillingness on the part of the branch managers of the numerous obsolescent units in each combine to accept the closure of inefficient works.

In the majority of cases such difficulties were eventually overcome by schemes involving the reconstruction of the ailing giants and by new methods of management,[4] and inasmuch as an increasing proportion of the larger firms came to be controlled by directors whose total shareholdings represented an ever-diminishing minority of the equity capital, the roots of managerial capitalism can dimly be perceived in Britain before the First World War as well as the eventual domination of the nation's economic structure by the corporate enterprise [23]. What is surprising is the tenacity throughout the nineteenth century – and beyond – of forms of business organisations characterised by a marriage of ownership and control almost as complete as that encountered during the Industrial Revolution [53: *173, 180–1*].

4 The Entrepreneur: Origins and Motivation

In 1948 Ashton showed that the pioneer industrialists 'came from every social class and from all parts of the country' [172: *16*; see also 204: *376–82*]. Although subsequent enquiries [notably 73; 84; 85; 108; 164; 174; 189; 194; 226] have vastly increased our knowledge of this entrepreneurial class and its geographical, social and occupational origins, generalisation regarding the relative contributions of each distinguishable group remains hazardous. Crouzet's estimates are undoubtedly the best and most comprehensive yet devised [181]. By collecting the overwhelming majority of the published data about the origins and careers of the men who pioneered the new industrial system, and by employing in their analysis realistic definitions of such concepts as occupation and social class, he confirms the growing belief that only a relatively small proportion of 'the true industrialists, the founders of relatively large undertakings' [181: *139*] came from the upper class or the lower orders. Recruits from the middle ranks of society, frequently with mercantile connections, appear to have predominated. Crouzet reveals that although many of the early industrialists had humble – though not proletarian – backgrounds, upward social movement did take place on such a scale and in such a way that it *is* possible to speak of the self-made man; that 'rags to riches' is not entirely a myth; that there was intra-class if not inter-class mobility. 'Most people who benefitted . . . rose *within* the middle class, from its lower strata (in some cases on the fringe of the working class) to a new stratum of wealthy, or at least well-to-do industrialists' [181: *142*]. Acknowledging that his carefully constructed sample is unscientific, Crouzet has concentrated upon the major figures 'about whose career[s] *some* information was available'. These were a minority, surrounded, in almost every branch of industry, by swarms of small firms, operated by men who can be assumed to have had more modest origins. They constituted, he aptly suggests, 'a reserve army of capitalists' from whose ranks a substantial proportion of successful industrialists arose. Crouzet believes that industry itself 'bred a large number of the leaders who "revolutionized" it', that a powerful process of endogenesis was at work. [181: *116*]

Essentially, these were Katrina Honeyman's conclusions. In each industry she examined, 'there was a paucity of new blood. Leadership was either entrenched because of the traditional nature of the industry [lead mining], or, in the case of the new industries, it was recruited from a less developed branch of the same industry [fustian masters and calico printing moved into spinning; silk merchants and manufacturers into hosiery]' [194: *166*]. For all that, the building up of 'samples' inevitably suffers from serious weaknesses. As Charlotte Erickson was to write of a later generation of industrialists in steel and hosiery, they 'represent the proportion of the whole population which the historical sources enabled us to study' [182: *7*]. What of the regiments of the anonymous; of those whom many economic historians have depicted 'as ants tirelessly maximising profits to lift the graph of economic growth'[5] by participating in short-lived partnerships, leaving perhaps only an entry in the docket books in the Court of Bankruptcy [44]?

It is because all the individual 'samples' embodied in Crouzet's study are themselves inherently biased towards the successful that dangers are involved in too ready an acceptance of the apparent correlation between Dissent and entrepreneurial activity. Flinn, who provides the best introduction to this long-debated topic, takes as a basic assumption 'a substantial disparity between the proportion of non-conformists in society and the proportion who were successful entrepreneurs' [187: *25*]; then, building on the work of McClelland [203] and Hagen [189], he seeks to explain this in terms of achievement motivation operating through systems of child upbringing which were themselves significantly influenced by religious persuasion. The argument is convincing, but the suspicion remains that the over-representation of non-conformists among the *entrepreneurs who attained prominence* may be explicable not in terms of their religious precepts, their superior education or their need for achievement, but because they belonged to extended kinship families that gave them access to credit which permitted their firms, and their records, to survive, while others, less well connected, went to the wall.

Be that as it may, the early entrepreneurs, whatever their geographical, occupational or social origins, were similarly motivated. They sought to enrich themselves. Yet as Perkin has observed, 'the limitless pursuit of wealth for its own sake is a rare phenomenon', and he quotes Adam Smith approvingly: '"to what purpose is all the toil and bustle of the world? . . . it is not vanity which urges us on . . . it is not wealth that men desire, but the consideration and good opinion that wait upon riches.". . . The pursuit of wealth was the pursuit of social status, not merely for oneself but for one's family' [208: *83*], and this often meant the acquisition of a landed estate, the purchase or building of a great house, and the quest for political power, either on the national or the local scene. It was always so, before, during and after the Industrial Revolution [234: *95ff*].[6] Only the relative attractiveness of land, the stately home, and the title of nobility or knighthood as symbols of social advancement appear to have varied over time;[7] and those who have argued that this pursuit of non-economic ends inevitably involved a haemorrhage of entrepreneurial talent as the nineteenth century progressed [237: *190–1*], should perhaps balance this against what might be called the demonstration effect of conspicuous consumption or social elevation on the new men crowding in to emulate those who had already succeeded.

One cannot help believing that many new thrusting firms would not have come into existence, or small established companies grown, had not their founders or owners, or their socially ambitious wives, seen or been aware of the tangible results of commercial or industrial success. In one sense there was a need for the 'frenetically tangled French Gothic skylines' of the palaces of the cottontot grandees, the Wagnerian retreat of Sir Titus Salt in the woods above Saltaire, the enormous Old English house built for Sir H. W. Peek,[8] and the metamorphosis of Mr Edward Strutt – who appears to have devoted much of his time to politics and government rather than the direct management of the firm established by his grandfather – into Lord Belper [210: *10–11*]. These manifestations of success served to encourage the others.

Similarly, many sought to establish firms so that the family name might be perpetuated. The attainment of this objective became easier during the nineteenth century. The unincorporated partnership, often embodying in its trading title the names of its more prominent members, was legally terminated with the death of any one of them. If reconstituted, a new collection of names would often replace those of the founders. With the joint-stock form the company could enjoy eternal life. If successful and well respected, commercial considerations dictated the retention of the original name, so that, for example, 'George Green & Co' would continue, albeit with the suffix 'Limited', even if the male members of the Green family – having attended Eton and Oxford – no longer played an active role in the business. They had inherited – and often greatly enlarged – family mansions, picked up a knighthood or even a peerage, perhaps for political services, and seen the fountainhead of their wealth prosper under the guiding hands of the new generation of professional executives, drawn sometimes from a less affluent branch of the family. There was no need to suffer any loss of identity.

Indeed, some economic historians, almost invariably citing the case of Marshall's of Leeds [326], have seen in this waning of the entrepreneurial energies of the founders' descendants a plausible reason for Britain's disappointing economic performance in the late nineteenth century [214: *563–4*; 45: *91–2*]. The seeds of ultimate decline of Rathbone Bros & Co merchants of Liverpool, for example, are clearly visible by the late 1860s when 'money ceased to be much of object [to the partners]' and the firm was 'gradually allowed to run down' so that the members of the family could more actively pursue their own interests in politics, education, philanthropy and religion [308: *120, 128, 131*]. This aspect of business history has been labelled 'the Buddenbrook syndrome' (from the novel by Thomas Mann) and undoubtedly a number of studies furnish some empirical support for it (e.g. [102; 147; 232; 233; 274; 276; 344]).[9] But, as Professor Coleman has observed, if one castigates some second- or third-generation businessmen for quitting their offices and factories one is only blaming them for following a long-established English tradition, and there are, moreover, numerous significant exceptions [278: *270–1*].

Indeed, as yet all too little is known about the age-structure of firms in the nineteenth century. Just how many firms remained under the control of the same family for three generations? And of those that did, what proportion did they consitute of any particular industrial or commercial sector? John Butt found that very few partnerships in the Scottish cotton industry during the industrial revolution were continued for longer than a decade [80: *120*]. 'Of the 135 firms in Leeds engaged in the sale and manufacture of woollens, worsteds and blankets [in 1830] only 21 houses had partners who could provide a direct link with those in 1782' [226: *115*]. In Oldham, it was said that of 138 concerns in existence in the town in 1846, only four had been in possession of the same firm or family before 1800 [89: *23*]; and in 1891 the Rev. M. Anstey of Leicester calculated that in the previous twenty-eight years, of 105 firms that began business in the hosiery trade, 27 had failed, 27 had closed down through making no profit, 13 had transferred their businesses into other hands, no information was available on 21 and only 17 firms were known still to be in business [168: *176*).[10] A comprehensive study of the early Scottish limited companies formed between 1856 and 1895 showed that the *average* length of life of those involved in manufacturing exceeded twenty years only in textiles, clothing and footwear (21.1 years); in chemicals and allied products, the average length of life was but ten years [52: *101*]. Facts such as these lead one to suspect that only a very small proportion of firms created and continued by deed of partnership in the first half of the nineteenth century or incorporated in the latter half of the century survived more than thirty years, a period insufficiently long to sustain more than two generations of a founding family [see 53: *190–2*; 154: *111*]. This is not to imply that the Buddenbrook syndrome does not exist – indeed, some interesting examples can be found [278: *270–1*] – but that its influence in the nineteenth century is of little significance.

When the data collected in the course of creating the *Dictionary of Business Biography* [198] and the *Dictionary of Scottish Business Biography* [219] are fully analysed,[11] they will almost certainly reveal *inter alia* that in the older firms control was increasingly exercised by those brought up to a life-style foreign to the founding fathers, and that during the course of the nineteenth century some degree of formal education became increasingly necessary for business success. But, above all, the relatively narrow base of British industry (cotton textiles, iron and steel, and heavy engineering) coupled with a slowly changing structure, made for the continuation – even strengthening – of the process of endogenesis. Certainly the provisional findings of David Jeremy [199] and Christine Shaw [218] strongly suggest this possibility. The great majority of those 'captured' by the *Dictionary of Business Biography* 'came from relatively prosperous backgrounds; were well educated by the standards of the day' and 'began their careers by working their way . . . in their family business' [218: *38, 16*].

This is in marked contrast to the general spirit of the assertion by Samuel Smiles who, in his famous work *Self-Help* (first published in 1859), observed that

> The instances of men ... who, by dint of persevering application and energy, have raised themselves from the humblest ranks of industry to eminent positions of influence in society, are indeed so numerous that they have long ceased to be regarded as exceptional [221: *47–8*]

If business leaders *were* drawn predominantly from the middle class during the pioneering period, how much more likely is it that the area of recruitment was similarly restricted as the nineteenth century advanced? There undoubtedly occurred a diminution in the opportunities open to those in the lower reaches of the middle class and a positive contraction of those confronting the artisans and the working class, if only because, as free grammar schools were converted into fee-charging schools and boarding schools and free places transformed into scholarships requiring expensive preparation, the chances that the educational system offered to the sons of manual workers became increasingly circumscribed. Upward mobility for the working class by this route was, Perkin has indicated, probably at its nadir in the second half of the nineteenth century [208: *426–7*]. Chapman and Gatrell can detect a constriction of the area of recruitment in the cotton industry from as early as the mid 1820s [89: *20*; 18: *124–5*] and Howe's study [196] reveals that the increasing capital size of enterprises in cotton enhanced the position of hereditary owners. Howe's

> review of the origins and recruitment of mid-century textile masters reveals ... a strongly hereditary nucleus. Approximately 54 per cent had succeeded to partnership in their father's firms or had been the sons of textile masters. [Even] where 'new men' entered, the evidence does not suggest a preponderance of lowly-born self-helpers ... but the entry of men from relatively prosperous commercial, industrial, and professional backgrounds. [196: *8–21*]

Although it is conceivable that some branches of engineering were not inimical to entry by talented persons of relatively humble origins throughout the century, it is almost certain that more typical was iron and steel which, Charlotte Erickson has shown, became increasingly closed, exclusive and patrician in its recruitment [182: *189, passim*; 208: *426*], and coal, where 'the social composition of the business élite . . . seems to have narrowed during the late nineteenth century . . . and business leadership became increasingly inbred' [94: *449–68*].

With the notable exception of what are generally known as the 'Oldham limited liability companies',[12] the public company probably suffocated the entrepreneurial aspirations of the lower middle strata of society. Possessing few, if any, shares; names which had no attraction for the potential investor; and at best only the most tenuous connections with other firms, there was no room for them on the board. Their career ceiling in such concerns was in the ranks of management. Even the railway companies, which, as Gourvish has shown [188), did much to raise the status and augment the role of the non-owning, salaried manager, appear to have recruited the majority of their chief executives from those who possessed considerable initial advantages of birth and education. Their origins were predominantly upper-middle and upper class; and it is not, therefore, too surprising to find that a high proportion of them gained seats on the board, for their social backgrounds were similar to those of their erstwhile employers.

Thus, the creeping dominance of the economy by corporate enterprise apparent at the turn of the century, coupled with the necessity of even larger initial capital stocks, even for relatively small-scale manufacturing partnerships, may have made for a situation in which what Chapman and Marquis aptly called 'the movement of work people against gravity' [178: *299*] became increasingly rare.

If much of the foregoing is offered, as Church has observed, 'in the subjunctive mood' [7: *20*], there seems to be general agreement upon Rubinstein's thesis that 'where there was commerce, finance or trade, money was made more readily than where there was manufacturing industry' [213: *619*]. If it is correct to argue that the entrepreneurs in the late eighteenth and nineteenth centuries sought to enrich themselves, then their chances of doing so appear to have been much greater in a London counting house than in a Lancashire factory or a Clydeside shipyard: 'it is clear that the wealthy earned their fortunes disproportionately in commerce, finance and transport – that is, as merchants, bankers, shipowners, merchant bankers and stock and insurance brokers – rather than as manufacturers and industrialists' [213: *605*; 7: *24*]. Although it is almost impossible not to be convinced of the essential accuracy of Rubinstein's argument (which seems likely to be confirmed by the findings of the *Dictionary of Business Biography* [198]), the case of William Todd Lithgow is a salutory reminder of the possible inadequacy of executry records in assessing the wealth of the industrialist [313].

5 The Quality of Entrepreneurial Performance

(i) THE INDUSTRIAL REVOLUTION: A CASE FOR REASSESSMENT?

The poverty of information on so many aspects of the study of British entrepreneurship has not inhibited economic historians from making assessments of the quality of entrepreneurial performance. Attention has mainly been directed to the closing decades of the nineteenth century, but a proper appreciation necessitates a much broader comparative view. To assert, as Aldcroft did in 1964, that '. . . entrepreneurial initiative and drive were flagging, particularly before 1900' rests partially on the assumption that 'the British entrepreneur had lost much of the drive and dynamism possessed by his predecessors of the classical industrial revolution' [227: *114*]. But is this assumption fully justified? And, furthermore, does a consideration of 'drive and enthusiasm' constitute an adequate basis for judgement? Surely, other criteria, such as knowledge and skill, are involved?

Such questions have so far attracted little systematic analysis. Perhaps the very paucity of scholarly business histories has inhibited such inquiries, but it is more likely that, overwhelmed by a belief that an economic transformation *did* take place between, say, 1780 and 1830, there has been too ready an acceptance of the idea that the entrepreneurs, the chief instruments of change, must deserve their reputations for courage and adventurousness, progressive efficiency, organisational ability and grasp of commercial opportunity, combined with a capacity need to exploit it. But do they? This is too large a theme for adequate treatment here, but recent studies raise the suspicion that the eulogistic aura enveloping the pioneers has been somewhat obscuring, if only because it is becoming increasingly clear that earlier assessments of the entrepreneur – which have been implicit rather than explicit – have reflected a biased sample. If nothing else, there is a possibility that the majority of records that have been located and 'worked' for this period – and these, it will be freely admitted, are few in number – are predominantly those of concerns that were sufficiently successful to have created conditions favourable for untypical longevity. Hence the survival of their archives.

On the basis of this biased sample, the temptation has been almost irresistible not merely to reconstruct a composite 'complete businessman', possessing all, or nearly all, the virtues, but to extrapolate these qualities not only to the many hundreds whose concerns have been mentioned in the county histories and the accounts of local clergy, but even to those whose names have *never* been recorded, to those in the ranks of the stage armies of 'early cotton manufacturers' or 'ironmasters' deployed by economic historians. It is possible that such a procedure is misleading. Recent research depicts the Industrial Revolution in a much more negative light than was the case even as recently as a decade or so ago. Crafts's work [11] lends weighty support to Cannadine's observation that the industrial revolution was 'a limited, restricted, piecemeal phenomenon, in which things did *not* happen or where, if they did, they had far less effect than was previously supposed' [4: *162*]. This is not the place to discuss the historiography of the industrial revolution; suffice it to say that if the economic significance of the period *c*. 1760–1830 has been diminished, so too has the status of its traditional heroes. The fundamental changes introduced in certain industries, so comprehensively surveyed by Pollard [209], cannot be denied, but the new interpretation of the 'heroic' period does strengthen the belief expressed in the first edition of this essay that many who succeeded in the early years may not have fared so well in later decades; that, in fact, the ancestors of the much maligned later Victorian businessmen may not have been superior entrepreneurs in every facet of business activity.

It should be remembered that many industrial pioneers operated in what was in some ways a uniquely favourable economic environment. They faced a buoyant domestic market buttressed, particularly in cotton textiles, by a flourishing overseas demand in the exploitation of which they enjoyed monopolistic advantages. So great were the profit potentials at the turn of the century that many entrepreneurs, such as Robert Owen [209: *246*], Benjamin Gott and his partners [115: *240, 277*] and George Newton and Thomas Chambers [70: *156–61*], who fortuitously caught a rising demand, could often amass sufficient funds to enable their companies to weather later economic storms [180: *162–222*]. The consequence was, as Lee has told us in his study of McConnel and Kennedy, that 'the young man with ability but necessarily endowed with capital could begin business . . . without being doomed to fail' [300: *145*]. Then, following a period of rapid capital accumulation made possible by high initial profits [18: *96, 100*], a policy of 'scrupulous caution' often permitted impressive growth in the size of the firm to take place. And those who have emphasised the risks involved in pioneering – pointing to crises induced by the weather, by the sudden collapse of inherently shaky financial institutions, and by disasters outside the control of the individual manufacturer – should perhaps give greater weight to the widespread existence of fraudulent practices [44: *366*] and to the fact that the severity of entrepreneurial difficulties was often exacerbated by feverish overproduction. 'Here as in England business is overdone; the Manchester houses have manufactured enough yarn to serve the world for four or five years', wrote one disappointed partner from Boston in 1809 [270: *286–7*]; an error of judgement so often encountered in the literature that it cannot but diminish any estimate of the commercial acumen of the cotton entrepreneurs, for all the difficulties encountered in obtaining the latest 'market intelligence'. It was the generally favourable demand situation which sometimes allowed the perpetration of the grossest errors to go unpunished by bankruptcy.

Jennifer Tann's investigation of the letters sent to Boulton and Watt clearly reveals that entrepreneurs with exceedingly little technical knowledge were prepared to risk large sums of money in manufacturing ventures and, having done so, to build a factory the size of which was determined not by rational calculation of power supply or transport costs but 'by the capital available for investment on a long-term basis and the maximum output that the entrepreneur thought he could achieve within that limit' [222: *27*; see also 86: *15*]. Not surprisingly, apparently suicidal imbalances of power supply, mill-capacity and potential demand for the product often resulted, and optimal factory layouts were rarely achieved. In Leeds, wrote William Brown in 1821, few flax mills were 'without some defect or other in the height, length, width or shape of the rooms and where irregularity exists in the building complications and confusion must be running in all directions and cards and frames standing in all positions' [222: *33*].

Some of these planning imperfections – which could conceivably have led to business failure later in the century – might have been remedied had more of the earlier industrialists developed accurate accounting techniques.[13] These could have served as a guide to costing, but even one of the more talented and efficient entrepreneurs, George Lee – responsible for the building and equipping of the Salford Twist Mill – was forced to admit to James Watt Jr that his production techniques had outrun his knowledge of 'keeping manufacturing Books – in the construction of machinery we never could reduce it to regular piece work or divide the labour of Making and Repairing it in such a manner as to determine the distinct cost of each' [222: *27, 39*]. And with a few exceptions, notably Josiah Wedgwood or Boulton and Watt, these plaintive words probably represent the unspoken views of the vast majority of entrepreneurs in all branches of economic activity. Pollard's explanation of the failure to develop to any considerable extent the use of accounts on guiding management decisions is significant: '. . . the problem calling for a solution was not widely or continuously felt . . . . Apart from certain crisis years, anyone with a better technique had no problem in selling, and new techniques were so obviously "better" that it did not need elaborate accounts to prove this' [209: *248*], but more plausible are Patricia Hudson's observations on the West Riding woollen manufactures whose 'desire for confidentiality and secrecy of affairs meant that most [of them] preferred to do their own accounting and the sheer burden which this involved militated against the adoption of more tedious profit calculations and double entry methods' [115: *236*]. In Wales only the larger firms had appointed 'accountants' by the 1820s [121: *89*] and there is some evidence, from the Crawshay ledgers, that 'in many ways there was less detailed [costing] information being disclosed in 1825 than in the early years of the firm's existence' [121: *136*].

These remarks are not intended to belittle the achievements of the entrepreneurs of the Industrial Revolution. Their object is twofold: to emphasise the need for more detailed comparative investigations of the responses of entrepreneurs to the difficulties that confronted them in the context of the overall economic environment within which they operated; and to suggest that the names that have become famous (Arkwright, Oldknow, Strutt, Peel, Owen, McConnel and Kennedy, Gott and Marshall in textiles; Crawshay, Lloyd, Reynolds, Roebuck, Walker, Wilkinson, Boulton,

Watt, Bramah, Maudslay in iron and engineering; Minton, Spode, Wedgwood in pottery; Dundonald, Garbett, Keir, Macintosh, Tennant in chemicals; Whitbread, Thrale, Truman in brewing) were not typical entrepreneurs. The majority of them conducted their operations on a scale much greater than their less well-known competitors; many of them owed their successful growth to some degree of monopoly power acquired through patent exploitation, the possession of some unique skill, or the differentiation of their products. Certainly, to generalise upon 'the British entrepreneur' on the basis of this sample is illegitimate, particularly if its purpose is to shed discredit upon their successors. It is not inconceivable that more representative were the Wilsons of Wilsontown Ironworks [282], the Needhams of Litton [307], the Austins of Wotton-under-Edge [131: *172, 183–5*], William Lupton of Leeds [226: *112–15*; 115: *passim*], and John Cartwright of Retford [222: *35*; 80: *107–9, 121*]; all of whose concerns suffered from serious entrepreneurial shortcomings coupled with gross mismanagement.

(ii) THE EARLY VICTORIAN DECADES: THE NEED FOR MORE INFORMATION[14]

If there is an inadequate and probably untypical collection of scholarly studies on which to base an assessment of the performance of the industrial pioneers, this aspect of the three or four post-1830 decades is currently even worse served. Neither is the immediate future position very promising. Whereas several collections of business records of the classic period of the Industrial Revolution have been carefully preserved and studied, the overwhelming majority of those of the early Victorian period have either been destroyed or have not yet attracted much attention. Analysis is thus either impossible or insubstantial. Not until the legal requirements associated with the adoption of corporate status guaranteed the retention of certain basic records by *going concerns* is it possible even to begin to assess the role of entrepreneur with any confidence, and even then the surviving sample of archives is unlikely to be representative simply because the records of those firms which were wound up or liquidated have usually disappeared.[15]

This is a grave misfortune. Many of the problems of the pioneers had been surmounted; relatively sophisticated managerial techniques evolved; and the markets of the world, many growing in depth, long remained open to British exploitation – for several decades competition from foreign manufacturers was of little significance. Such was the development of the home and overseas markets, the former enjoying a remarkable buoyancy with the coming of the railway and gradually rising living standards, that the British entrepreneur had no great inducement to alter the basic economic structure painfully evolved in the pioneering period; textiles and iron remained supreme. Not without reason Samuel Smiles was able to write: 'Anybody who devotes himself to making money, body and soul, can scarcely fail to make himself rich. Very little brains will do' [220: *107*].[16]

Even Marshall argued that

> rich old firms could thrive by their mere momentum, even if they lost the springs of energy and initiative. Men whose childhood had been passed in the hard days before the repeal of the Corn Laws; who had come to business early in the morning and stayed late in the afternoon; who had been full of enterprise and resource, were not infrequently succeeded by sons who had been brought up to think life easy, and were content to let the main work of the business be carried out by salaried assistants on the lines laid down in a previous generation. But yet so strongly were such men supported by the general inflation of prices, that in most cases they made good profits and were satisfied with themselves. Thus an extraordinary combination of favourable conditions induced undue self-complacency. [45: *91–2*]

But how far are Marshall's strictures correct, or even fair?

Immediately, the question arises of how many concerns were in fact controlled by the sons or nephews of the founders. The point has already been made that all too little is known about the age-structure of firms in this, or indeed in any other, period of the nineteenth century. With the ever-changing internal power structure of partnerships and the high rates of dissolution and liquidation [48; 52], it is possible that the controlling interest in relatively few firms remained in the hands of the founder's immediate family beyond two generations. We are perhaps too eager to generalise from the records of those that did, forgetting that our inadequate sample is far from random. This is not to say that entrepreneurial weaknesses did not exist – though this is as yet unconfirmed, it is simply to argue that it is potentially dangerous to set too much weight on any proposition that is dependent upon the mere passage of generations.

It has already been noted that the absence of any dramatic change in the scale of operations, the relatively slow enlargement of the labour forces of individual enterprises, and the close coincidence of firm and plant, coupled with the fact that the majority of large companies were but 'private firms converted', meant that the nature of entrepreneurship and the structure of the firm changed but little in the middle decades of the nineteenth century. Influenced no doubt by the relatively high rate of economic growth, burgeoning exports and apparently rapid technological diffusion, there has been little or no retrospective criticism of the early Victorian entrepreneur. Yet the decline of a number of hitherto leading firms can be traced to this period. 'The Final Phase' of Marshall's of Leeds set in during the mid 1840s, though this once great firm was destined to linger on for another forty years, by which time many of its leading competitors in flax spinning had already gone: Benyons in 1861, John Morfitt and John Wilkinson a few years later and others, including W. B. Holdsworth, soon following [326: *199, 229*].

The Ashworth cotton enterprises, built up between 1818 and 1834 by Henry and Edward Ashworth – 'among the most renowned of the men who followed the great inventors and . . . took the cotton industry forward by "assiduity, perseverance, attention to detail, minor improvement"' – began their relative decline in the 1840s, when the partners' will to expand withered away before diversifying interests, growing internal tensions, and low profits and even losses. In 1846 George Binns Ashworth, Henry's son, noted that:

> in the new Eagley Weaving Shed there were no costings, no control of quality, no regular stock-takings; customers suffered from late delivery, and often the lengths of cloths were shorter than had been ordered. Owing to technical and managerial defects the looms now ran for hardly half the working day and total production was much below that of their competitors.

Although this was perhaps the worst of the firm's periodic managerial lapses, after 1847 things improved, but the firm never regained its earlier technical pre-eminence: 'Fortunes now will only be made by intense plodding and keenness', noted George Binns Ashworth in his diary [263: *14, 42, 31*].

One who failed to 'plod' was James Thompson of the Primrose Works, near Clitheroe. Perhaps the leading firm in the calico-printing trade, his exclusive prints – in the design of which he called upon 'the talent even of Royal Academicians' – were specifically manufactured 'for the upper hundreds, and not for the millions'. Heedless of warnings by the young Lyon Playfair, who became chemical manager of the works in 1841, that the business was doomed unless he changed the character of his product, Thompson refused to abandon his short runs. 'His products were known all over Europe for their high excellence, and he could not bear to lower . . . their quality.' 'It was a common saying of Thompson that "once you become a Calico printer there are but two courses before you – the *Gazette* or the grave".' In the event, he died a disappointed man, in 1859, but a few months before his famous works were closed [324: *43–4, 52–6; 78–81*]. Other calico printers had, however, attempted to produce for the million instead of the few and to do so had cut their costs to the bone by the debasement of design and by trying to convert 'herds of Lancashire boors into drawers, cutters, printers, machine workers, etc.' at appallingly low wages. Not surprisingly the products were execrable and failures numerous. As John Dugdale, owner of the Lowerhouse Print Works, near Burnley, observed in 1847: 'If yo'll look back for th' last six years, yo'll find half o' th' Printers are brocken – an' half o' those that are left canno' break, for nobody'll trust 'em, and the rest get on as weel as they con' [165: *73*].

Courtaulds got on very well. When Samuel III went into semi-retirement in the mid 1860s, the partners (now George Courtauld III, Harry Taylor and John Warren) enjoyed enormous incomes – the fruits of the efforts of an earlier generation – while allowing the firm to fall technically far behind other silk throwsters and manufacturers. Indeed, George Courtauld III 'contributed virtually nothing but inertia to the family business'. Only a buoyant and inelastic demand for its main product, ritual mourning crepe, coupled with falling raw silk prices, permitted the enterprise to make its handsome returns on capital at a time when its senior partner brought to the family firm none of 'those qualities of vigour, perception, intelligence, and enterprise' to which it owed its establishment by his uncle [278 vol. I; *174–7, 213*].

In iron, Joshua Walker & Co. did not long survive the end of the Napoleonic Wars, its steel trade being formally wound up in 1829, and the iron trade finally wasting away by the early 1830s [296: *29–31*]. Other ironmasters fared little better. John Darwin, sometime associate of Peter Stubs and one of the leading Sheffield industrialists, had gone bankrupt by 1828 [260: *41–2*; 75: *161–2*]; many vanished in the middle decades of the nineteenth century, among them Lloyd, Foster & Co., of Wednesbury, the first exploiters of host-blast and, later, the Bessemer process in the Black County [75: *156*]. Even the Coalbrookdale Company, bereft of managerial guidance when Abraham and Alfred Darby retired (in 1849) and Francis Darby died (in 1850), faltered, sustained only by sheer momentum and a continuing demand for the products of its foundry [320: *270*]. In South Wales, William Crawshay II, regarding his family as 'Iron Kings and Cyfarthfa as the crown they wore, wanted to dictate terms and force his own ideas upon the buyers'. The Guests of Dowlais 'might send agents to Russia to canvas for orders but Crawshay sat in his counting house and orders came [or failed to come] to him' [256: *120–6*].

Though these examples could be multiplied nothing can be proved by them. They are mentioned merely to indicate the desirability of additional research into the quality of entrepreneurship in the staple British industries during the decades following the heroic age of the Industrial Revolution, and to suggest the possibility that many more firms would have gone down in this period had they been confronted by the degree of competition encountered by their successors; that, in fact, 'a decline in entrepreneurship' can be selectively exemplified at almost every time and in almost every well-established branch of trade. Certainly the closing decades of the century possess no monopoly of this phenomenon.

Nevertheless, in one respect there *may* have been a difference between the pre-1870 and post-1870 decades. Towards the end of the latter period, whatever ingenious defences the 'new' economic historians have engineered to re-establish our faith in the quality of British entrepreneurship in cotton, coal, and iron and steel, there is no gainsaying the belated recognition of the growth and profit-potential of motor cars, some branches of chemicals, electrical engineering and the like. Few such significant failures to appreciate the *new* can be perceived in earlier years.

Take the possibilities for entrepreneurial resource engendered by the boundless demand associated with the coming of the railways. The number of patents taken out relating to railway equipment in the middle decades of the century was enormous. Everywhere, the engineers of the railway companies and freelance inventors developed their own devices to provide greater efficiency, safety and comfort, and the manufacture of many of their gadgets was taken up both by railway companies and by outside firms, some of which were literally brought into being to exploit railway patents. George Spencer & Co., for example, was created to work Spencer's own conical rubber buffer, draw and bearing spring patents of 1852 and 1853 and those granted to P. R. Hodge, J. E. Coleman and Richard Eaton. Similarly, John Brown of Sheffield, quickly perceiving the need for more powerful buffers as locomotive rolling stock outgrew plain wooden headstocks or horse-hair pads confined by metal bands, was already building his fortune on the manufacture of steel helical or volute buffer springs and, as early as 1855, was said to dispense no less than £5000 annually in 'getting people to uphold' his product, a sales technique which, coupled with a willingness to provide long credits and even take payments in shares, made him Spencer's most formidable rival in the ensuing decades [318: *2–3, 73–4*].

Other firms owed their origins to success in the desperate scramble to gain sole licences to work the patents of the host of railway inventors. Forges and brass- and iron-foundries came into being or were expanded in order to make innumerable fittings for locomotives and carriages, signals and lights, which, since they were specified for use in the construction of a particular locomotive or carriage design, the railway company workshop, locomotive builders or carriage and wagon manufacturers had no option but to 'buy in' [318: *138–41*]. Indeed, the engine and rolling stock works, spawned by the dozen in the middle decades of the century by the railway companies themselves and by outside initiatives, were the pioneers in the process whereby complicated machines and vehicles came to be assembled from a wide range of component parts of metal, wood, leather, glass, textile and rubber, for the most part manufactured by a host of suppliers working to exact specifications and, in the case of moving parts, to very close tolerances [103].

There was, in this instance, apparently no hesitation in taking up new things, adopting new production techniques, devising new modes of organisation, and fashioning new and flexible marketing organisations and techniques. Is this rapid appreciation of the new perhaps the *only* significant difference between the middle years of the nineteenth century and the two or three decades preceding the First World War? Or is this too an illusion, a consequence of the non-existence of competitive economies elsewhere against which to measure the mid-Victorian achievement? Indeed, how does one measure entrepreneurial capacity? 'The answer', as Saul has argued, 'may lie in a series of international comparisons' [248: *394*], but what if this technique is, as in the present case, inappropriate? Can one then employ the concept of export market shares? Hardly, in a period when Britain was virtually in a monopolistic position, enjoying the benefits of an early start. It might be possible to analyse deviations from what is apparently best practice in particular industries, though here one runs the real danger of equating 'best' with 'most recent'. It is enough to say that at this juncture there is insufficient information to assess mid-Victorian entrepreneurship in any meaningful sense.

Some firms which traced their origins to the Industrial Revolution were declining in relative importance; some were disappearing altogether; others were crowding in to take their chances in both old and new fields of enterprise. There were many who shared with Josiah Mason, the steel-pen maker and pioneer of electro-plating, a 'quickness in seizing a new idea . . . sagacity in realising the possibilities of development, and . . . courage in bringing it within the range of practical application' [257, vol. I: *151*], though few shared his great success. Yet an economic historian is ill-equipped to judge the technical feasibility of the thousands of inventions whose specifications – often deliberately obscure in their wording – line the walls of the Patent Office. How can one estimate what profitable opportunities went unexploited? It is not enough to say what had been done; it is necessary to assess what might have been done and was not. Not until the Americans, the Germans and the Belgians were in a position to undertake a range of manufacturing activities comparable with that of the British can innovatory negligence even begin to be appraised, though one would guess that in the middle decades of the nineteenth century such cases were few in number.[17]

But to point to the enthusiasm for taking up patents as an indication of energetic and adventurous entrepreneurial behaviour may be partially misleading, for it is equally capable of illustrating the adoption of tactics designed to permit survival rather than innovation and growth. The refusal of so many family concerns even to contemplate the adoption of the joint-stock organisation condemned the majority of them to remain limited in size. Given that many branches of economic activity experienced growing competition in the middle decades of the century, an increasing number of firms attempted to differentiate their products, frequently by concentrating on lines at the top end of the price range that exhibited craftsmanship and individual character. Alternatively, or even additionally, they could specialise in the manufacture of goods 'protected' – however dubiously – by a patent. Immediately the product was endowed with an inalienable uniqueness.

Almost equally powerful a weapon of sales strategy was the adoption of a distinctive trade mark of 'brand'. There was nothing new in this technique – once again it was well known to Wedgwood – but it seems to have been increasingly adopted in the middle decades of the century.[18] It must have received a considerable boost from the Great Exhibition of 1851, as a result of which the names of many firms and their products first became known nationally, even internationally. By advertising the medals won, by announcements in newspapers, by posters on railway stations, and above all by the 'pushing' of commercial travellers and commission agents, the product could sometimes attain a reputation for superiority over the basically similar offerings of competitors. (For case-studies, see [318: *95–113*; 122: *251*; 262: *29–331*; 339].)

By increasing specialisation designed to exploit marginal differences in quality or design, and by creating the impression that the differences were greater than they were in reality, many British firms were able to secure a degree of oligopoly power. This attempt to insulate themselves from the pricing policies of their rivals was in several instances sufficiently successful to permit some concerns to reap relatively high profits on a relatively small capital and turnover, even if this involved the exploitation of regional rather than national or international markets.

The policy of product differentiation, however, may well have had the consequence of depressing the national rate of economic growth. Many small firms were able to make comfortable profits, and were strengthened in their resolve not to increase the scale of their operation beyond the size which would have involved partially entrusting their businesses to managers recruited from outside the family circle. But having consciously decided to restrain the growth of the firm within the limits of existing managerial resources, such concerns were often ill-equipped to exploit overseas markets, even when it was considered desirable or necessary to do so.

At home a number of travelling salesmen might be employed to 'cover' the intended market and, since their remuneration was usually partly dependent upon the volume of sales, there was every likelihood that they would 'push' the firm's product vigorously. However, a permanent sales force of this kind was apt to be expensive, particularly in the early days of a firm's existence, and it was often supplemented by a network of strategically located commission agents. Selling through agents was particularly attractive to the relatively small concerns anxious to minimise direct selling costs and desirous of stabilising marketing expenses as a percentage of sales, particularly when the market for the product was characterised by seasonal or cyclical fluctuations. Furthermore, commission agents often enjoyed greater accessibility to certain trades because of previous or current experience with a related line.

Nevertheless, this mode of marketing possessed inherent disadvantages in the British context. So many British firms were small that agents would rarely act solely for one manufacturer. This often inhibited the continuous promotion of specific products; the agent varying his effort in accordance with the relative salability of the lines he represented in order to maximise his own income rather than the sales of the products of any one of his clients. Indeed, there is a possibility that a commission agent will deliberately refrain from maximising sales volume for fear that he will be replaced by a salesman when a certain level of business has been obtained. The inherent weaknesses involved in the use of commission agents were greater in overseas than in domestic trade where, because of distance, language difficulties and unfamiliarity with the market, the manufacturer had even less control over the agent sales force than at home. Partial representation was more likely since overseas agents tended to act for a greater number of firms, and the direct contact between the manufacturer and buyer was often so attenuated that inadequate market intelligence sometimes led to defective or apparently lethargic entrepreneurial response.[19]

In many cases, of course, there was no direct contact between manufacturer and consumer. Many manufacturers were wholly or partly dependent on wholesaling factors and merchants for the distribution of their goods.[20] This was the case, for example, in hardware, tinplate and many kinds of textiles. Furthermore, it is clear that many intermediaries required that their trademarks be put on goods manufactured by their suppliers, whose manoeuvrability and marketing strength must thereby have been greatly weakened, if not completely surrendered. Not the least important consequence of the manufacturers' dependence on 'the wholesale people' was the multiplicity of shapes, sizes and designs that they were expected to produce, for it was in the interests of the wholesale merchants to be able to offer a comprehensive 'range'. This method of marketing also made possible the continued existence of numerous small, often weakly-financed family concerns, many of whom chose to specialise in the exploitation of but a limited portion of the full spectrum of demand for related products.[21]

It would appear that the majority of British firms – whether their products were sold directly to the consumer or through intermediaries – became increasingly specialised during the middle decades of the nineteenth century. It was an ideal way to get started and, having become established, to survive. But as the author has argued elsewhere:

> specialisation, for whatever cause, tends to become increasingly irreversible, for there takes place a concomitant growth of special mercantile relationships, highly skilled labour forces and the evolution of particular types of managerial talent that makes any return to an earlier, more flexible, position more expensive and difficult. Thus, all too many British entrepreneurs ceased even to consider the possibilities of diversification, of branching out into entirely new lines of production where more profitable opportunities may have existed. Faced with an apparently limited market for the existing range of products, failure to grow was often incorrectly attributed to demand conditions rather than to the limited nature of entrepreneurial resources. The firm's resources, both material and entrepreneurial, had, in fact, become characterised by a high degree of "specificity". In many cases this inevitably involved a limitation of the firm's horizon of expectations and this constituted a barrier to further growth. (51: *525*]

It is apparent from the records of many of the West Riding wool textile firms [115: *251–2, 311*, note 50] and from the private ledgers of several Scottish firms that investment expenditures shifted from activities within the firm to investment in the equity of unrelated outside companies (for an interesting example, see [128: *13–15*]).

Growth did not constitute a major desideratum of the majority of British firms; they wished to remain small enough to permit supervision and control by the family. And if their profits were considered adequate – and product differentiation often meant relatively higher profits per unit of output – can they be criticised for so doing? It is unrealistic to suppose that entrepreneurs should be completely immune from experiencing an increasing desire to substitute leisure or political power, or prestige from philanthropic works, for income maximisation after a certain conventionally acceptable income level had been attained or a fortune acquired.[22] The danger involved is not only that the national rate of economic growth will fall below its potential or even optimum level – since, as Hobsbawm has emphasised, there is no necessary correspondence between the interest of the individual firm and the economy [25: *187–91*] – but that any future acceleration will be jeopardised.

It is arguable that in the mid nineteenth century British industrial organisation, characterised by the family firm, became partly ossified at a relatively immature level of development, and that this structure remained largely undisturbed even when the legal obstacles to the growth of firms were removed in the mid 1850s. The consequence would have been less severe had it not been for the fact that to combat foreign competition successfully in the closing decades of the century demanded large units enjoying lower unit costs, and marketing arrangements more sensitive than those that were an inevitable corollary to the small-scale firm.

(iii) 1870–1914: THE CRITICAL PERIOD?

One of the most stimulating debates by economic historians in the last two decades concerned the competence of entrepreneurs in late-Victorian and Edwardian Britain. Exercised by the need both to understand and to explain the declining rate of growth of industrial production, the relative deterioration in the international position and the sluggish rise in productivity, there has been an almost overwhelming temptation to adopt – in varying degrees – the suggestion of many critics that 'to an indefinable but considerable extent leadership was not wrested from Britain, but fell from her ineffectual grasp' [140: *230*]. Even those who have vigorously denied this proposition have reluctantly conceded that there might be something in it. 'It may be', wrote Saul, in an earlier study in this series, 'that after all is said and done, the entrepreneur and his shortcomings remain to provide the residual explanation for Britain's weaknesses' [55: *51*].

In summarising the case for the prosecution, Landes, acknowledging an element of caricature, found that British enterprise reflected a:

> combination of amateurism and complacency. Her merchants, who had once seized the markets of the world, took them for granted; the consular reports are full of the incompetence of British exporters, their refusal to suit their goods to the taste and pockets of the client, their unwillingness to try new products in new areas, their insistence that everyone in the world ought to read in English and count in pounds, shillings, and pence. Similarly, the British manufacturer was notorious for his indifference to style, his conservatism in the face of new techniques, his reluctance to abandon the individuality of tradition for the conformity implicit in mass production. [241: *564*]

Aldcroft, in his first tentative exploration of the role of the British entrepreneur, reached the 'inescapable' conclusion that 'the British economy could have been made more viable had there been a concerted effort on the part of British enterprise to *adapt itself more readily*' [227: 134]; and Levine, after examining a number of possible explanations of industrial retardation, concluded that 'technical and organisational lag in British industry was, more than anything else, a question of entrepreneurial responses' [243: *150*].

In this brief essay it is impossible to do justice to these authors. Their works all repay close study; and Landes's sophisticated reasoning is especially compelling. Indeed, his contribution to the *Cambridge Economic History of Europe* (subsequently reprinted with minor revisions and chronologically extended to the present day as *The Unbound Prometheus*) represents the high-water mark of the critical school. Although Habakkuk's remarkable essay, *American and British Technology in the Nineteenth Century* [237] – which drew attention to the possibility that British entrepreneurial shortcomings could be explained as a consequence of a slow rate of market growth, and that lack of adventurousness and dynamism in many branches of British industry was a logical response to demand conditions – provoked Landes into a brilliant rearguard action in 1965 [242], the hypothesis of entrepreneurial failure took 'quite a beating' in the late 1960s [246: *393*].

The attack on this hypothesis took several forms. It was pointed out that the student was being asked to accept a quantitative conclusion – that the detrimental effect of entrepreneurial deficiencies on the performance of the British economy was highly significant – on the basis of a qualitative argument; one moreover that rested on a somewhat narrow basis of fact. McCloskey and Sandberg emphasised Landes's heavy dependence on illustrations drawn from Burn's and from Burnham and Hoskins's studies of the British steel industry, and, less fairly, on 'a few . . . cases in chemicals, electrical engineering and a handful of other industries' [247: *97*]; and Sigsworth noted that Aldcroft's assertion that 'studies of the individual business firms confirm the belief that entrepreneurial initiative and drive was flagging, particularly before 1900' rests upon four such case-histories [252: *21*].

Characteristically, the response of British economic historians was to re-examine and broaden the factual base. Thus, Charles Wilson enlarged the scope of the enquiry by drawing attention to the entrepreneurial activities of those beyond the 'frontiers of pig iron and cotton stockings' to those engaged in the 'new industries, where the factory was encroaching on old craft, and the multiple on . . . the village shop', to the manufacturers of soap, patent medicines, mass-produced foodstuffs and confectionery; to the great publishers – George Newnes and Alfred Harmsworth – and to a miscellaneous collection of international freebooters who were carving out commercial empires abroad [255: *194–5*]. Although Saul's comment on this argument 'by example' was that it was hardly convincing [55: *62*], he was guilty of adopting a similar approach, albeit one with much greater analytical depth and penetration. His armour-piercing bullets – compared with Wilson's buckshot – were, appropriately, directed at the machine tool and mechanical engineering industries, which he found displayed many praiseworthy features. He made it plain that their very real commercial and technological successes had been generally underestimated [152; 153; 154; 229; and see the discussion by Floud, 107].

Meanwhile, the authors marshalled by Aldcroft [229] to examine a number of major British industries in an endeavour to refine his own earlier critical evaluation of the British entrepreneur were beavering away among the reports of government Commissions and Select Committees, trade journals, business histories and all manner of secondary sources to discover (perhaps to the editor's, perhaps to their own, surprise?) that really hard evidence of entrepreneurial failure was remarkably elusive. Indeed, Sigsworth, faced with this survey of British manufacturing industry, asked:

> can we still continue to generalise with such certainty about the characteristics of "the British entrepreneur" between 1870 and 1914? It is not simply that as *between* industries, British entrepreneurial performance was "patchy" and that a patchiness existed in "old" industries as well as "new", but that *within* industries (e.g. engineering, iron and steel, glass, wool textiles), there existed marked differences in performance between different sections and, within sections, between different firms. And if the diversity of experience appears even stronger than has hitherto been conceded, can we continue to accept generalised explanations about characteristics which, in so far as they amounted to 'shortcomings" or even "failure", were so variously distributed? [252: *129*]

And the relevance of these questions was enhanced by studies of the British boot and shoe [91], leather [93], and cycle industries [112].

But the British approach of piling case upon case, despite the increasing sophistication of the analyses, was unsatisfactory to those American scholars who were convinced that the measures of performance employed by Landes, Aldcroft and his associates, Wilson, Church and Harrison, were inadequate on theoretical grounds: 'measures of output because they confound influences of demand with those of supply and the measures of indicative innovations because they neglect the variability in the advantage to be gained from different innovations in different countries' [246: *100–1*]. Essentially, their argument was that the only legitimate way to arrive at a quantitative conclusion concerning the relative importance of entrepreneurial failure – if such proved to exist – was by quantitative methods, the selection of which should be determined by the application of explicit economic models.

As McCloskey and Sandberg, two of the leading proponents of this approach, argued in a very useful paper [247], since assertions of British entrepreneurial failure imply a comparison with superior performance elsewhere, usually in Germany or America, the first desideratum is some yardstick to measure the distance between British and foreign performance. That chosen was the profit forgone by choosing British over foreign methods. In other words:

> The adoption of foreign methods . . . is viewed as a potential investment, and entrepreneurial failure as a failure to make such investments as were profitable. The existence of profitable but unexploited investments is used to gauge whether British entrepreneurs could have done better, and the size of the foregone earnings to gauge the significance for economic growth of their failures to do so. [247: *102*][23]

Perhaps the most rigorous application of the new methodology to British experience was McCloskey's study of the iron and steel industry [129], an industry which had to a special degree encouraged generalisation concerning the economy as a whole. McCloskey argued that the slow adoption of the basic steel-making process (which has been called 'the most notable single instance of entrepreneurial failure') is explicable in terms of technological developments, and that the much-criticised neglect of phosphoric Lincolnshire ores was a rational response in a competitive market to the location of the ores. He was convinced that the British iron and steel masters exploited the potentialities of world technology before the First World War as well as, if not better than, their much lauded American competitors. 'Late Victorian entrepreneurs in iron and steel did not fail. By any cogent measure of performance in fact, they did very well indeed' [129: *127*]. And, in a much slighter and less convincing examination of the British coal industry, McCloskey found that 'the case for a failure of masters and men in British coal mining before 1913 . . . is vulnerable to a most damaging criticism; there was clearly no failure of [labour] productivity' [248: *295*].

Lars Sandberg also returned to the nineteenth-century staples, examining Britain's lag in adopting ring-spinning. Although this has usually been taken as a sign of technological conservatism, not to say backwardness, after a careful analysis of the differences that existed in the benefits to be derived from replacing mules with rings in the United States and the benefits to be derived from doing so in Great Britain, Sandberg concluded that under the conditions then prevailing with regard to factor costs, as well as the technical capabilities of the ring spindles then being built, the British may well have been acting rationally [150: *46*]. Furthermore, the same author found no evidence that firms installing automatic looms at the time the cotton textile industry was beginning to be criticised for ignoring them, in the first decades of the twentieth century, expanded faster or made larger profits than their more conservative competitors [150: *82–4*].

Indeed, of all the revisions employing econometric methods, only Lindert and Trace – using a cost-benefit calculation to measure the private profits forgone by a non-optional choice of techniques in the chemical industry – discovered an unambiguous case of entrepreneurial deficiency: among those alkali producers who clung to the Leblanc process long after the superiority of the ammonia process, patented by Solvay, was apparent [246: *239–74*; for the industrial context, see Warren, 167].

On the basis of these and other studies, McCloskey expressed the belief that there was 'little left of the dismal picture of British failure painted by historians' [247: *459*]. But doubts remained. Nicholas questioned the very basis of the methodology employed by the neo-classical cliometricians to show that no productivity failure occurred [250]. Locke criticised their failure to analyse sufficiently the factors involved in calculating cost, profit and productivity [244; 245] and, after reviewing the course of the debate, Crouzet remarked in 1982 that although McCloskey and Sandberg 'thought that they had saved the Victorian entrepreneur from damnation and assured his reputation. . . . Perhaps the wisest solution lies somewhere halfway – leaving many late Victorian entrepreneurs in some sort of Purgatory, undamned but still unredeemed' [12: *412*].

So much depended upon what yardsticks were used for the measurement of success or failure: international productivity comparisons? the rapidity of technological diffusion? profitability? the dispersion among various industries of the rate of return to capital? So much of the argument turned upon a consideration of aggregative measures. The firm, which in the nineteenth century was, after all, the engine of economic progress, and the individual entrepreneur tended to get lost. Only Floud applied economic methods (regression analysis) to assess performance at the level of the individual British enterprise – Greenwood & Batley, a leading firm of machine tool makers – and even in this case, with fairly complete statistical data, the findings were somewhat inconclusive if only because it was impossible to determine the precise significance of the growth rate in labour productivity (2.3 per cent per annum) which this firm achieved in the latter part of the century [246: *313–37*].

Nevertheless, one feels that the key to an understanding of the role of the entrepreneur and hence a proper assessment of his performance must be in the analysis of the business records that are now, after decades of neglect, increasingly being located and properly calendared and preserved [349–368]. As Richardson observed, 'what makes a progressive entrepreneur is how he acts in a *given set of conditions*' [229: *276*], and to discover these conditions, which are often highly specific and extremely complex, it is imperative to analyse the letter books, the bundles and files of incoming correspondence, the account books and the internal memoranda of individual firms, and compare the results with those derived from the records of similar firms in the same line of business operating in the same markets.

Only a decade or so ago such a course of action seemed almost utopian; now it becomes increasingly plausible. That formidable difficulties are involved is undeniable, but the effort should be made if only because entrepreneurial behaviour can only be assessed within the context of the individual firm, and an assessment so derived inevitably gains in significance with comparative enquiries into competing firms.[24] There has been all too much criticism based upon social and/or general criteria. To draw once again upon Richardson's pertinent discussion:

> If innovations do not yield reductions in average unit costs, then it would be irrational for a businessman to introduce them even if the innovations would benefit the future growth of the economy. The individual businessman cannot be expected to estimate external economies. The net social returns from investment in innovations may be higher than the private returns, with the result that a capitalistic environment may produce a rate of innovation well below the social optimum [229: *275*];

an argument echoed in Hobsbawm's widely read study *Industry and Empire* [25: *187*].

But the procedure of investigating in detail the surviving records of individual enterprises cannot answer all the questions. One serious deficiency is that it cannot fully reveal why some potentially profitable avenues of enterprise – in, say, some branches of chemicals and pharmaceuticals, electric engineering, domestic equipment, and the like – were either apparently neglected or ignored,[25] simply because inactivity, by definition, can leave no written testimony. In his stimulating survey of *Economic Growth in France and Britain 1851–1950*, Kindleberger has argued that 'social values' must be given the greatest weight in explanations of why new enterprises failed to elbow their way to the forefront in Britain after 1880.

> As business became more complex, the amateur ideal of British society became less sought through accumulation and more through the liberal professions, the civil services, and politics. The attention of people in business drew back from income maximisation. Those outside either found themselves satisfied with social acceptance in a class structure which emphasised cosiness or sought to achieve the upper-middle-class ideal in other ways. The hungry outsiders – immigrants, Quakers, Jews, and lower-class aspirants to wealth – diminished either in numbers or in the intensity of their drive. [32: *133*]

And Coleman's elegant series of variations on the earlier part of this theme, 'Gentlemen and Players' [234], is both thought-provoking and convincing.

There seems little question that many known cases of neglect have correctly been ascribed to the fact that 'the Englishman . . . [had] yet to learn that an extended and systematic education up to and including the methods of original research [was] now a necessary preliminary to the fullest development of industry' [217: *17*]. Landes has pointed to the:

> library of lament and protest about the failure of British educational institutions to turn out applied scientists in numbers and of a quality comparable to those produced in Germany; the failure of British enterprise to use such scientific personnel as were available; the scorn of the body of entrepreneurs for innovations in this domain; and the misuse of such scientists as were employed. [242: *28*][26]

And Coleman [234], Levine [243], Locke [202] and Sanderson [217] have, in their different ways, gone far to explaining these failures, the significance of which seems undeniable, if unmeasurable. Nevertheless, the student of economic history does well to heed Hobsbawm's warning of the dangers of being seduced by 'simple sociological explanations' [25: *189*]. Kindleberger implies a diminution in the supply of potential entrepreneurs, but there is no evidence of any such shortage, rather the reverse. It is possible that there were too many entrepreneurs in late-nineteenth-century Britain.

It is not without significance that much of the criticism of the quality of British entrepreneurship is based upon the consular reports, which constitute a veritable 'compendium of derogatory information on British trade' [240, II:*26*].[27] Even allowing for the fact that 'the consuls reporting were less interested in the aggregate of British exports, or even the total of exports to their own areas, than in the fortunes of specific commodities, the outcome of given contract negotiations, the success of a particular businessman or syndicate' – that, in fact, their accounts 'tended to emphasise the unfavourable news' – there is a verisimilitude about some of the complaints that it would be foolish to deny. One thing is certain: there was 'no phase of the question of foreign competition with British trade abroad on which so much unanimity appears to prevail on the part of Her Majesty's representatives as that of the scarcity of the British commercial traveller'.[28] Why was this? Why was a marketing system so successfully employed in the home market apparently so woefully under-utilised abroad?[29]

The explanation is not simply to be found in the Englishman's traditional abysmal ignorance of, or inability to learn foreign languages. It is more deep-rooted than that. It is related to the structure of British industry itself. The representative British firm was too small to be able to afford a vigorous selling effort in world markets by means of a salaried force of commercial travellers.[30] Hence the continued dependence upon commission agencies and large-scale merchant importers, who, as has been explained, were by no means as 'pushing' as the American and German salesmen employed by much larger manufacturing enterprises.[31] There is no need to labour this point. It is mentioned again simply because it emphasises the necessity – if foreign competition abroad was to be more successfully combated – of an increase in the scale of the average unit in many branches of British industry.

This was not be be: firstly, because of the limitation on growth inherent within the closely controlled private company; and secondly, because many firms were able to avoid losing their identities through amalgamation by means of membership of a trade association. From the viewpoint of enlarged scale this was a double loss. The amalgamation movement was inhibited and the size of the median firm remained small. Furthermore, the industry as a whole 'carried' a number of manifestly inefficient firms. As one witness to the Committee on Trusts explained, although 'it was a law of progess that the inefficient should go . . . in practice progress was impeded because he would not go, so instead of trying to kill him' off, he was pensioned off, 'since that cost far less'.[32]

This policy might have had less detrimental effect on economic growth and less debilitating effects on the export trade if any of the numerous associations which the committee on Trusts revealed had come into being at the close of the nineteenth century had adopted some form of central selling agency, but none of them had. There was 'no counterpart in Great Britain of the German Kartell'[33] whose diligent representatives so impressed the consular officials. Thus the British economy was characterised by relatively small firms whose ability to compete abroad – when, indeed, they made any attempt to do so – was inherently weak,[34] a weakness which was exacerbated by the widespread policy of product differentiation, the successful implementation of which demands continuous personal representation in the market. At home, or in limited regional areas, this could be done; overseas, it was impossibly expensive for the small firm, and of the 'giant companies' that came into existence at the close of the century, few could equal J. & P. Coats, under the redoubtable German salesman, O. E. Phillipi [219: *389–92*], in the efficiency of their marketing organisations.

Instead, resort was made to meeting the most perverse specifications in order to satisfy the customer's often unreasonable demands. British steelmakers offered a multiplicity of shapes and sections [229: *80–1*]; the locomotive and carriage and wagon builders went to almost ridiculous lengths to satisfy the whims of consulting engineers [318; see also 82: *192*]; rarely did a shipbuilder send two similar vessels down the slipways of the Clyde or the Tyne; while at the level of the firm, C. & J. Clark of Street offered literally hundreds of types of boots, shoes and slippers [338: *96–7*]; the number of varieties of biscuits produced by Huntley and Palmers exceeded 400 by the end of the century, many of them specifically for the export trade to which the firm was giving absolute priority [279: *159*]; the early pattern books of the United Turkey Red Company of Alexandria, founded in 1898, contain examples of thousands of prints designed to appeal to the varied tastes of customers throughout the world [362: *52*]; 'Greenwood & Batley made, in the period from 1856 to 1900, 793 differently named machine tools, of which 457 were ordered only once during the period' [246: *321*].

Clearly, in these cases, there was vigour, a responsiveness to the vagaries of demand and the requests of the customers. What is less certain is how representative these examples are. One suspects that the records of the smaller concerns in most industries would reveal a disproportionate concentration on the home market, not because of any lack of trade to be obtained overseas, but because of an intrinsic weakness in the small firm's ability to exploit it. It may be that during the nineteenth century exporting vigour and overseas selling was in direct relationship to the size of the firm, and that the size of the average British firm in most industrial categories was relatively small. If Britain lost her pre-eminence in international trade during the latter part of the nineteenth century more quickly than she need have done (in itself an almost endlessly debatable proportion), this was doubtless partly due not to any general decline in entrepreneurial ability but to a surfeit of individual entrepreneurs, a multitude of aggressively independent firms, each pursuing their own self-interest where any increase in the rate of economic growth demanded more co-operation.[35] But that, as Hobsbawm might put it, could not be expected of an unplanned capitalistic economy.

Only if, as Allen and Lazonick – basing their arguments on brilliant analyses of the North-east Coast pig iron [68][36] and the British cotton industry [123–7] – have argued we abandon the concept of the entrepreneur as a neo-classical manager optimising his profits subject to given constraints, and embrace a Schumpeterian definition of the entrepreneur as one who fundamentally changes these constraints – by, for example, accelerating the speed with which he adopted improved technology (Allen) or by altering the organisational structure that determines technological choices and profitable opportunities, and hence transforming his industrial environment (Lazonick) – can British industrialists be condemned.

Lazonick accuses them of entrepreneurial failure because they failed 'to confront institutional constraints innovatively' [15: 2]. To Lazonick only the replacement of the atomistic, competitive organisation of British industry by a corporate, concentrated, managerial structure capable of superseding the market as an allocative mechanism could British decline be halted or even reversed.

In focusing attention on the question of institutional adaptation, Lazonick and Elbaum have, in effect, given substance to the generalities of Mancur Olsen[37], and doubtless much future work will necessarily be involved with illustrating, refining and assessing their approach, which represents a major advance in understanding Britain's relative decline. It is less clear whether it will further knowledge of the role of the entrepreneur in this decline since it is dependent upon the acceptance of a definition of entrepreneurship which is at variance with that upon which the debate has hitherto been conducted (see the interesting discussion by Harvey [192]).

Recent explorations make it unrealistic to condemn the great majority of British businessmen for the way they behaved *within the context of their individual firms*. Even Lazonick agrees that they 'performed admirably as neo-classical managers – they took the conditions facing them as given and tried to do the best they could' [125:236]. It is difficult to accept his corollary that to merit the use of the appellation 'entrepreneur', they *should* have transformed their industrial environment. That they did not do so is not to be explained by reference to 'cultural conservatism', as Wiener has so elegantly argued [253].[38] The questions that need to be answered are: 'How could they?'[39] and equally, if not more important, 'Why should they?', when the problems confronting those who tried were, as Elbaum indicates in his study of the early steel industry [15: 51– 81][40] all but insuperable; the cost – in profits foregone and the horrendous physical and mental strain involved – so high; and the rewards so uncertain.

Furthermore, would Lazonick's restructuring of the British economy *before the First World War* have retarded Britain's economic decline? It is impossible to say, but the question does suggest a more recent analogy. With the recent and continuing mania for mergers in Great Britain, there is no doubt that institutional rigidities are being eroded. Will British industry be revitalised by the massive restructuring currently underway? It remains to be seen, but it requires the exercise of considerable optimism to believe that the present increase in industrial concentration will necessarily lead to the regeneration of the British economy.

Be that as it may, it is undeniable – as Allen implies [68] – that the rate of British economic growth in the decades before the First World War would have been enhanced had *more* businessmen developed new technologies or new industries possessing high potential levels of productivity. The reason why the British economy failed to generate this desirable response was not so much the fault of the entrepreneur but stemmed largely from the British educational system. Certainly, this was the belief of Herbert Gray and Samuel Turner writing in 1916 [236], and echoed most recently by Correlli Barnett [3] and, even more specifically, by R. R. Locke, whose study demonstrates that the relative decline of the British economy since 1880 can be explained by our inferior and inappropriate educational system [202]. By emphasising the needs of technologically-based industries (and it was here that the British lagged so grievously) and the nature of the new professional skills and business organisations that the growth of the large-scale firm demanded, Locke shows that higher education in Germany – and to a lesser extent in the United States – met these requirements far more successfully than did the British and French systems. It is, moreover, arguable that Britain's education system – and here we are focusing particularly on the primary and secondary level – was also socially more divisive than elsewhere, and that it therefore contributed to the continuance of attitudes and social relations between managers and workers hostile to the development of an efficient, modern economy.

It is not implausible that at a critical time an important sector of the British labour force was, paradoxically, too well-trained (as opposed to being too well-educated), too disciplined and skilled to encourage their employers to abandon handicraft techniques, which in any case were consistent with the tactics of product differentiation. The long-run economic significance of skilled labour, initially postulated by C. K. Harley [238], has received powerful support from W. Lewchuk who, in his studies of the British motor vehicle industry, had emphasised the importance of the associated tradition of labour independence on the shop floor which made it necessary for management to exercise only partial control over labour effort and to depend upon the motivation provided by piece-rates to secure a relatively high and acceptable profit despite low productivity, the malign consequences of which were not fully exposed until the 1960s [15: *135–61*]. It was, moreover, the skill of the British labour force, combined with their appreciation of the 'rules of the game', that inhibited innovation – as Donald Coleman and Christine MacLeod have revealed [235], and as Lazonick has demonstrated in the case of cotton [124] – and so contributed to the relatively low level of investment in Great Britain which, perhaps as much as any other factor, retarded British economic growth.

Additional reasons for the low level of investment in manufacturing activity were undoubtedly the relative attractiveness of the service sector which, it is plain, did not fail to recruit new entrepreneurs [255] and the fact – demonstrated by Rubinstein [213–216] – that money could be made so much more easily in finance than in industry, a point vividly exemplified by Davenport-Hines' masterly study of *Dudley Docker* [280] and by numerous entries in the *Dictionary of Business Biography* [198]. Clive Lee's work [35–38] makes it clear that the expansion of the service sector *during the late-Victorian period* possessed highly beneficial consequences for economic growth and that this growth was neither directly nor in spatial terms immediately dependent upon manufacturing. Thus, the movement into services, to which Charles Wilson drew attention in 1965 [255], provides positive evidence of entrepreneurial perspicacity and vigour in the closing decades of the nineteenth century, and this verdict has recently been strengthened by a number of specific illustrations, among the more notable of which have been those provided by William Rubinstein [198, Vol. 11: *248–64*], Edwin Green and Michael Moss [286], T. R. Nevett [137], Asa Briggs [264], J. W. Reader [322], Clive Trebilcock [341] and Charles Wilson himself [347].

In the context of this exploration of entrepreneurship and British relative economic decline, this movement into services is of the utmost importance. If the 'British entrepreneur' is to be criticised for failing constructively to confront the organisational constraints that were progressively strangling him in the staple industries (industries which were so labour-intensive that Clive Lee has described them collectively as the apogee of proto-industrialisation, rather than the products of an Industrial Revolution), and if he is to be criticised for failing more vigorously to enter new manufacturing industries, then surely this same 'British entrepreneur' deserves some praise for moving into the service sector, whose relatively rapid rate of output growth and high productivity, certainly between c. 1870–1913, was so much superior to the old staples that its expansion provided what little buoyancy there was in Britain's aggregate economic growth.[41]

Were, then, the four decades preceding the First World War a critical period of entrepreneurship? The answer must be 'no'. It was simply that with the development of competitive economies, British entrepreneurial errors and hesitation, *always present*, even in the period of the classic Industrial Revolution, became more apparent, and the belabouring of the businessmen who seemed inadequate in their responses mollified the frustrations of those who believed that British industrial supremacy before the mid 1870s was somehow normal and her accelerating relative decline thereafter, abnormal. Rather was it that the whole complex of circumstances that produced British pre-eminence before 1873 was fortuitous. To see the course of British economic development in the nineteenth century in terms of the dissipation of an initial fund of entrepreneurialship is untenable.

6 Conclusions

The one certain conclusion that can be drawn from this all too brief survey is that there is much more to be discovered about the British entrepreneur in the nineteenth century. Charles Wilson's observation remains valid: 'let us not be in too much of a hurry to reach for the black cap: there is more evidence to come'.[42] It is still dangerous to speak of *'the British entrepreneur'*. No such person exists. Over the century there were countless different entrepreneurs in a remarkable variety of trades and industries. Some, perhaps the majority at any one time, were first-generation entrepreneurs, striving to establish a manufacturing firm, a merchant house, a shipping line, and doubtless – if recent enquiries into the small firm are any guide[43] – imbued with enthusiasm and adventuousness; others were the descendants of the founders, apparently less 'pushing', more concerned with order, stability and the sheer mechanics of organisation, to whom the firm was less all-consuming of energy and time; and, during the closing decades of the century, there was a growing number of managers, perhaps from a different socio-economic background, operating within a different institutional framework, and apparently increasingly concerned with the attainment of different objectives.

Indeed, it may be that one element in the lethargic response of some British entrepreneurs to foreign competition in the decades before the First World War was that at the very period when such competition became significant, Britain's industrial structure was being transformed, and that in this transitional stage, during which the dominance of the private company was giving way to the large-scale joint-stock company with limited liability, there was insufficient expertise available to manage the emergent 'giant' enterprises that possessed the potential capacity to grapple with American, German and Belgian competitors (see, for example, the penetrating studies by Locke, [202; 244; 245]). What little is known about the internal organisations of the burgeoning large-scale firms – especially those created by amalgamation and merger – inspires scant confidence in their ability to formulate a swift or appropriate response to conditions of difficulty [52: *534–5*].

But when one attempts to understand the specific problems that were being encountered by industrial firms – and this often involves a degree of technical insight with which historians are rarely generously endowed – one can seldom fault the solution arrived at in the light of the available information at the disposal of the entrepreneur or the board at the time of the decision. As Platt has justly observed: 'As historians, we would be unwise to assume that we can judge business decisions by a kind of macro-economic hindsight, by broad economic trends, by developments which may be clear enough to us now but which at the time covered more than a man's working lifetime' [142: *309*]. Yet the consequence of envisaging businessmen as neo-classical managers optimising profits subject to given constraints is that it has not been difficult to give them 'a clean bill of health' [190: *121*], despite Britain's relatively slow rate of economic growth between the 1880s and the inter-war years and the deterioration of her international position. Should then the application of the term 'entrepreneur' be forbidden to all who failed to lead in the internal transformation of their chosen industries? It seems pedantic to do so, especially when the empirical evidence correlating increased industrial concentration and corporate capitalism to economic growth is so ambivalent.[44]

The current state of the debate on British entrepreneurs before 1914 appears to indicate that as a whole they did not fail, although in certain industrial sectors there appears to have been a failure of entrepreneurship. Such an epigrammatic conclusion is far from satisfactory but it does reveal the desirability of, and scope for further inquiry. The analysis of the data by the editors of the *Dictionary of Business Biography* and the *Dictionary of Scottish Business Biography* [198: 219] should go some way towards extending Charlotte Erickson's work [182] on the social, educational and religious backgrounds of entrepreneurs and top management; but there is still a need to discover more about the motivations of entrepreneurs and the changes in their motivation over time [179]; the longevity of firms in different industries; the influence of institutional arrangements upon entrepreneurial goals; the relationship between size of firm and marketing policies; the possibility, suggested by Checkland, that firms 'cannot adjust to change continuously, but must reach some critical level of vulnerability before a response is forthcoming'.[45] These are but a handful of the themes whose exploration would be enhanced by more evidence. Such comparative investigations are inherently complex, and the less ambitious or less experienced student should remember the continuing need for detailed narratives in a wide variety of business endeavour; analytical case-studies, particularly for the middle decades of the century; and the provision of data permitting inter-firm productivity and profitability comparisons. The range of questions is almost endless; the raw material for research is assuming awesome proportions; new and more precise methods of inquiry are being evolved. One day it may be less hazardous to generalise about different categories of British entrepreneurs. Currently, it is still as dangerous a pursuit as it was a dozen years ago when the first edition of this essay was published, but perhaps therein lies its continuing fascination.

Notes and References

1. Arthur Shadwell, *Industrial Efficiency*, new edn (1909) p. 653. That Shadwell's criticisms were not without foundation is apparent in several recent studies; see, for example, Mary Rose on Edward Hyde Greg [333: *92–5*] Richard Wilson on Sir Walter Greene [198, vol. II: *673*], and Maurice Kirby on Joseph Whitwell Pease [299: *55*].

2. For an interesting discussion of entrepreneurship, business performance and industrial development, see Alford [231]; Casson's economic theory of the entrepreneur [177] is valuable.

3. My own researches into the files of the early Scottish companies [52] makes me very sceptical of Kennedy's argument that '*at the root of this very hesitant development* lay the fact that the legal requirements governing managerial behaviour and the disclosure of company affairs under limited liability were so minimally drawn as to place the company's directors in virtually unchallengeable and unchecked possession of the company's assets' [31: *113*, emphasis supplied].

4. Although, as Lazonick [34: *119–39*] has recently emphasised, this took a remarkably long time.

5. The phrase used by Richard Wilson [226: *122*] which, he asserts, bears no resemblance to the activities of the Leeds merchants.

6. There are, of course, exceptions. For an interesting – if not necessarily typical – example, see Minchinton's study of the tinplate makers of West Wales [134: *106–7*].

7. It has to be said that the motives which inspired some industrialists to invest in land were not confined to the quest for prestige. Mary Rose has shown that the Gregs purchased land because it was safe investment, and 'far from being a hindrance to the millowner, land might prove a positive advantage, by making mortgages easier to obtain in time of need, or by improving the return on capital' [332: *79–88*]; and Hudson has emphasised the importance of the ownership of landed property in gaining access to credit [115: *269*].

8. Details of some of the houses built for Victorian entrepreneurs

are provided by Mark Girouard's fascinating study, *The Victorian Country House* (Oxford, 1971); for examples cited, see pp. 7, 8, 184, 186–7.

9. Byres has shown how the Bairds of Gartsherrie conformed to the Buddenbrook dynamic. Control of their great firm passed out of the hands of the family after the impressive efforts of the second generation had given it a position of supremacy in the Scottish iron industry [232, vol. II: *802–6*]. One particularly odious member of the third generation, 'Squire Baird' as he was nicknamed, a backer of prizefighters, had the dubious, if appropriate, distinction of being accorded a pen-picture by the scurrilous Frank Harris in *My Life and Loves* (1964), vol. 3, ch. XIII.

10. It was observed by G. d'Eichthal in 1828 that: 'Throughout Lancashire no family survives longer than two generations. Children brought up to habits of luxury and idleness are incapable of salvaging their business when fortune turns against them' (quoted by Gatrell [18: *117*]). Data on the West of England cloth industry in the first half of the century show a very high mortality rate, and even the names of the relatively few surviving firms may have concealed a change of partners [131: *104–5*]. The volatility of firms in the cotton industry in the early nineteenth century, 'with high exit rates compensated by high entry rates', is demonstrated by Lloyd-Jones and Le Roux [41: *147*].

11. In both cases it is intended to subject the data collected by the galaxy of authors to computer-assisted analysis.

12. For these unique companies, see Roland Smith [160], R. E. Tyson [342; 343], W. A. Thomas [162: *145–68*] and, particularly, D. A. Farnie [104: *244–73*].

13. That some attempted to do so is evident from the pioneering study by Haydn Jones of *Accounting, Costing and Cost Estimation [in] Welsh Industry: 1700–1830* [121].

14. After the first edition of this study appeared, Roy Church subjected this section to protracted critical examination [7: *19–43*]. Since several of his strictures and suggested modifications are not only tangential but rest on foundations 'only marginally less flimsy' than my own, I have retained my original treatment of this period in the hope that it may continue to stimulate constructive debate and inspire further empirical inquiry. I would add only that my own explorations since the early 1970s, primarily into Scottish business archives [141; 52], have proved to be consistent with the majority of

the hypotheses put forward in the following pages.

15. Of the *surviving* 1200 companies of the 30,000 firms registered as companies in London between 1856 and 1889, the majority are concerned with banking, insurance, food, drink and leisure or are professional associations. Industrial concerns are relatively rare. See Richmond and Stockford [365].

16. Professor Church regards this opinion 'as quite simply untenable' [7: *38*] and chastises me for citing it. It must be confessed that I found it irrisistible! This is not the place to pursue our differing interpretations of the period, suffice it to say that the differences between us on the question of profits are briefly discussed by Mokyr [249: *866–9*].

17. It must be confessed that this observation is founded on an acquaintance with a fairly limited range of railway equipment, the technical understanding of which took all too long to acquire.

18. Considerable evidence on this practice is contained in the Minutes of Evidence of the *Select Committee on Trade Marks*, 1862 (212, xii, pp. 431–627). See also Redford [146: *42*], Alexander [65: *114–15, 126, 149*], Jefferys [117: *passim*].

19. For a brief but cogent discussion of the advantages and disadvantages of employing commission agents both at home and overseas, see Stephen Nicholas, 'Agency Contracts, Institutional Modes, and the Transition to Foreign Direct Investment by British Manufacturing Multinationals before 1939', *Journal of Economic History*, XLIII (1983), 677–9.

20. As Platt argues, for the small manufacturer this often made good sense. '"Never thou put salt water between thee and thy money" was the advice which the British manufacturer received from his cradle' [142: *142*].

21. The foregoing argument – based upon a reading of a variety of business archives supplemented by numerous hints in secondary sources – is set down as an hypothesis requiring more rigorous empirical testing. Needless to say, it is only our general ignorance of marketing – and the significance attached to it by the author – which makes its inclusion permissible in a study such as this.

22. As William Rathbone of Liverpool wrote to his wife in July 1869: 'My feeling with a merchant was that when he got over £200,000 he was too rich for the Kingdom of Heaven' [308: *3*].

23. It might be helpful to emphasise a point made by McCloskey and Sandberg:

The opportunities foregone in neglecting the best technique have been expressed in a variety of ways and this gives a misleading impression of heterogeneity of purpose in the new work. The various measures used are essentially identical. Higher profits can be achieved if more output can be produced with the same inputs, that is if productivity can be raised. The measuring rod for entrepreneurial failure, then, can be expressed indifferently as the money amount of profit foregone, as the proportion by which foreign exceeded British productivity, as the distance between foreign and British production functions, or as the difference in cost between foreign and British techniques. All of these give the same result and each can be translated exactly into any one of the others. [247; 103]

For a criticism of the methodological technique involved, see Nicholas [250].

24. It is the consistent appraisal of entrepreneurial efficiency, using a variety of techniques, that makes the studies of shipping companies by Hyde and his colleagues at the University of Liverpool so valuable [293; 294; 308; 309].

25. A formidable list of new inventions and innovations more quickly taken up by Americans and Europeans than by the British was compiled in 1916 by H. G. Gray (a member of the Mosely Educational Commission to the United States in 1903) and Samuel Turner [236].

26. Byatt has illustrated the fact that in the electrical industries, 'British businessmen were not very good at using their engineers' [82: *190*], and Pollard and Robertson that in shipbuilding, 'few builders maintained even rudimentary laboratory facilities or employed *any* scientists' [144: *137*, emphasis supplied].

27. The study by Ross J. S. Hoffman [239] is heavily reliant on this source. It is interesting to compare his findings with those of Platt [142: *136–72*], whose analysis of the same material is much more understanding of economic realities. See also Alfred Marshall [45: *135–6*] and, for a more favourable view of the British overseas marketing performance in the decades before 1914, Nicholas [251].

28. *Opinions of H.M. Diplomatic and Consular Officers on British Trade Methods*, Cd.9078 (1898) p. 5. See the discussion by Aldcroft [230: *295–9*].

29. For comparative figures of travellers in the Swiss market at the

close of the century, see Chapman [6; 253].

30. Some idea of the expenses incurred in overseas representation is given by Platt [142: *143–4*]. See also Payne [318: *190*], Davis [281: *33–5*] and Hoffman [239: *87*]. J. H. Fenner & Co's principal foreign representative, operating in southern and south-eastern Europe, was so generously remunerated with salary and commission that in 1910–13 he was earning more than the company's managing director [281: *33*].

31. For an interesting example – the way in which Singers built up its European markets – see R. B. Davis, '"Peacefully Working to Conquer the World": The Singer Manufacturing Company in Foreign Markets, 1854–1889', *Business History Review*, XLIII (1969) especially 306–11.

32. Ministry of Reconstruction, *Report of the Committee on Trusts*, Cd.9236 (1918), p. 3.

33. *Ibid.*, p. 22. See *Report of the Departmental Committee appointed by the Board of Trade to consider the position of the Textile Trades after the War*, Cd.9070 (1918), p. 113.

34. This argument, based upon business archives to which the author has had access, receives some support from the Bolton Report, *Report of the Committee of Inquiry on Small Firms*, Cmnd.4811 (1971) pp. 37–9.

35. This point was made in a number of reports of the committees set up to consider the position of several trades after the war of 1914–18. See, for example, *Report of the Departmental Committee appointed by the Board of Trade to consider the position of the Shipping and Shipbuilding Industry after the War* Cd.9092 (1918), p. 31, paras. 89–90: 'Whilst individualism has been of inestimable advantage in the past, there is reason to fear that individualism by itself may fail to meet the competition of the future in Shipbuilding and Marine Engineering, as it has failed in other industries. We are convinced that the future of the nation depends to a large extent upon increased co-operation in its great industries.' How the existence of many mutually suspicious firms could constitute a formidable barrier to improvement in an industry is perhaps best illustrated in tinplate [134: *87–8, 198*].

36. Although the central thrust of Allan's article [68] is both sound and stimulating, it can and has been criticised in detail. I am grateful to Dr Gordon Boyce for allowing me to read his unpublished manuscript entitled 'The Development of the Cargo Fleet Iron Co.,

1900–1914: A Study of Entrepreneurship, Planning, and Production Costs in the Northeast Coast Basic Steel Industry'.

37. Mancur Olson, *The Rise and Decline of Nations: Economic Growth, Stagflation, and Social Rigidities* (New Haven, Conn., 1982), see especially pp. 77–87.

38. See the criticisms of Wiener's thesis by Saul [55: *69–70*]; Coleman and MacLeod [235: *599–600*]; McKendrick [42: *101, 103*]; and J. M. Winter [42: 185–6].

39. This is not the place to take up this major question but it is worthy of note that Kennedy [22: *151–83*; 30; 31] implies that even entrepreneurs of Schumpeterian stature would have found it difficult to achieve rapid structural change in the late Victorian economy because of the inadequacies of the capital market, cf. the cogent, if brief, discussion by Lee [37: *66–70*].

40. It is not without significance that Elbaum, Lazonick's co-editor of *The Decline of the British Economy*, remarks in the course of his illuminating paper: 'That British firms none the less lagged behind their competitors was less the result of entrepreneurial failure – *as the term is conventionally understood* – than of the constraints on individual entrepreneurial action posed by market conditions and a rigid institutional environment' [15: *54*, emphasis supplied].

41. Manufacturing labour productivity in the United Kingdom in 1870 was only 71 per cent of that in services; in 1913, only 46 per cent [38, Table 1]. Even so, an important component of the service industries, insurance, has not escaped criticism from Trebilcock for entrepreneurial failings in the late Victorian period [42: *137–72*].

42. C. Wilson, 'Canon Demant's Economic History', *Cambridge Journal*, VI (1953–4), p. 286.

43. See Jonathan Boswell, *The Rise and Decline of Small Firms*, (1973), pp. 36, 68–74; Donald A. Hay and Derek J. Morris, *Unquoted Companies* (1984).

44. See, for example, K. Cowling, P. Stoneman *et al.*, *Mergers and Economic Performance* (1980).

45. S. G. Checkland, review of Coleman's *Courtauld's* in *Economic History Review*, 2nd ser. XXIII (1970), 559–60.

Select Bibliography

Such has been the flood of books and articles on different aspects of entrepreneurship in the past decade that it is impossible fully to recommend a general bibliography to both the subject and the period covered in this essay. That compiled by David Landes for the *Cambridge Economic History of Europe, Vol. VI: The Industrial Revolution and After*, ed. H. J. Habakkuk and M. Postan (Cambridge, 1965) remains valuable; A. E. Musson's list in *The Growth of British Industry* (1978) is useful, as are the 'Notes' to Crouzet's *The First Industrialists* (Cambridge, 1985) and the footnotes to Coleman and MacLeod [197a].

The purpose of this brief bibliography is to provide references to the secondary works upon which this essay is based; to furnish a guide to further reading; and to indicate a number of basic sources which might profitably be consulted by those students seeking to pursue research into those business archives which may, in time, serve to confirm or to deny some of the arguments advanced by those who have rushed to judge the British entrepreneur. The bibliography is roughly divided into six main sections which are not mutually exclusive. The second of these, 'Studies of Particular Industries, Trade and Regions', is particularly selective, the works cited being those which have special relevance to this exploratory essay.

The place of publication is London unless otherwise stated.

I GENERAL WORKS AND THOSE CONCERNED WITH INDUSTRIAL STRUCTURE AND ORGANISATION

[1] T. S. Ashton, 'The Growth of Textile Businesses in the Oldham District, 1884–1924', *Journal of the Royal Statistical Society*, LXXXIX (1926).
[2] W. Ashworth, 'Changes in the Industrial Structure, 1870–1914', *Yorkshire Bulletin of Economic and Social Research*, XVII (1965).

[3] Corrrelli Barnett, *The Audit of War* (1986).
[4] David Cannadine, 'The Present and the Past in the English Industrial Revolution, 1880–1980', *Past and Present*, No. 103 (1984).
[5] A. D. Chandler, 'The Growth of the Transnational Industrial Firm in the United States and the United Kingdom: A Comparative Analysis', *Economic History Review*, 2nd Ser., XXXIII (1980).
[6] S. J. Chapman, *Work and Wages, Pt I: Foreign Competition* (1904).
[7] Roy Church (ed.), *The Dynamics of Victorian Business* (1980).
[8] J. H. Clapham, *An Economic History of Modern Britain*, 3 vols (Cambridge, 1926–38).
[9] P. Lesley Cook, *Effects of Mergers: Six Studies* (1958).
[10] P. L. Cottrell, *Industrial Finance, 1830–1914. The Finance and Organisation of English Manufacturing Industry* (1980).
[11] N. F. R. Crafts, *British Economic Growth during the Industrial Revolution* (1985).
[12] Francois Crouzet, *The Victorian Economy* (1982).
[13] A. B. Dubois, *The English Business Company After the Bubble Act, 1720–1800* (New York, 1938).
[14] R. S. Edwards and H. Townsend, *Business Enterprise. Its Growth and Organisation* (1958).
[15] Bernard Elbaum and William Lazonick (eds), *The Decline of the British Economy* (Oxford, 1986).
[16] P. Fitzgerald, *Industrial Combination in England* (1927).
[17] P. S. Florence, *Ownership, Control and Success of Large Companies* (1961).
[18] V. A. C. Gatrell, 'Labour, Power and the Size of Firms in Lancashire Cotton in the Second Quarter of the Nineteenth Century', *Economic History Review*, 2nd Ser., XXX (1977).
[19] H. J. Habakkuk, *Industrial Organisation since the Industrial Revolution. The Fifteenth Fawley Foundation Lecture* (Southampton, 1968).
[20] Tom Haddon, *Company Law and Capitalism* (1972).
[21] Leslie Hannah, 'Mergers in British Manufacturing Industry, 1880–1918', *Oxford Economic Press*, New Ser., XXVI (1974).
[22] Leslie Hannah (ed.), *Management Strategy and Business Development. An Historical and Comparative Study* (1976).
[23] Leslie Hannah, *The Rise of the Corporate Economy* 2nd edn (1983).

[24] A. E. Harrison, 'Joint-stock Company Flotation in the Cycle, Motor-vehicle and Related Industries, 1882–1914', *Business History*, XXIII (1981).
[25] E. J. Hobsbawm, *Industry and Empire* (1969).
[26] B. C. Hunt, *The Development of the Business Corporation in Britain 1800–1967* (Cambridge, Mass., 1936).
[27] P. Ireland, 'The Rise of the Limited Liability Company', *International Journal of the Sociology of Law*, XII (1984).
[28] J. B. Jeffreys, 'The Denomination and Character of Shares, 1855–1885', *Economic History Review*, XVI (1946).
[29] J. B. Jeffreys, *Trends in Business Organisation in Great Britain Since 1856* (New York, 1977).
[30] William P. Kennedy, 'Economic Growth and Structural Change in the United Kingdom, 1870–1914' and see the appended 'Discussion' by Ben Baack and Donald McCloskey. *Journal of Economic History*, XLII (1982).
[31] William P. Kennedy, 'Notes on Economic Efficiency in Historical Perspective: The Case of Britain, 1870–1914', *Research in Economic History*, vol. 9 (1984).
[32] C. P. Kindleberger, *Economic Growth in France and Britain, 1851–1950* (Cambridge, Mass., 1964).
[33] D. S. Landes, 'The Structure of Enterprise in the Nineteenth Century. The Cases of Britain and Germany', Comité International des Sciences Historiques, XL Congrès Internationale des Sciences Historiques, Stockholm, *Rapports V: Histoire Contemporaire*, Uppsala, 1960.
[34] William Lazonick, 'Strategy, Structure and Management Development in the United States and Britain' in K. Kobayashi and H. Morikawa (eds), *Development of Managerial Enterprise* (Tokyo, 1986).
[35] C. H. Lee, 'Regional Growth and Structural Change in Victorian Britain', *Economic History Review*, 2nd Ser., XXXIV (1981).
[36] C. H. Lee, 'The Service Sector, Regional Specialization, and Economic Growth in the Victorian Economy', *Journal of Historical Geography*, 10 (1984).
[37] C. H. Lee, *The British Economy since 1700: A macroeconomic perspective* (1986).
[38] C. H. Lee, 'Growth and Productivity in Services in the Industrial Economies' (forthcoming).

[39] H. Levy, *Monopolies, Cartels and Trusts in British Industry* (1927).
[40] R. Lloyd-Jones and A. A. Le Roux, 'The Size of Firms in the Cotton Industry, 1815–41', *Economic History Review*, 2nd Ser., XXXIII (1980).
[41] R. Lloyd-Jones and A. A. Le Roux, 'Marshall and the Birth and Death of Firms: The Growth and Size Distributions of Firms in the Early Nineteenth Century Cotton Industry', *Business History*, XXIV (1982).
[42] Neil McKendrick and R. B. Outhwaite (eds), *Business Life and Public Policy. Essays in Honour of D. C. Coleman* (Cambridge, 1986).
[43] H. W. Macrosty, *The Trust Movement in British Industry* (1907).
[44] Sheila Mariner, 'English Bankruptcy Records and Statistics before 1850', *Economic History Review*, 2nd Ser., XXXIII (1980).
[45] Alfred Marshall, *Industry and Trade*, 4th edn (1923).
[46] W. H. Marwick, 'The Limited Company in Scottish Economic Development', *Economic History*, III (1937).
[47] Peter Mathias, 'Conflicts of Function in the Rise of Big Business: The British Experience' in H. F. Williamson (ed.), *Evolution of International Business Structures* (Newark, New Jersey, 1975).
[48] M. S. Moss and J. R. Hume, 'Business Failure in Scotland, 1839–1913: A Research Note', *Business History*, XXV (1983).
[49] T. B. Napier, 'The History of Joint Stock and Limited Liability Companies', in *A Century of Law Reform* (1901).
[50] Tony Orhnial (ed.) *Limited Liability and the Corporation* (1982).
[51] P. L. Payne, 'The Emergence of the Large-scale Company in Great Britain', *Economic History Review*, 2nd Ser., XX (1967).
[52] P. L. Payne, *The Early Scottish Limited Companies, 1856–1895* (Edinburgh, 1980).
[53] P. L. Payne, 'Family Business in Britain: An Historical and Analytical Survey' in Akio Okochi and Shigeaki Yasuoka (eds), *Family Business in the Era of Industrial Growth* (Tokyo, 1984).
[54] S. J. Prais, *The Evolution of Giant Firms in Britain* (1976).
[55] S. B. Saul, *The Myth of the Great Depression, 1873–1896*, 2nd edn (1985).
[56] J. Saville, 'Sleeping Partnerships and Limited Liability, 1850–1856', *Economic History Review*, 2nd Ser., VIII (1956).
[57] H. A. Shannon, 'The Coming of General Limited Liability', *Economic History*, II (1931).

[58] H. A. Shannon, 'The First Five Thousand Limited Companies and their Duration', *Economic History*, II (1932).
[59] H. A. Shannon, 'The Limited Companies of 1866 and 1883', *Economic History*, IV (1932–3).
[60] Christine Shaw, 'The Large Manufacturing Employers of 1907', *Business History*, XXV (1983).
[61] John M. Stopford, 'The Origins of British-based Multinational Manufacturing Enterprises', *Business History Review*, XVLIII (1974).
[62] Geoffrey Todd, 'Some Aspects of Joint-stock Companies, 1844–1900', *Economic History Review*, IV (1932–33).
[63] M. A. Utton. 'Some Features of the Early Merger Movements in British Manufacturing Industry', *Business History*, XIV (1972).
[64] E. Welbourne, 'Bankruptcy Before the Era of Victorian Reform', *Cambridge Historical Journal*, IV (1932).

II STUDIES OF PARTICULAR TRADES, INDUSTRIES AND REGIONS

[65] David Alexander, *Retailing in England during the Industrial Revolution* (1970).
[66] G. C. Allen, *The Industrial Development of Birmingham and the Black Country* (1929).
[67] R. C. Allen, 'International Competition in Iron and Steel, 1850–1913', *Journal of Economic History*, XXXIX (1979).
[68] R. C. Allen, 'Entrepreneurship and Technical Progress in the North-east Coast Pig Iron Industry: 1850–1913', *Research in Economic History*, 6 (1981).
[69] P. S. Andrews and E. Brunner, *Capital Development in Steel* (Oxford, 1952).
[70] T. S. Ashton, *Iron and Steel in the Industrial Revolution*, 2nd edn (Manchester, 1951).
[71] T. C. Barker and J. R. Harris, *A Merseyside Town in the Industrial Revolution: St Helens, 1750–1900* (Liverpool, 1954).
[72] J. N. Bartlett, 'The Mechanisation of the Kidderminster Carpet Industry', *Business History*, IX (1967).
[73] J. N. Bartlett, *Carpeting the Millions. The Growth of Britain's Carpet Industry* (Edinburgh, 1978).
[74] Joyce M. Bellamy, 'Cotton Manufacture in Kingston Upon Hull', *Business History*, IV (1982).

[75] Alan Birch, *The Economic History of the British Iron and Steel Industry, 1784–1879* (1967).
[76] D. Bremner, *The Industries of Scotland. Their Rise, Progress and Present Condition* (1869).
[77] D. L. Burn, 'The Genesis of American Engineering Competition', *Economic History*, II (1931).
[78] Duncan Burn, *The Economic History of Steel Making, 1867–1939* (Cambridge, 1961).
[79] T. H. Burnham and G. O. Hoskins, *Iron and Steel in Britain, 1870–1930* (1943).
[80] John Butt, 'The Scottish Cotton Industry during the Industrial Revolution 1780–1840', in *Comparative Aspects of Scottish and Irish Economic and Social History, 1600–1900* (ed. L. M. Cullen and T. C. Smout) (Edinburgh, 1980).
[81] Neil K. Buxton, *The Economic Development of the British Coal Industry* (1978).
[82] I. C. R. Byatt, *The British Electrical Industry, 1875–1914. The Economic Returns of a New Technology* (Oxford, 1979).
[83] R. H. Campbell, *The Rise and Fall of Scottish Industry, 1707–1939* (Edinburgh, 1980).
[84] S. D. Chapman, *The Early Factory Masters* (Newton Abbot, 1967).
[85] S. D. Chapman, 'Fixed Capital Formation in the British Cotton Industry, 1770–1815', *Economic History Review*, 2nd Ser., XXIII (1970).
[86] S. D. Chapman, 'The Cost of Power in the Industrial Revolution: The Case of the Textile Industry', *Midland History*, I (1971).
[87] S. D. Chapman, 'Enterprise and Innovation in the British Hosiery Industry, 1750–1850', *Textile History*, V (1974).
[88] S. D. Chapman, 'Financial Restraints on the Growth of Firms in the Cotton Industry, 1790–1850', *Economic History Review*, XXXII (1979).
[89] S. D. Chapman, 'Working Capital in the British Cotton Industry, 1770–1850', *Mimeo* (undated, *c.*1977).
[90] Sydney J. Chapman, *The Lancashire Cotton Industry. A Study in Economic Development* (Manchester, 1904).
[91] R. A. Church, 'The Effect of the American Export Invasion on the British Boot and Shoe Industry, 1885–1914', *Journal of Economic History*, XXVIII (1968).

[92] R. A. Church, 'Labour Supply and Innovation, 1800–1860. The Boot and Shoe Industry', *Business History* XII (1970).

[93] R. A. Church, 'The British Leather Industry and Foreign Competition 1870–1914', *Economic History Review*, 2nd Ser., XXIV (1971).

[94] R. A. Church, *The History of the British Coal Industry. vol. 3: 1830–1913: Victorian Pre-eminence* (Oxford, 1986).

[95] J. H. Clapham, The Woollen and Worsted Industries (1907).

[96] Archibald and Nan L. Clow, *The Chemical Revolution. A Contribution to Social Technology* (1952).

[97] D. C. Coleman, *The British Paper Industry, 1495–1860* (Oxford, 1958).

[98] W. H. B. Court, *The Rise of Midland Industries, 1600–1838* (1938).

[99] Ian Donnachie, *A History of the Brewing Industry in Scotland* (Edinburgh, 1979).

[100] Baron F. Duckham, *History of the Scottish Coal Industry, vol. I, 1700–1815* (Newton Abbot, 1970).

[101] M. M. Edwards, *The Growth of the British Cotton Trade, 1780–1815* (Manchester, 1867).

[102] Cyril Ehrlich, *The Piano. A History* (1976).

[103] C. Hamilton Ellis, *Nineteenth Century Railway Carriages* (1949).

[104] D. A. Farnie, *The English Cotton Industry and World Markets, 1815–1896* (Oxford, 1979).

[105] Michael Flinn, *The History of the British Coal Industry, vol. 2, 1700–1830: The Industrial Revolution* (1984).

[106] Roderick Floud, *The British Machine and Tool Industry, 1850–1914* (1976).

[107] R. C. Floud, 'The Adolescence of American Engineering Competition, 1860–1900', *Economic History Review*, 2nd Ser., XXVII (1974).

[108] J. H. Fox, 'The Victorian Entrepreneur in Lancashire' in S. P. Bell (ed.), *Victorian Lancashire* (Newton Abbot, 1976).

[109] F. J. Glover, 'The Rise of the Heavy Woollen Trade of the West Riding of Yorkshire in the Nineteenth Century', *Business History*, IV (1961).

[110] L. F. Haber, *The Chemical Industry during the Nineteenth Century* (Oxford, 1958).

[111] Henry Hamilton, *An Economic History of Scotland in the Eighteenth Century* (Oxford, 1963).

[112] A. E. Harrison, 'The Competitiveness of the British Cycle Industry, 1890–1914', *Economic History Review*, 2nd Ser., XXII (1969).
[113] A. E. Harrison, 'Joint-stock Company Flotation in the Cycle, Motor-vehicle and Related Industries, 1882–1914', *Business History*, XXIII (1981).
[114] Elijah Helm, 'The Alleged Decline of the British Cotton Industry', *Economic Journal*, II (1892).
[115] Pat Hudson, *The Genesis of Industrial Capital. A Study of the West Riding wool Textile industry c.1750–1850* (1986).
[116] Charles K. Hyde, *Technological Change and the British Iron Industry 1700–1870* (Princeton, N.J., 1977).
[117] J. B. Jefferys, *Retail Trading in Britain, 1850–1950* (Cambridge, 1954).
[118] D. J. Jenkins and K. G. Ponting, *The British Wool Textile Industry, 1770–1914* (1982).
[119] A. H. John, *The Industrial Development of South Wales* (Cardiff, 1950).
[120] A. H. John and G. Williams (eds), *Glamorgan Country History, vol. V, Industrial Glamorgan from 1700 to 1970* (Cardiff, 1980).
[121] Haydn Jones, *Accounting, Costing and Cost Estimation, Welsh Industry: 1700–1830* (Cardiff, 1985).
[122] S. R. H. Jones, 'Price Associations and Competition in the British Pin Industry, 1814–40', *Economic History Review*, 2nd Ser., XXVI (1973).
[123] William Lazonick, 'Factor costs and the diffusion of ring-spinning in Britain prior to World War I', *Quarterly Journal of Economics*, XCVI (1981).
[124] William Lazonick, 'Production Relations, Labour Productivity and Choice of Technique: British and US Cotton Spinning', *Journal of Economic History*, XLI (1981).
[125] William Lazonick, 'Industrial Organisation and Technical Change: The Decline of the British Cotton Industry', *Business History Review*, LVII (1983).
[126] William Lazonick, 'Rings and Mules in Britain: Reply [to Sandberg, 151]', *Quarterly Journal of Economics*, XCIX (1984).
[127] William Lazonick and William Mass, 'The Performance of the British Cotton Industry, 1870–1913', *Research in Economic History*, 9 (1984).
[128] Bruce Lenman and Kathleen Donaldson, 'Partners' Incomes,

Investment and Diversification in the Scottish Linen Area, 1850–1921', *Business History*, XIII (1971).
[129] Donald M. McCloskey, *Economic Maturity and Entrepreneurial Decline: British Iron and Steel, 1870–1913* (Cambridge, Mass., 1973).
[130] Neil McKendrick, 'The Victorian View of the Midland Potteries', *Midland History*, I (1971).
[131] J. de L. Mann, *The Cloth Industry in the West of Scotland from 1640 to 1880* (Oxford, 1971).
[132] J. D. Marshall, *Furness and the Industrial Revolution* (Barrow, 1958).
[133] R. C. Michie, *Money, Mania and Markets. Investment, Company Formation and the Stock Exchange in Nineteenth-Century Scotland* (Edinburgh, 1981).
[134] W. E. Minchinton, *The British Tinplate Industry: A History* (Oxford, 1957).
[135] Michael S. Moss and John R. Hume, *Workshop of the British Empire. Engineering and Shipbuilding in the West of Scotland* (1977).
[136] A. E. Musson and E. Robinson, 'The Origins of Engineering in Lancashire' *Journal of Economic History*, XX (1960).
[137] T. R. Nevett, *Advertising in Britain. A History* (1982).
[138] G. A. North, *Teeside's Economic Heritage* (Cleveland, 1975).
[139] J. L. Oliver, *The Development and Structure of the Furniture Industry* (1966).
[140] T. G. Orsagh, 'Progress in Iron and Steel: 1870–1913', *Comparative Studies in Society and History*, III (1960–1).
[141] P. L. Payne, *Colvilles and the Scottish Steel Industry* (Oxford, 1979).
[142] D. C. M. Platt, *Latin America and British Trade, 1806–1914* (1973).
[143] Sidney Pollard. 'British and World Shipbuilding, 1890–1914: A Study in Comparative Costs', *Journal of Economic History*, XVII (1957).
[144] Sidney Pollard and Paul Robertson, *The British Shipbuilding Industry, 1870–1914* (Cambridge, Mass., 1979).
[145] Arthur Redford, *Manchester Merchants and Foreign Trade, 1794–1858* (Manchester, 1934).
[146] Arthur Redford, *Manchester Merchants and Foreign Trade, 1850–1939* (Manchester, 1956).

[147] A. J. Robertson, 'The Decline of the Scottish Cotton Industry', *Business History*, XII (1970).

[148] D. J. Rowe, *Lead Manufacturing in Britain: A History* (1983).

[149] Lars G. Sandberg, 'American Rings and English Mules: The Role of Economic Rationality', *Quarterly Journal of Economics*, LXXXIII (1969).

[150] Lars G. Sandberg, *Lancashire in Decline. A Study in Entrepreneurship, Technology and International Trade* (Columbus, Ohio, 1974).

[151] Lars G. Sandberg, 'The Remembrance of Things Past: Rings and Mules Revisited', *Quarterly Journal of Economics*, XCIX (1984).

[152] S. B. Saul, 'The American Impact on British Industry, 1895–1914', *Business History*, III (1960).

[153] S. B. Saul, 'The Motor Industry in Britain' *Business History*, V (1962).

[154] S. B. Saul, 'The Market and Development of the Mechanical Engineering Industries in Britain, 1860–1914', *Economic History Review*, 2nd Ser., XX (1967).

[155] S. B. Saul, Research and Development in British Industry from the end of the Nineteenth Century to the 1960s', in T. C. Smout (ed.), *The Search for Wealth and Stability* (1979).

[156] G. R. Saxonhouse and G. Wright, 'New Evidence on the Stubborn English Mule and the Cotton Industry, 1878–1920', *Economic History Review*, 2nd Ser., XXXVII (1984).

[157] Seymour Shapiro, *Capital and the Cotton Industry* (Ithaca, New York, 1967).

[158] E. M. Sigsworth, 'The West Riding Wool Textile Industry and the Great Exhibition', *Yorkshire Bulletin of Economic & Social Research*, IV (1952).

[159] Anthony Slaven, *The Development of the West of Scotland* (1975).

[160] Roland Smith, *The Lancashire Cotton Industry and the Great Depression, 1873–1896*, Unpublished Ph.D. thesis, University of Birmingham, 1954.

[161] A. J. Taylor, 'Concentration and Specialisation in the Lancashire Cotton Industry 1825–50', *Economic History Review*, 2nd Ser., I (1949).

[162] W. A. Thomas, *The Provincial Stock Exchange* (1973).

[163] S. Timmins (ed.), *The Resources, Products and Industrial History of Birmingham and the Midland Hardware District* (1866).

[164] Barrie Trinder, *The Industrial Revolution in Shropshire* (1973).
[165] G. Turnbull, *A History of the Calico Printing Industry of Great Britain* (Altrincham, 1951).
[166] R. H. Walters, *The Economic and Business History of the South Wales Steam and Coal Industry, 1840–1914* (New York, 1977).
[167] Kenneth Warren, *Chemical Foundations: The Alkali Industry in Britain to 1926* (Oxford, 1980).
[168] F. A. Wells, *The British Hosiery Trade* (1935).
[169] O. M. Westall (ed.), *The Historian and the Business of Insurance* (Manchester, 1984).

III THE ENTREPRENEUR: DEFINITION, MOTIVATION, RECRUITMENT AND ROLE

[170] H. G. H. Aitken, 'The Future of Entrepreneurial Research', *Explorations in Enrepreneurial History*, 2nd Ser., I (1963).
[171] E. Ames and N. Rosenberg, 'Changing Technological Leadership and Industrial Growth', *Economic Journal*, LXXIII (1963).
[172] T. S. Ashton, *The Industrial Revolution* (1948).
[173] J. W. Atkinson and B. F. Hoselitz, 'Entrepreneurship and Personalilty', *Explorations in Entrepreneurial History*, X (1958).
[174] Reinhard Bendix, *Work and Authority in Industry. Ideologies of Management in the Course of Industrialisation* (New York, 1956).
[175] Reinhard Bendix, 'A Study of Managerial Ideologies', *Economic Development and Cultural Change*, V (1957).
[176] N. M. Bradburn and D. E. Berlew, 'Need for Achievement and English Industrial Growth', *Economic Development and Cultural Change*, X (1961).
[177] Mark Casson, *The Entrepreneur. An Economic Theory* (Oxford, 1982).
[178] S. J. Chapman and F. J. Marquis, 'The Recruiting of the Employing Classes from the Ranks of the Wage-Earners in the Cotton Industry', *Journal of the Royal Statistical Society*, LXXV (1912).
[179] A. H. Cole, 'An Approach to the Study of Entrepreneurship' *Journal of Economic History*, VI Supplement (1946).
[180] François Crouzet (ed.), *Capital Formation in the Industrial Revolution* (1972).

[181] François Crouzet, *The First Industrialists: The Problem of Origins* (Cambridge, 1985).
[182] Charlotte Erickson, *British Industrialists: Steel and Hosiery, 1850–1950* (Cambridge, 1959).
[183] G. H. Evans Jr., 'The Entrepreneur and Economic Theory: A Historical and Analytical Approach', *American Economic Review*, XXXIX (1949).
[184] G. H. Evans Jr, 'Business Entrepreneurs, Their Major Functions and Related Tenets', *Journal of Economic History*, XIX (1959).
[185] D. E. C. Eversley, 'The Home Market and Economic Growth in England, 1750–1780', in *Land, Labour and Population in the Industrial Revolution. Essays Presented to J. D. Chambers* (ed. E. L. Jones and G. Mingay) (1967).
[186] M. W. Flinn, *Origins of the Industrial Revolution* (1966).
[187] M. W. Flinn, 'Social Theory and the Industrial Revolution' in *Social Theory and Economic Change* (ed. T. Burns and S. B. Saul) (1967).
[188] T. R. Gourvish, 'A British Business Elite: the Chief Executive Managers of the Railway Industry, 1850–1923' *Business History Review*, XLVII (1973).
[189] E. E. Hagen, *On the Theory of Social Change* (Homewood, Illinois, 1964).
[190] Leslie Hannah, *Entrepreneurs and the Social Sciences: An Inaugural Lecture* (1983).
[191] R. M. Hartwell, 'Business Management in England during the period of Early Industrialisation: Inducements and Obstacles', in *The Industrial Revolution* (ed. R. M. Hartwell) (Oxford, 1970).
[192] Charles E. Harvey, 'Business History and the Problem of Entrepreneurship: The Case of the Rio Tinto Company, 1873–1939', *Business History*, XXI (1979).
[193] David Hey, *The Rural Metalworkers of the Sheffield Region: A Study of Rural Industry Before the Industrial Revolution* (Leicester, 1972).
[194] Katrina Honeyman, *Origins of Enterprise: Business Leadership in the Industrial Revolution* (Manchester, 1982).
[195] B. F. Hoselitz, 'Entrepreneurship and Capital Formation in France and Britain since 1700', in National Bureau of

Economic Research, *Capital Formation and Economic Growth* (Princeton, 1956).
[196] A. Howe, *The Cotton Masters, 1830–1860* (Oxford, 1984).
[197] Hester Jenkins and D. Caradog Jones, 'Social Class of Cambridge University Alumni of the 18th and 19th Centuries', *British Journal of Sociology*, I (1950).
[198] David J. Jeremy (ed.), *Dictionary of Business Biography*, 5 vols (1984–86).
[199] David J. Jeremy, 'Anatomy of the British Business Elite, 1860–1980', *Business History*, XXVI (1984) (based on the careers of 270 individuals in Volume I of the *DBB*, with surnames beginning with the letters A to C).
[200] Peter Kilby (ed.), *Entrepreneurship and Economic Development* (New York, 1971).
[201] Roy Lewis and Rosemary Stewart, *The Boss, The Life and Times of the British Business Man* (1961).
[202] R. R. Locke, *The End of the Practical Man: Entrepreneurship and Higher Education in Germany, France and Great Britain, 1880–1940* (1984).
[203] D. C. McClelland, *The Achieving Society* (Princeton, New Jersey, 1961).
[204] P. Mantoux, *The Industrial Revolution in the Eighteenth Century* (1923).
[205] Robin Marris, *The Economic Theory of 'Managerial' Capitalism* (1964).
[206] W. M. Mathew, 'The Origins and Occupations of Glasgow Students, 1740–1839', *Past and Present*, No. 33 (April 1966).
[207] Edith Penrose, *The Theory of the Growth of the Firm* (Oxford, 1959).
[208] Harold Perkin, *The Origins of Modern English Society* (1969).
[209] S. Pollard, *The Genesis of Modern Management* (1965).
[210] R. E. Pumphrey, 'The Introduction of Industrialists into the British Peerage: A Study in Adaptation of a Social Institution', *American Historical Review*, LXV (1959).
[211] W. J. Reader, *Professional Men* (1966).
[212] F. Redlich, 'Economic Development, Entrepreneurship and Psychologism: A Social Scientist's Critique of McClelland's *Achieving Society*', *Explorations in Entrepreneurial History*, 2nd Ser., I (1963).

[213] W. D. Rubinstein, 'The Victorian Middle Classes: Wealth, Occupation and Geography', *Economic History Review*, 2nd Ser., XXX (1977).

[214] W. D. Rubinstein, 'Wealth, Elites and Class Structure in Britain', *Past and Present*, No. 76 (1977).

[215] W. D. Rubinstein, *Wealth and the Wealthy in the Modern World* (1980).

[216] W. D. Rubinstein, *Men of Property: The Very Wealthy in Britain since the Industrial Revolution* (1981).

[217] Michael Sanderson, *The Universities and British Industry, 1850–1970* (1972).

[218] Christine Shaw, 'Characteristics of British Business Leaders: Findings from the *Dictionary of Business Biography*' (based on a random sample of 188 cases taken from Volumes 1–4 (A–R) of the DBB [165a]). Paper presented to the Anglo-Japanese Conference on Business History, 1986, *mimeo*.

[219] Anthony Slaven and Sydney Checkland (eds), *Dictionary of Scottish Business Biography, Vol I: The Staple Industries* (Aberdeen, 1986).

[220] Aileen Smiles, *Samuel Smiles and his Surroundings* (1956).

[221] Samuel Smiles, *Self-Help*, Centenary edition (1958).

[222] Jennifer Tann, *The Development of the Factory* (1970).

[223] E. P. Thompson, *The Making of the English Working Class* (1963).

[224] E. P. Thompson, 'Time, Work-Discipline and Industrial Capitalism', *Past and Present*, No. 38 (December 1967).

[225] L. Urwick and E. F. L. Brech, *The Making of Scientific Management* 2 vols (1949).

[226] G. Wilson, *Gentlemen Merchants. The Merchant Community in Leeds, 1700–1830* (Manchester, 1972).

IV THE ENTREPRENEUR: GENERAL ASSESSMENTS OF PERFORMANCE

[227] D. H. Aldcroft, 'The Entrepreneur and the British Economy, 1870–1914', *Economic History Review*, 2nd Ser., XVII (1964).

[228] D. H. Aldcroft, 'Technical Progress and British Enterprise 1875–1914', *Business History*, VIII (1966).

[229] D. H. Aldcroft (ed.), *The Development of British Industry and Foreign Competition, 1875–1914* (1968).

[230] D. H. Aldcroft, 'Investment in and Utilization of Manpower: Great Britain and her rivals, 1870–1914', in Barrie M. Radcliffe (ed.), *Great Britain and Her World, 1750–1914* (Manchester, 1975).

[231] B. W. E. Alford, 'Entrepreneurship, Business Performance and Industrial Development', *Business History*, XIX (1977).

[232] T. J. Byres, *The Scottish Economy During the Great Depression, 1873–1896*, unpublished B.Litt. thesis, University of Glasgow, 1962.

[233] T. J. Byres, 'Entrepreneurship in the Scottish Heavy Industries, 1870–1900', in *Studies in Scottish Business History*; see [362] below.

[234] D. C. Coleman, 'Gentlemen and Players', *Economic History Review*, 2nd Ser., XXVI (1973).

[235] D. C. Coleman and Christine MacLeod, 'Attitudes to New Techniques: British Businessmen, 1800–1950', *Economic History Review*, 2nd Ser., XXXIX (1986).

[236] H. G. Gray and Samuel Turner, *Eclipse or Empire?* (1916).

[237] H. J. Habakkuk, *American and British Technology in the Nineteenth Century* (Cambridge, 1962).

[238] C. K. Harley, 'Skilled Labour and the Choice of Technique in Edwardian Industry', *Explorations in Economic History*, XI (1974).

[239] Ross Hoffman, *Great Britain and the German Trade Rivalry, 1875–1914* (Philadelphia, 1933).

[240] D. S. Landes, 'Entrepreneurship in Advanced Industrial Countries: The Anglo-German Rivalry', in *Entrepreneurship and Economic Growth*. Papers presented at a Conference sponsored jointly by the Committee on Economic Growth of the Social Science Research Foundation and the Harvard University Research Centre in Entrepreneurial History, Cambridge, Massachusetts, 12–13 November 1954.

[241] D. S. Landes, 'Technological Change and Development in Western Europe, 1750–1914', in *The Cambridge Economic History of Europe*, VI. *The Industrial Revolutions and After*, Part I (ed. H. J. Habakkuk and M. Postan) (Cambridge, 1965), subsequently reprinted and extended as *The Unbound Prometheus* (Cambridge, 1969).

[242] D. S. Landes, 'Factor Costs and Demand: Determinants of Economic Growth', *Business History*, VII (1965).

[243] A. L. Levine, *Industrial Retardation in Britain, 1880–1914* (1967).
[244] R. R. Locke, 'New Insights from Cost Accounting into British Entrepreneurial Performance, c.1914', *The Accounting Historians Journal*, VI (1979).
[245] R. R. Locke, 'Cost Accounting: an Institutional Yardstick for Measuring British Entrepreneurial Performance, c.1914', *The Accounting Historians Journal*, VI (1979).
[246] Donald N. McCloskey (ed.), *Essays on a Mature Economy: Britain After 1840. Papers and Proceedings of the M.S.S.B. Conference on the New Economic History of Britain, 1840–1939* (1971).
[247] Donald N. McCloskey and Lars G. Sandberg, 'From Damnation to Redemption: Judgements on the Late Victorian Entrepreneur', *Explorations in Economic History*, IX (1971).
[248] Donald N. McCloskey, 'Did Victorian Britain Fail?', *Economic History Review*, 2nd Ser., XXIII (1970). See the later comment by N. F. R. Crafts and the reply by McCloskey, *Economic History Review*, 2nd Ser., XXXII (1979).
[249] Joel Mokyr, 'Prosperous Interlude', *Economic Development and Cultural Change*, 30 (1982).
[250] Stephen J. Nicholas, 'Total Factor Productivity and the Revision of Post-1870 British Economic Growth', *Economic History Review*, 2nd Ser. XXXV (1982).
[251] Stephen J. Nicholas, 'The Overseas Marketing Performance of British Industry, 1870–1914', *Economic History Review*, 2nd Ser., XXXVII (1984).
[252] Eric M. Sigsworth, 'Some Problems in Business History, 1870–1914', in *Papers of the Sixteenth Business History Conference*, ed. Charles J. Kennedy (Lincoln, Nebraska, 1969).
[253] Martin J. Wiener, *English Culture and the Decline of the Industrial Spirit, 1850–1980* (Cambridge, 1981).
[254] Charles Wilson, 'The Entrepreneur in the Industrial Revolution in Britain', *Explorations in Entrepreneurial History*, III (1955).
[255] Charles Wilson, 'Economy and Society in Late Victorian Britain', *Economic History Review*, 2nd Ser., XVIII (1965).

V STUDIES OF PARTICULAR FIRMS AND ENTREPRENEURS

[256] J. B. Addis, *The Crawshay Dynasty. A Study in Industrial Organisation and Development, 1756–1867* (Cardiff, 1967).
[257] Anon. [various authors] *Fortunes Made in Business*, 3 vols (1884–7).
[258] Anon. *James Finlay and Company Ltd., Manufacturers and East India Merchants, 1750–1950* (Glasgow, 1957).
[259] T. S. Ashton, 'The Records of a Pin Manufacturer, 1814–21', *Economica*, V (1925).
[260] T. S. Ashton, *An Eighteenth Century Industrialist: Peter Stubs of Warrington, 1756–1806* (Manchester, 1939).
[261] T. C. Baxter, *The Glassmakers, Pilkington: 1826–1976* (1977).
[262] J. N. Bartlett, 'Alexander Pirie & Sons of Aberdeen and the Expansion of the British Paper Industry c. 1860–1914', *Business History*, XXII (1980).
[263] Rhodes Boyson, *The Ashworth Cotton Enterprise. The Rise and Fall of a Family Firm, 1818–1880* (Oxford, 1970).
[264] Asa Briggs, *Wine for Sale: Victoria Wine and the Liquor Trade, 1860–1984* (1985)
[265] R. H. Campbell, *Carron Company* (Edinburgh and London, 1961).
[266] J. A. Cantell, *James Nasmyth and the Bridgewater Foundry. A study of entrepreneuship in the early engineering industry* (Manchester, 1984).
[267] W. H. Chaloner, 'Robert Owen, Peter Drinkwater and the Early Factory System in Manchester, 1788–1800', *Bulletin of the John Rylands Library*, XXXVII (1954).
[268] Dennis Chapman, 'William Brown of Dundee, 1791–1864: Management in a Scottish Flax Mill, *Explorations in Entrepreneurial History* IV (1952).
[269] S. D. Chapman, 'The Peels in the Early English Cotton Industry', *Business History* XI (1969).
[270] S. D. Chapman, 'James Longsdon (1745–1821), Farmer and Fustian Manufacturer: The Small Firm in the Early English Cotton Industry', *Textile History*, I (1970).
[271] Stanley Chapman, *Jesse Boot of Boots the Chemists* (1974).
[272] S. G. Checkland, *The Mines of Tharsis* (1967).
[273] S. G. Checkland, *The Gladstones. A Family Biography, 1764–1851* (Cambridge, 1971).

[274] R. A. Church, 'An Aspect of Family Enterprise in the Industrial Revolution', *Business History*, IV (1962).
[275] R. A. Church, 'Messrs Gotch & Sons and the Rise of the Kettering Footwear Industry', *Business History*, VII (1966).
[276] R. A. Church, *Kenricks in Hardware. A Family Business, 1791–1966* (Newton Abbot, 1969).
[277] Roy Church, *Herbert Austin and the British Motor Car Industry to 1914* (1979).
[278] D. C. Coleman, *Courtaulds. An Economic and Social History*, 3 vols (1969, 1980).
[279] T. A. B. Corley, *Quaker Enterprise in Biscuits: Huntley and Palmers of Reading, 1822–1972* (1972).
[280] R. P. T. Davenport-Hines, *Dudley Docker, The Life and Times of a Trade Warrior* (Cambridge, 1984).
[281] Ralph Davis, *Twenty-One and a Half Bishop Lane: A History of J. H. Fenner & Co Ltd., 1861–1961* (1961).
[282] I. L. Donnachie and J. Butt, 'The Wilsons of Wilsontown Ironworks (1779–1813): A Study in Entrepreneurial Failure, *Explorations in Entrepreneurial History*, IV (1966–7).
[283] D. A. Farnie, 'John Rylands of Manchester', *Bulletin of the John Rylands University Library of Manchester*, LVI (1973).
[284] R. S. Fitton and A. P. Wadsworth, *The Strutts and the Arkwrights, 1758–1830* (Manchester, 1958).
[285] James Foreman-Peck, 'Diversification and the Growth of the Firm: The Rover Car Company to 1914', *Business History*, XXV (1983).
[286] Edwin Green and Michael Moss, *A Business of National Importance: The Royal Mail Shipping Group, 1902–1937* (1982).
[287] Robert G. Greenhill, 'The Royal Mail Steam Packet Company and the Development of Steamship Links with Latin America, 1875–1900', *Maritime History*, II (1973).
[288] A. E. Harrison, 'F Hopper & Co – The Problems of Capital Supply in the Cycle Manufacturing Industry, 1891–1914', *Business History*, XXIV (1982).
[289] Charles E. Harvey, 'Business History and the Problems of Entrepreneurship: The Case of the Rio Tinto Company, 1873–1939', *Business History*, XXI (1979).
[290] Charles E. Harvey, *The Rio Tinto Company: An Economic History of a Leading International Mining Concern, 1873–1954* (Penzance, 1981).

[291] H. Heaton, 'Benjamin Gott and the Industrial Revolution in Yorkshire', *Economic History Review*, III (1931–2).
[292] John R. Hume and Michael S. Moss, *Beardmore. The History of a Scottish Industrial Giant* (1979).
[293] F. E. Hyde assisted by J. R. Harris, *Blue Funnel: A History of Alfred Holt and Company of Liverpool from 1865 to 1914* (Liverpool, 1956).
[294] F. E. Hyde, *Shipping Enterprise and Management, 1830–1939* (Liverpool, 1967).
[295] R. J. Irving, 'New Industries for Old? Some Investment Decisions of Sir W G Armstrong, Whitworth & Co Ltd., 1900–1914, *Business History*, XVII (1975).
[296] A. H. John (ed.), *The Walker Family, Ironfounders and Lead Manufacturers, 1741–1893* (1951).
[297] A. H. John, *A Liverpool Merchant House: Being the History of Alfred Booth and Company, 1863–1958* (1959).
[298] S. R. H. Jones, 'Hall English & Co., 1913–41. A Study of Entrepreneurial Response in the Gloucester Pin Industry', *Business History*, XVIII (1976).
[299] M. W. Kirby, *Men of Business and Politics. The Rise and Fall of the Quaker Pease Dynasty of North-east England, 1700–1943* (1984).
[300] C. H. Lee, *A Cotton Enterprise, 1795–1840. A History of M'Connel and Kennedy, Fine Cotton Spinners* (Manchester, 1972).
[301] John C. Logan, 'The Dumbarton Glass Works Company: A Study in Entrepreneurship', *Business History*, XIV (1972).
[302] Neil McKendrick, 'Josiah Wedgwood: An Eighteenth-Century Entrepreneur in Salesmanship and Marketing Techniques', *Economic History Review*, 2nd Ser., XII (1960).
[303] Neil McKendrick, 'Josiah Wedgwood and Factory Discipline', *Historical Journal*, IV (1961).
[304] Neil McKendrick, 'Josiah Wedgwood and the Factory System', *Proceedings of the Wedgwood Society*, No. 5 (1963).
[305] Neil McKendrick, 'Josiah Wedgwood and Thomas Bentley: An Inventor-Entrepreneur Partnership in the Industrial Revolution', *Transactions of the Royal Historical Society*, XIV (1964).
[306] Neil McKendrick, 'Josiah Wedgwood and Cost Accounting in the Industrial Revolution', *Economic History Review*, 2nd Ser., XXIII (1970).

[307] M. H. MacKenzie, 'Cressbrook and Litton Mills, 1779–1835', *Derbyshire Archaeological Journal*, LXXXVIII (1968).
[308] Sheila Marriner, *Rathbones of Liverpool, 1845–74* (Liverpool, 1961).
[309] Sheila Marriner and Francis E. Hyde, *The Senior: John Samuel Swire: 1825–98* (Liverpool, 1967).
[310] John J. Mason, 'A Manufacturing and Bleaching Enterprise during the Industrial Revolution: The Sykeses of Edgeley, *Business History*, XXIII (1981).
[311] Peter Mathias, *Retailing Revolution: A History of Multiple Retailing in the Food Trades based upon the Allied Supplies Group of Companies* (1967).
[312] Jocelyn Morton, *Three Generations in a Family Textile Firm* (1971).
[313] Michael S. Moss, 'William Todd Lithgow – Founder of a Fortune', *Scottish Historical Review*, LXII (1983).
[314] A. E. Musson, 'An Early Engineering Firm: Peel, William & Co. of Manchester', *Business History*, III (1960).
[315] A. E. Musson, *Enterprise in Soap and Chemicals, Joseph Crosfield & Sons Ltd., 1815–1965* (Manchester, 1965).
[316] A. E. Musson, 'Joseph Whitworth and the Growth of Mass-Production Engineering', *Business History*, XVII (1975).
[317] Robert Owen, *The Life of Robert Owen, written by Himself*, (1857).
[318] P. L. Payne, *Rubber and Railways in the Nineteenth Century* (Liverpool, 1961).
[319] S. Piggott, *Hollins: A Study of Industry, 1784–1949*, (Nottingham, 1949).
[320] A. Raistrick, *Dynasty of Iron Founders* (Newton Abbot, 1970).
[321] W. J. Reader, *Imperial Chemical Industries, A History*, vol. I, *The Forerunners, 1870–1926* (1970).
[322] W. J. Reader, *A House in the City: A Study of the City and the Stock Exchange based on the records of Forster and Braithwaite, 1825–1975* (1985).
[323] Goronwy Rees, *St Michael: A History of Marks and Spencer* (1969).
[324] Sir Wemyss Reid, *Memoirs and Correspondence of Lyon Playfair* (1900).
[325] H. W. Richardson and J. M. Bass, 'The Profitability of Consett Iron Company Before 1914', *Business History*, VII (1965).

[326] W. G. Rimmer, *Marshalls of Leeds, Flax Spinners, 1788–1886* (Cambridge, 1960)
[327] A. J. Robertson, 'Robert Owen, Cotton Spinner: New Lanark, 1800–1825' in *Robert Owen, Prophet of the Poor*, ed. S. Pollard and J. Salt (1971).
[328] Eric Robinson, 'Boulton & Fothergill, 1762–1782, and the Birmingham Export of Hardware', *University of Birmingham Historical Journal*, VII (1959).
[329] Eric Robinson, 'Eighteenth Century Commerce and Fashion: Matthew Boulton's Marketing Techniques', *Economic History Review*, 2nd Ser., XVI (1963).
[330] E. Roll, *An Early Experiment in Industrial Organisation, Being a History of Boulton and Watt, 1775–1805* (1930).
[331] Mary Rose, 'The Role of the Family in providing Capital and Managerial Talent in Samuel Greg & Co., 1784–1840', *Business History*, XIX (1977).
[332] Mary Rose, 'Diversification of Investment by the Greg Family, 1800–1914', *Business History*, XXI (1979).
[333] Mary B. Rose, *The Gregs of Quarry Bank Mill. The rise and decline of a family firm, 1750–1914* (Cambridge, 1986).
[334] J. D. Scott, *Vickers. A History* (1962).
[335] Eric M. Sigsworth, *Black Dyke Mills* (Liverpool, 1958).
[336] A. Slaven, 'A Glasgow Firm in the Indian Market: John Lean & Sons, Muslin Weavers', *Business History Review*, XLIII (1969).
[337] Roland Smith, 'An Oldham Limited Liability Company, 1875–1896' *Business History*, IV (1961).
[338] G. B. Sutton, 'The Marketing of Ready Made Footwear in the Nineteenth Century. A Study of the Firm of C. & J. Clark', *Business History*, VI (1964).
[339] G. B. Sutton, *A History of Shoemaking in Street, Somerset: C. & J. Clark, 1833–1903* (1979).
[340] Clive Trebilcock, *The Vickers Brothers: Armaments and Enterprise, 1854–1914* (1977).
[341] Clive Trebilcock, *Phoenix Assurance and the Development of British Insurance, vol. I: 1782–1870* (Cambridge, 1986).
[342] R. E. Tyson, *The Sun Mill Company Limited: A Study in Democratic Investment, 1858–1959*, unpublished M. A. Thesis, University of Manchester, 1962.
[343] R. E. Tyson, 'William Marcroft (1822–94) and the Limited Liability Movement in Oldham', *Transactions of the Lancashire and Cheshire Antiquarian Society*, 80 (1980).

[344] David Wainwright, *Broadwood by Appointment* (1982).
[345] R. A. Wells, *Hollins and Viyella. A Study in Business History* (Newton Abbot, 1968).
[346] Charles Wilson, *The History of Unilever*, 2 vols (1954).
[347] Charles Wilson, *First with the News: A History of W. H. Smith, 1792–1972* (1985).
[348] Charles Wilson and William Reader, *Men and Machines. A History of D. Napier & Sons, Engineers Ltd., 1808–1858* (1958).

VI GUIDES TO BUSINESS ARCHIVES AND BUSINESS HISTORIES

[349] David Allen, 'Surveys of Records in the British Isles', *Aslib Proceedings* (1971).
[350] T. C. Barker, R. H. Campbell, P. Mathias and B. S. Yamey, *Business History*, Rev. edn (1971).
[351] Joyce M. Bellamy (ed.), *Yorkshire Business Histories: A Bibliography* (Bradford, 1970).
[352] H. A. L. Cockerill and Edwin Green, *The British Insurance Business, 1547–1970* (1976).
[353] B. R. Crick and M. Alman, *A Guide to Manuscripts Relating to America in Great Britain and Ireland* (1961).
[354] Charles Harvey, 'Business Records at the Public Record Office', *Business Archives*, No. 52 (November, 1986).
[355] S. Horrocks, *Lancashire Business Histories* (Manchester, 1971).
[356] Patricia Hudson, *The West Riding Wool Textile Industry: A Catalogue of Business Records* (Edlington, Wiltshire, 1975).
[357] Joan Lane, *Register of Business Records of Coventry and Related Areas* (Coventry, 1977).
[358] Jane Low, *A Guide to Sources in the History of the Cycle and Motor Industries in Coventry, 1880–1939* (Coventry, 1982).
[359] Sheila Marriner, 'Company Financial Statements as Source Material for Business Historians', *Business History*, XXII (1980).
[360] P. Mathias and A. W. H. Pearsall (eds), *Shipping: A Survey of Historical Records* (Newton Abott, 1971).
[361] E. R. J. Owen and Frank Dux, *A List of the Location of Records belonging to British Firms and to British Businessmen active in the Middle East, 1800–1950* (Oxford: Middle East Centre, 1973).
[362] P. L. Payne (ed.), *Studies in Scottish Business History* (1967).

[363] L. S. Pressnell and J. Orbell (eds), *A Guide to the Historical Records of British Banking* (Aldershot, 1985).
[364] T. Rath, 'Business Records in the Public Record Office in the Age of the Industrial Revolution', *Business History*, XVII (1975).
[365] Lesley Richmond and Bridget Stockford, *Company Archives. The Survey of the Records of 1000 of the First Registered Companies in England and Wales* (Aldershot, 1986).
[366] L. A. Ritchie, *Modern British Shipbuilding. A Guide to Historical Records* (Maritime Monographs and Reports, No.48, 1980).
[367] R. A. Storey (ed.), *Sources of Business History in the National Register of Archives: First Five-year Cumulation* (Historical Manuscripts Commission, 1971).
[368] Peter Walne (ed.), *A Guide to Manuscript Sources for the History of Latin America and the Caribbean in the British Isles* (1973).

An annual list of new accessions of business records in county record offices and other repositories reporting to the National Register of Archives is published in *Business Archives, The Journal of the Business Archives Council*, which also carries a useful list of business histories. In 1984, it was announced in *Business History*, XXVI (1984), 80, that, as a preliminary to the preparation of a published guide to manuscript sources for the history of business and industry in the nineteenth and early twentieth centuries, the Royal Commission on Historical Manuscripts had constructed an index of all relevant information that it possessed about the records of individual companies. The index is available for public consultation and use in the Commission's search room. Those particularly concerned with Scottish business should consult the Newsletter of the Business Archives Council of Scotland, an occasional publication superseded in 1976 by *Scottish Industrial History*. Useful information on archives and sources and ongoing research is contained in the *Business History Newsletter* produced by the Business History Unit of the University of London.

Proto-Industrialization: The First Phase of Industrialization?

*Prepared for
the Economic History Society by*

L. A. CLARKSON
Queen's University, Belfast

Acknowledgements

This book was accepted by the Economic History Society when Professor Smout was editor of the series but was finished after I had taken over. Accordingly, I have turned to others to scrutinize my text. I am grateful to Dr. R. B. Outhwaite for sceptical comments characteristic of Cambridge; to my colleague, Dr. K. D. Brown, for exercising skills sharpened by his editorial duties with another series; and to another colleague, Mr J. McAllister, whose perception of what students will tolerate is matched only by his unrivalled knowledge of the early-modern period. I have accepted some of their advice; the faults remaining are my own. I wish to thank, also, Sr Anne McKernan, O.P. of the University of Michigan for discussing with me her researches on the linen industry in County Armagh.

Note on References

References in the text within square brackets relate to the numbered items in the Bibliography, followed, where necessary, by the page numbers in italics, for example [1,7–9].

1 'Proto-industrialization': The urge to generalize

In the early 1970s an ugly new word – 'proto-industrialization' – entered the literature of economic history and since then has rapidly colonized books, articles and even undergraduate essays, spawning additional abstractions as it goes along. A new historical generalization had arrived, chiefly through the efforts of Franklin Mendels [64].

The concept of proto-industrialization is a contribution to the long debate on the origins of the industrial revolution and, more generally, on the genesis of industrial capitalism. In the fashion of the time the concept is sometimes given a quasi-scientific status by its proponents who refer to it as a model. When historians use the word 'model' in preference to the more old-fashioned 'hypothesis' they have two objectives in mind. First, they are simply coining a descriptive label to fasten on to a bundle of historical events. All students of economic history are familiar with such labels as 'industrial revolution' and 'capitalism'; although often the first faltering step to wisdom is the realization that identical labels can mean different things to different historians [see 17; 41]. The second purpose of a model is to provide a set of generalized explanations of historical developments. This is done by observing regularities in the data and then, by a process of induction, establishing reasons for them.

In the present case proto-industrialization is concerned with the fact that in Europe before the industrial revolution manufacturing industries supplying national and international markets were often located in the countryside. Production was organized in cottage workshops where men, women and children combined the manufacture of textiles, leather goods, metal wares and similar items with farming. Not all industry, of course, was organized in this way. This form of organization was not found, for example, in the mining or metal-smelting industries, or in activities such as milling or tanning which required a relatively large investment in fixed capital. There were also dozens and scores of full-time craftsmen in every market town producing clothing, household goods, saddlery, pots and pans, and the like, for the local market. Nevertheless there were many regions of Europe where cottage workers combined the production of industrial goods, overwhelmingly textiles, with the cultivation of the soil or the grazing of sheep and cattle. The essence of cottage industries was that labour employed in this manner was cheap; therefore the goods produced were competitive in national and international markets.

As a description, therefore, proto-industrialization points to a common feature of the economy of pre-industrial Europe: the existence of industries in the countryside. In its dynamic, or explanatory, aspect proto-industrialization postulates that cottage industries contained the conditions for the eventual development of factory-based industries; it analyses the way in which during the eighteenth and nineteenth centuries the factory system grew out of rural industry. It is because cottage industry preceded and sometimes led on to modern industry that it has been labelled proto-industry, that is, 'the first phase of industrialization'. In some instances, however, the second phase did not occur and instead rural industry decayed, so producing 'deindustrialization'.

Proto-industrialization also explores other aspects of industrial development. For example, considerable attention is paid to 'proletarianization' whereby once independent farmer-manufacturers were turned into wage-earners as a result of their increasing reliance on merchant-capitalists who supplied them with raw materials and who bought their manufactured goods for resale in distant markets. Accompanying proletarianization was 'immiseration', said to afflict cottage workers as they were metamorphized into wage workers, thereby suffering a fall in their social and economic status and spending their miserable earnings on alcohol and other debasing consumption goods. Finally, proto-industrialization suggests that the growth of cottage industry and its eventual evolution into factory industry affected the formation, size, structure and functioning of households and families, and the rate of population growth, a theme that by some oversight has failed to be christened 'socialization'.

Historical models can be used as research tools to point to issues that are worth investigating. Proto-industrialization has initiated comprehensive studies of rural industries geared to distant markets in eighteenth and nineteenth-century Europe and also elsewhere as scholars have come to appreciate that they were not purely a European phenomenon [see 28; 75]. Bolder spirits among historians also claim that the concept of proto-industrialization does more than merely reveal facets of the past. It also contains lessons for those interested in strategies of economic development at the present time and in the future. As Charles and Richard Tilly have written, 'our eventual hope is to specify the relevance and irrelevance of European history both for general theories of economic development and for projections of economic change in contemporary countries' [89, *195*].

As we have remarked, proto-industrialization and its attendant neologisms are part of the study of the development of industrial civilization. When Arnold Toynbee delivered his lectures in 1880–1 on the industrial revolution in England, so launching the phrase into the stream of historical consciousness, he treated it as an almost complete break with the past: 'the essence of the industrial revolution [was] the substitution of competition for the medieval regulation which had previously controlled the production and distribution of wealth'. In its more narrowly manufacturing aspects, 'the all-prominent fact ... [of the industrial revolution was] the substitution of the factory for the domestic system' [91, *58*, *63*]. The point was put even more dramatically by Charles Beard in 1901 when he wrote that 'suddenly, almost like a thunderbolt from a clear sky, were ushered in the storm and stress of the Industrial Revolution' [quoted 30, *3*].

Such an explosive interpretation of industrial development was unlikely to survive the erosion of empirical research, and it was eventually replaced by a story of slow evolution. Two works more than any others established a more gradualist view into the historiography of the industrial revolution. In 1926 the first volume of Sir John Clapham's *An Economic History of Modern Britain* demonstrated how incomplete industrialization was by 1830 when 'the country [still] abounded in ancient types of industrial organization and in transitional types of all variety' [15, *I*, *143*]. Even more influential was T. S. Ashton's *The Industrial Revolution, 1760–1830* (1948) which summed up a generation of historical research by pointing out that 'the system of human relationships that is sometimes called capitalism had its origins long before 1760, and attained its full development long after 1830; there is a danger of overlooking the essential fact of continuity' [3, *2*].

At about the same time as Clapham was writing an alternative picture of industrial development was being painted, primarily in the works of J. U. Nef. In a massive book on the British coal industry published in 1932 he wrote that 'the late sixteenth and seventeenth centuries may have been marked by an industrial revolution only less important than that which began towards the end of the eighteenth century' [72, *I*, *165*]. In successive publications his tentative industrial revolution of the sixteenth and seventeenth centuries hardened into an event 'no less' important than its more famous successor, and other authors have added to it a series of revolutions stretching from the Bronze Age to the twentieth century [see 17].

The concept of proto-industrialization has little in common with views of economic development as a series of revolutions. It is more akin to the evolutionary tradition but it differs from it in one important respect: it sees earlier forms of industry, not merely as preceding factory industry, but as being causally related to it. As such it has affinities with various 'stage' theories of economic development that were propounded first by the German historical economists writing between the 1840s and the First World War. Although differing from one another on points of detail, all stressed the importance of the economic changes taking place during the sixteenth, seventeenth and eighteenth centuries in laying the foundations of industrial society in the nineteenth [see 45]. Much later, W. W. Rostow revived the stage approach and identified five stages of economic growth, of which two – the 'pre-conditions for take-off', and the 'take-off' proper – approximate to the phases of proto-industry and factory industry [80; 81]. Mendels, the main begetter of proto-industrialization, however, might protest that his model is more specific than Rostow's in explaining how one stage leads to the next.

Proto-industrialization also has points of similarity with that other German tradition, of Marxist writings dealing with the transition from feudalism to capitalism. One of the most influential publications of this kind in English has been Maurice Dobb's *Studies in the Development of Capitalism* (1946). The crucial stages of development according to the Marxist model are the feudal mode of production which disintegrated during the fifteenth and sixteenth centuries, and the 'definite triumph of capitalism at the end of the eighteenth century' [43, *162*]. Between these two stages existed an indeterminate period described by Dobb as 'an early and still immature stage of Capitalism' during which 'capital began to penetrate production on a considerable scale, either in the form of a fairly matured relationship between capitalist and hired wage-earners or in the less developed form of the subordination of domestic handicraftsmen, working in their own homes, to a capitalist on the so-called "putting-out system"' [29, *18, 19*].

Without using the word, Dobb was outlining the proto-industrial stage of industry and it is not surprising that recent Marxist writers have adopted the concept with enthusiasm. Thus, the editors of a recent volume devoted to *Industrialization before Industrialization* claim that 'proto-industrialization ... belonged to the second phase of the great transformation from feudalism to capitalism. It was indeed one of the driving forces during this second phase' [54, 7]. As if to emphasize its affinity to the Marxist scheme, one of the contributors, Peter Kriedte, refers to 'a crisis in the proto-industrial mode of production' that caused this first phase of industry to give way to the second, just as the 'crisis in the feudal mode of production' in the Marxist model propelled society from feudalism to capitalism [54, *137*]. There are differences, of course. The literature on proto-industry has concentrated on the eighteenth and nineteenth centuries whereas Marxists range much more widely. More important, the Marxist debate has had little to say about the connexions between industrialization and population growth [see 40], a theme central to proto-industrialization, although recently there has been some attempt to incorporate demography into Marxist explanations of long-run economic change [see 83]. On the whole, though, Marxists put much greater stress on class relationships as a cause of economic change [see 12]. In the proto-industrial literature, on the other hand, class relationships are treated more as the outcome of industrial developments.

Historical models, like industrial revolutions, rarely appear like thunderbolts from a clear sky but have their antecedents in earlier writings. Before Mendels explicitly formulated the features of proto-industrialization in 1972 they had been foreshadowed in a number of articles. In 1961 Joan Thirsk published an important essay in which she drew attention to 'semi-farming, semi-industrial communities' supplying national and international markets with textiles. Their common feature was that they possessed abundant supplies of labour, although she explicitly denied any intention of propounding 'a theory for the situation of rural handicraft industries which can be applied mechanistically to them all' [87, *86*]. At about the same time Rudolph Braun in a study of eighteenth-century Switzerland traced the effects that the introduction of cottage industry had on the process of family formation in agrarian communities [10].

A little later E. L. Jones pointed to the regional specialization developing within European agriculture from the later seventeenth century whereby some districts devoted themselves to the commercial production of cereals, while 'less-favoured areas tended to concentrate on livestock production and to switch into rural industry' [50, *138–9*]. Finally, in 1969 D. C. Coleman, writing of the development of new drapery production in England at the end of the sixteenth century, referred to 'a commercialization of peasant techniques' whereby cheap fabrics once made by farmers for their own use were now manufactured to satisfy the demands of expanding international markets [18, *421*]. All the elements of 'industrialization before the factory system' existed in print before Mendels finally fitted them together into a generalized account of industrial development.

Just why proto-industrialization was finally constructed in the early 1970s is a matter of speculation. The knowledge of rural industries was hardly new; they had been discussed at length, for example, by the pioneer English historians, Cunningham and Unwin, a century ago [26; 93], as well as by the German historical economists from whom they drew much of their inspiration. The decisive difference in the 1970s was probably that rural industries were now being studied by scholars trained in economics and familiar with concepts developed to analyse the workings of labour markets in agrarian-based economies [see 48; 59]. Such scholars shared an interest in the problems of promoting growth in present-day underdeveloped countries. A knowledge of how proto-industries were transformed into factory industries in western Europe in the eighteenth and nineteenth centuries would, they hoped, demonstrate how the process might be repeated today. The model of proto-industrialization was thus the creation of economically-trained historians. They were not, moreover, simply borrowing the economists' tools, but were attempting to forge new ones helpful to the understanding of present-day and future economic development [see 70, *xiii–xiv*]. Just how successful they have been we shall be better able to judge when we have considered the component parts of the model.

2 The Features of Proto-industry

Before the industrial revolution there existed throughout Europe a myriad of small workshops producing basic consumer goods. They were located mostly in towns where they catered for the demands of the local urban population and the agrarian community of the surrounding countryside, and included the tailors, dressmakers, shoemakers, bakers, butchers, carpenters, braziers and others, who made up a quarter or a third of the working population of pre-industrial towns. Some craftsmen – tanners, blacksmiths and the like – also worked in the countryside where their activities complemented those of local farmers. Here and there, too, were dotted larger-scale units of production in such processes as iron-smelting, corn-milling and paper-making where capital requirements and technical skills extended beyond the resources of cottage workshops [see 19].

None of these activities would be recognised as examples of proto-industry by the proponents of the concept since their markets were local and they did not evolve into factory production. Rather, proto-industrialization was, in the words of Mendels, 'a first phase [of industrialization] which preceded and prepared modern industrialization proper' [64, *241*].

Proto-industries were marked by four features which, in the right circumstances, led to the development of factory-based industry. First, proto-industrial craftsmen produced goods for markets beyond the regions where they lived; often these markets were overseas and the products of one region competed with the products of another. Second, the industrial products were made by peasant-manufacturers who combined, say, weaving or stocking-knitting with farming. Manufacturing slotted into the slack periods of the farming year, and it fitted in particularly well with pastoral farming which was less labour-intensive than corn-growing. Labour employed in this way was cheap since, in the absence of industry, farmers and their families would be idle for part of the year. In the language of economics, the opportunity costs of the labour of peasant-manufacturers were low. Cottage industry also made minimal demands on fixed capital, for no special industrial premises were required and the machinery used –

spinning wheels, looms and anvils, for example – was usually small and inexpensive: small enough to be housed in domestic cottages and cheap enough to be owned by poor farmers. Relatively expensive machines such as stocking-knitting frames were sometimes rented but in general industries requiring large and expensive equipment were not suited to a domestic form of organization. Neither were processes using materials of high value such as gold and silver.

The third important characteristic of proto-industrialization, it is argued, was that rural manufacturing stimulated commercial farming by creating a market for food. Proto-industrial workers did not grow enough food for their own needs, either because their farms were too small or too barren to begin with, or because manufacturing expanded to take up so much of their time that they neglected their farms. They were therefore obliged to buy supplies from other producers. This brings us to the fourth feature of proto-industrialization. Towns located in manufacturing zones were principally centres of trade and commerce. The merchants who supplied raw materials to cottage manufacturers lived in towns, and finishing processes – the dyeing of woollen cloth, for example – were sometimes carried out there by skilled workmen. Weekly or bi-weekly markets were held in towns and were attended by merchants who came to buy manufactured goods for export, and also by farmers and dealers who travelled from districts of commercial farming to sell their produce.

Regions of proto-industry were extensive throughout eighteenth-century Europe: for example, 'in Maine, Picardy, and Languedoc in France, Westphalia, Silesia, and southern Saxony in Germany, Flanders and Twente in the Low Countries, Ulster, the West Riding, the Cotswolds and East Anglia in Great Britain and many more' [27, *105*; see also 52; 76]. The cloth industries – wool, linen, cotton and silk – were the most important of the proto-industrial crafts. Textile production had been widespread throughout the economy of Europe in the middle ages and early-modern period, but from the later seventeenth century regional specialization became more pronounced. Thus the first of the features of proto-industrialization emerged.

The reason for the greater development of proto-industrial zones in the century or so before the industrial revolution was that market conditions were altering [see 50]. They were changing because within Europe population that had been growing from the end of the fifteenth century had now ceased to increase, so causing a widespread sluggishness in demand for basic consumer goods such as textiles. At the same time, though, new market opportunities were opening up outside Europe in areas of overseas settlement [see 42]. Both developments placed a premium on inexpensive products: within Europe as merchants struggled to maintain or even increase sales in stagnant markets by selling cheaper goods; outside Europe because demand was concentrated on lower-value products. Since labour was the largest element in the cost of manufacturing textiles and many other products, merchants sought out goods that had been made by the cheapest available labour. Those regions of the countryside possessing supplies of labour in excess of the requirements of agriculture were well placed to take advantage of these opportunities that changing market conditions afforded.

This part of the proto-industrialization thesis can be illustrated by the example of the West Riding of Yorkshire. Cheap woollen cloths had been made in the region from at least the fifteenth century, principally for the home market, and in 1700 the West Riding produced roughly one-fifth of total English cloth output. As an exporting district, however, it had been overshadowed by the Wiltshire-Gloucestershire woollen industry and by East Anglia. During the eighteenth century the position changed dramatically. Total English production doubled or trebled, but in the West Riding output rose eightfold, the greater part of the increase occurring in worsteds, the manufacture of which was concentrated in the north-west of the Riding. The production of traditional woollen cloths also rose, chiefly in the south-eastern parts of the district. Cloth was now produced chiefly for the export market, the West Riding having advantages over the older exporting regions of the West of England and East Anglia. These advantages may have included lower labour costs – the literature is not conclusive on this point – but some weight also has to be attached to the many varieties of cloths produced, adapted to the requirements of particular markets, and to the entrepreneurial skills and superior organization of producers in the region [see 37; 47; 95].

An even more striking example of an export-led expansion of a rurally located textile industry occurred in Ireland during the eighteenth century. Poor-quality linens for domestic consumption had been made in Ireland for centuries, but at the end of the seventeenth century an influx of English and continental expertise into the province of Ulster, coupled with the opening up of the

English market to Irish producers, resulted in a commercialization of traditional techniques and an improvement in quality. From insignificant levels at the beginning of the eighteenth century, linen cloth exports rose to over 40 million yards by 1800. The bulk of the output came from farmer-weavers living in parts of the Ulster countryside. As a contemporary wrote in 1819:

> it is not at all necessary to the advancement of that trade [i.e. linen], that either the spinners or the weavers should be collected into overgrown cities, or congregated into crowded and unwholesome factories. Those branches of the linen business, which are their particular concern, can be perfectly well managed in their respective cabins. [84, *467*]

According to an estimate made in 1770 there were then 42,000 weavers in Ulster. Taking account of household members also involved in linen production, as many as 200,000 persons may have been connected with the industry, the equivalent to a quarter of the province's population [24; 25; 32].

Turning to continental Europe, the spinning and weaving of flax developed as important activities in Flanders during the eighteenth century, displacing an older woollen industry. The linen-manufacturing zone lay in the interior of the country and was bounded on the west by a coastal strip devoted to commercial farming, and to the east by an area specializing in the cultivation of flax used by the linen manufacturers. The growth of output during the eighteenth century was less spectacular than in Ulster during the same period, but the proportion of the population employed in the linen industry – nearly all of them living in the countryside – was greater. More than 80 per cent of output was exported, much of it to Spain and the Spanish-American colonies. In the words of Mendels, 'the economic history of Flanders from the late seventeenth to the late eighteenth century adequately fits...a phase of "proto-industrialization"' [65, *203*].

In Germany the Rhineland offers a different example of rural industry. The area bounded by Krefeld, Aachen, Cologne and the Wupper valley was a mixed textile and metal-working zone producing mainly silks around Krefeld, woollens in the vicinity of Aachen, and linen, silks and cottons in the Wupper valley. The textile crafts were not exclusively rural, but during the eighteenth century the most rapid expansion occurred in those branches of production supplying distant markets and employing cheap country labour. Around Krefeld, for example, 'a thriving silk industry had taken root. Drawing upon the labour of underemployed linen weavers in the vicinity it was able to keep costs low and thus successfully compete in foreign markets.' Similarly, at the end of the seventeenth century the woollen industry in the city of Aachen had broken loose of restrictions imposed by urban gilds and was spreading into the countryside. The outcome of the developments was that:

> on the eve of the French Revolution the lower Rhine textile trades had become an integral part of the 'Atlantic economy' and fully shared the benefits of its buoyancy. Low costs of production, making it possible to meet the challenge of foreign competition, assured the industries of the region this favourable position. [53, 557; see also 6]

The cases cited so far refer to textiles, and the literature of proto-industrialization generally is dominated by discussions of woollens and linen. Rural industry, though, was not confined to textiles. In England, for instance, there were two important metal-working zones in the later seventeenth and eighteenth centuries that have some claim to be regarded as 'proto-industrial' in that they employed part-time agricultural labour, produced for export markets, and eventually became centres of factory production. In the vicinity of Walsall and Birmingham in the West Midlands a considerable proportion of the rural population combined farming with the manufacture of nails, knives, scythes, locks and the like. Much of the output was destined for the American market where the log cabins of the frontiersmen were fastened together by Birmingham nails. Similarly, in the Sheffield region of south Yorkshire knives, scythes and cutlery were manufactured for export by 'farmer-craftsmen [who] followed a dual occupation combining agriculture and metal-working' [38, 18; see also 23; 82). On the Continent there were important metal-working regions in the Liège Basin and the Rhineland.

The model of proto-industrialization stresses that the labour of peasant-manufacturers was cheap, although we should note in passing that very often in the literature this cheapness is assumed rather than demonstrated empirically. There has been considerable discussion, however, of why country-based labour was low-cost labour. In towns competing demands by employers pushed up wages; and in the case of self-employed craftsmen, gild restrictions on recruitment into the crafts they controlled served to keep the price of labour high. Rural labour was cheaper because there industrial production was undertaken by workers who would otherwise be periodically underemployed. Nevertheless, rural labour was not equally cheap in all regions and proto-industry therefore was not found everywhere in the countryside. Even within a particular proto-industrial zone, manufacturing was unevenly distributed: the populations of some parishes might be heavily involved with industry and in others hardly at all.

Joan Thirsk has noted three conditions that could result in supplies of cheap labour in a region. First, she suggests that low-cost labour was more likely to be found in pastoral regions than in areas of cereal farming with their more intensive demand for labour. Second, underemployed, and therefore cheap, farm labour was commonly available in communities composed of small freeholders living in areas unfettered by manorial control. In those villages where manor courts exercised a strict supervision of tenures – by, for example, preventing the subdivision of farms – and restricted the settlement of newcomers in the village, there was little likelihood that a labour supply in excess of the requirements of agriculture would emerge to any great extent. But where manorial control was weak or absent, farms were often subdivided; and where there were no community restrictions on immigration the population was likely to grow and outrun the employment opportunities available locally in agriculture. Finally, cheap labour was prevalent in upland and moorland districts with infertile soils and extensive commons. Such regions tended to become overpopulated, partly because the land was too barren to support a large population by arable farming to begin with, but also because the very availability of extensive grazing land – married to an absence of weak community controls on settlement – attracted emigrants from elsewhere [87].

Thirsk supports her general propositions by evidence drawn from several English textile regions. Thus, in Wiltshire, Gloucestershire and Somerset, textile manufacture was concentrated in the dairying regions but was unimportant in the sheep-corn areas. In Suffolk, similarly, cloth production was located mainly in the dairying district of the county. This was the wood-pasture region to the south where manorial organization was weak. Turning to Kent, there had been a vigorous textile industry in the seventeenth century concentrated in the Weald, a heavily populated pastoral region, although it was in decline during the eighteenth. Further north, Westmorland, a county of mountain and moor, was a considerable producer of coarse woollen cloth and knitted stockings, the labour coming from the densely populated lowland valleys. In the dales bordering Westmorland and north Yorkshire farming communities eked out a precarious existence by combining the grazing of cattle and sheep with hand knitting woollen hosiery for the London market.

Some other English studies confirm Thirsk's generalizations. To cite just one, about one-third of the West Riding of Yorkshire was composed of upland grazing and was inhabited by numerous small freeholders who combined subsistence farming with the manufacture of worsteds. Near to the market towns the farms were generally more fertile and their occupants were occupied with the production of food and with weaving woollen cloths. Finally, to the east of the Riding there was an area of tillage where industry was unimportant and the main purpose of agriculture was growing grain for the textile districts [47].

An association between proto-industrialization and regions of pastoral farming or infertile soils as suggested by proponents of the concept thus seems well-founded [see 66]. Nevertheless, it was not the only possible relationship and there are examples of rural industry concentrated in areas more concerned with cereal farming than with pasture or rough grazing. In Ulster, for example, County Armagh was at the very heart of the linen-producing zone, but 'notwithstanding the minute subdivision of land which is the natural result of these peculiar circumstances [i.e. linen manufacture] the farmers ... are more than competent to supply its population with vegetable [i.e. cereals and potatoes], though not with animal food ...' [84, *467*]. Cultivation, though, was often neglected in favour of linen weaving and Arthur Young remarked that the county displayed 'the worst husbandry I have met with' [97, *I, 127*]. We can hardly argue that the opportunity costs of the labour of farmers who neglected their fields to concentrate on weaving were negligible, but their priorities were economically rational since they were an attempt to maximize family income. On the Continent, to take another example, the Pays de Caux in Upper Normandy was a crop-growing area which from the 1720s developed an extensive rurally-located cotton industry.

Manufacturing was organized by cotton merchants based in Rouen and it provided a large number of landless people in the Caux with a valuable supplement to the incomes they earned as agricultural labourers [see 34].

The importance of social structure in influencing the geographical distribution of rural industry can be illustrated by the example of framework-knitting (i.e. the manufacture of woollen hosiery on knitting frames) in late seventeenth and eighteenth-century Leicestershire. The crucial social distinction was between 'open' and 'closed' parishes. Framework-knitting was located mainly in the former where the land was occupied by a large number of small cultivators who needed an industrial activity to supplement their meagre agricultural incomes; some cultivators even mortgaged their farms to raise money to buy a stocking frame. Before the mid-eighteenth century stocking knitters were usually independent producers, but as the population grew in the parishes devoted to knitting, there emerged a class of poor men who were unable to afford frames and who therefore worked for already established knitters or for merchants who supplied them with yarn and from whom they rented knitting frames. By contrast, in the 'closed' parishes the land was owned by a few large landlords who leased out their estates in large farms which were devoted to commercial farming. The landlords paid the poor rate and they therefore placed strict controls on cottage building, permitting their tenant farmers to erect only as many as necessary to house essential farm labourers. In the absence of housing and alternative employments, landless labourers in the closed parishes faced the choice of working for large farmers or moving away from the parish. Some went to the open parishes in search of employment in the knitting industry [see 58; 67].

The behaviour of landlords in the closed parishes of Leicestershire contrasts with that of landlords in the linen zones of Ulster, Silesia and Flanders. In the former farmer-weavers normally leased their farms from landlords but they were subject to very little regulation in matters of subdivision, cottage building, or farming practices. However, landlords encouraged linen production by establishing markets so that their tenants could earn money to pay the rent. In Silesia, which was still largely feudal in the eighteenth century, landlords were happy for their tenants to take up weaving so that they could afford the many feudal obligations heaped upon them [53]. In Flanders, landlords in the linen regions encouraged their tenants to subdivide holdings as a way of increasing their total rent incomes [9].

There is a common assumption in the literature of proto-industrialization that peasant-manufacturers were, or soon became, wage-earners employed by capitalist merchants who supplied them with raw materials to process in their own cottages, nevertheless retaining ownership of the materials throughout the various stages of manufacture. But this was only one possibility. Another was that peasant-manufacturers were self-employed craftsmen growing or buying their own raw materials and selling their finished goods to dealers who, in turn, dispatched them to their final destinations. We must not push the distinction between a self-employed craftsman and a wage-earner too far, however, for a man could be both simultaneously; or he might be independent at one point in time and an employee at another. As Ramsay [77] and others have pointed out, relations between manufacturers and dealers before the industrial revolution took many forms that defy modern categories of employer and employee. It is a criticism of the proto-industrialization model that 'the immense variety of organisational and industrial structures is ignored and the corresponding diversity of accumulation and change is glossed over' [47, 37].

Some examples will demonstrate the complexities. In the West Riding woollen industry the typical producer in the eighteenth century was a self-employed farmer-weaver who owned his own tools, grew his own wool, or purchased it locally, and sold his output to dealers who travelled around the urban cloth markets. In the worsted branch of the industry, by contrast, spinners and weavers were usually employees of merchant clothiers. In Ulster most linen producers were independent farmer-weavers who grew flax on their own farms which was harvested and prepared by family labour, spun by the women and woven by the men. Weavers with insufficient flax could buy it, or yarn, from the many petty dealers who visited the linen markets. These same markets were attended by drapers and bleachers who bought the linen webs and prepared them for the final markets. In the words of Stuart, writing in 1819, weavers were not employees but 'free agents whose employments are diversified and rational' [84, 467]. Only towards the end of the century did a class of wage-earning weavers emerge. On the Continent most linen weavers appear to have been self-employed, although wage-earners were widespread in the woollen and metal crafts. In the metal-working trades in the English West

Midlands self-employed workers and wage-earners were both common, with the former predominating among the more prosperous scythe-makers and the latter among poor nailers (32; 47; 53; 65; 82].

Just as the proto-industrialization literature glosses over the many variations in organization, so it provides no very convincing explanation of *why* some peasant manufacturers were self-employed and others were wage-earners. The most ingenious reason is that offered by Millward who suggests that wage-labour emerged under two conditions. The first is 'when there is a demand for high volumes of standardized middle-quality products'. The second is where 'there was a distinct innovation in the mix of materials [e.g. the new draperies]' [68, 28–9]. In these circumstances, Millward argues, merchants found it easier to obtain the quantities and qualities of goods they required in order to satisfy demand by supplying employees with raw materials than by buying manufactured wares from large numbers of self-employed craftsmen. The argument works well enough for, say, worsteds and metal-wares where the volume of demand was high and there was a large variety in the types and qualities of goods produced. But this was true, too, with linen and woollens which were often made by independent producers. Some additional explanation is called for. It is noticeable that it was often the most impoverished producers who became wage-earners: those too poor to buy raw materials and in need of an industrial wage for their subsistence.

In Marxist literature on capitalist development there is an arcane debate on whether 'a section of producers themselves accumulated capital and took to trade', or whether 'a section of the existing merchant class began to "take possession directly of the means of production"' [29, *123*; 85, *52–6*]. The proponents of the concept of proto-industrialization do not have much to say explicitly on this subject, perhaps because empirical studies of rural industries suggest a complex set of arrangements that cannot easily be generalized. Throughout southern England, as Ramsay has pointed out, the cloth export trade from the sixteenth century was dominated by London and the important figure in trade was the clothier. He might own a loom or two, he probably put out materials to spinners and weavers in their own cottages, but 'his crucial responsibility lay in the delivery of the cloth to the London market and finding a purchaser there' [77, *23*]. Clothiers lived among the weavers and spinners and may well have evolved from their ranks. In the West Midlands nail trade, also, marketing enterprise seems to have developed initially within the region although as a substantial trade grew up with the American end of the business it increasingly passed into the hands of London-based ironmongers and merchants [23]. But there are also examples of external interests coming into a region seeking out manufactured goods for export. In Ulster, for example, linen production was harnessed to overseas markets by English settlers and landlords [24; 25]; in Silesia, also, locally produced linen was bought by merchants who came from elsewhere [53]. Turning to a different trade, London-based merchants sent their agents into the English East Midlands to buy footwear and hosiery more cheaply than they could get them in the capital [13].

As we have noted, proto-industrialization postulates that rural industry develops in association with commercial agriculture. Commercial farming and rural manufacturing were, in fact, often found in close proximity. In Wiltshire, for example, there were two distinct but contiguous farming regions: 'the enclosed, non-manorial countries – the cheese and butter countries – [which] were the lands of family farmers and self-employed persons', and 'the manorialized, champion, sheep-and-corn countries ... [which] were the main field for the development of agrarian capitalism and for the agricultural revolution' [quoted 87, 74]. The former was the home of cloth manufacturers and the latter of commercial farmers. In Ulster, where much of the linen zone was a fertile region, weavers and farmers lived cheek-by-jowl. Nevertheless, much of the food consumed by linen manufacturers came from 'great importations' from other parts of Ireland, 'besides what comes occasionally from England and Scotland' [97, *I*, *133*].

Proto-industrialization draws a clear distinction between countryside and town: manufacturing was done principally in the former, with the latter being centres of trade and commerce. The functions of towns are well illustrated by the example of Ulster where, in the late eighteenth century, there were about sixty places scattered throughout the province serving as weekly linen markets. Most were small and the bulk of trade was concentrated in the three major towns of Armagh, Lisburn and Lurgan. From there cloths were dispatched to the bleach yards before being transported to Dublin, Newry, Belfast or Londonderry for export [32]. Similarly, in the West Riding of Yorkshire, 'the eighteenth century towns, especially the smaller ones, functioned chiefly as trading centres. Such towns as Dent, Bedale, Skipton, Cawood, Aberford, and the like spent the greater part of the year in slumber, only awakening for the annual fairs or the more frequent market-days' [37, *385*]. A few strategically placed centres grew to larger importance: Wakefield from the mid-seventeenth century; Leeds from the end of the seventeenth century, with growing competition from Halifax and Huddersfield during the eighteenth. On the Continent, the towns in Flanders actually decayed as manufacturing centres during the eighteenth century at the same time as they increased their concentration on the marketing of cloth. Thus, the number of looms at work in Ghent fell by 25 per cent between 1700 and 1780, but the quantity of linen passing through the Ghent market doubled in the same period [65].

Ultimately, the dichotomy between urban and rural industry perceived by historians of proto-industrialization is somewhat strained, unless 'urban' is interpreted in a strictly legalistic sense to mean a place possessing borough status [see 'Introduction' to 8]. It may be generally true that before the industrial revolution towns were primarily centres of trade and distribution. Nevertheless, they also contained a fair sprinkling of industrial workers, some of whom were employed in a very similar fashion to rural craftsmen. The Ulster town of Lisburn, for example, was the home of skilled damask weavers working on complex looms too large to be accommodated in rural cottages. There were also a large number of spinners and plain linen weavers working in their own homes [16]. In England the best known example of a city possessing a substantial textile industry in the seventeenth and eighteenth centuries is Norwich [see 22]. Conversely, there were rural communities – such as Shepshed in Leicestershire with its heavy commitment to framework-knitting – that became so involved in manufacturing during the eighteenth century that they became *de facto* urban centres [see 58].

To sum up, the essence of proto-industrialization was that industries producing for export markets became established in regions of the countryside possessing supplies of cheap labour. The workers might be self-employed or they might be wage-earners working for town-based capitalists; in either case the home was the workshop and the household the unit of production. A further characteristic of proto-industrialization was the interdependence of zones of rural industry and zones of commercial farming. The dynamic of proto-industrialization was provided by the force of the market: without the stimulus of large and competitive markets, rural manufacturers vegetated quietly in the countryside, supplying household and local needs, but untroubled by the pressures of commercial capitalism. In some regions the demands of the market became so strong that manufacturing outstripped the available labour supply, so inducing changes in industrial organization and techniques. Proto-industry was then transformed into the second stage of modern, factory based, industry. The transformation did not take place everywhere, however; some rural-industrial zones instead slipped gently into obscurity. To the problems of industrialization and deindustrialization we now turn.

3 Industrialization and Deindustrialization

Why and how did cottage industry become metamorphized into modern factory industry? According to Mendels [64] there were five links between the first and second stages of industrialization.

The most important was that industries in the countryside became the victims of their own success. The prime reason for their development in the first place was the low cost of labour arising from the widespread underemployment in certain types of agrarian economies. However, supplies of labour were not totally elastic. As increasing numbers of cultivators moved into manufacturing – or devoted a larger part of their time to industry and a lesser part to farming – so the productivity and hence the earnings of those remaining in agriculture rose. It now cost more to entice them into industry; in economic terms, their opportunity costs had increased.

There is a logical difficulty at this point because the concept of proto-industrialization postulates that cottage industry stimulated the growth of population and hence of the labour supply (see Chapter 4). So an assumption must be made that the demand for labour eventually grew more rapidly than its supply. Faced with rising labour costs, merchants and employers cast their net over ever widening areas. This had the further effect of increasing distribution and supervision costs, and there came a point where it was cheaper to reorganize production methods and employ labour in centralized workshops where it could be supervised and also to devise or introduce machinery which would raise the productivity of labour.

Production in centralized workshops was more capital-intensive than cottage production. Buildings were needed to accommodate the machinery that had once competed for space with bed and board in farm cottages and to house the workforce. Centralized workshops contained more elaborate machinery, perhaps powered by a water wheel or a steam engine, developed to replace the labour that had become too expensive, so adding to the demands for capital. This brings us to the second link between the first and second stages of industry outlined by the model: the capital came from the proto-industrial merchants. As Mendels puts it, 'proto-industrialization had created an accumulation of capital in the hands of merchant employers, making possible the adoption of machine industry with its (relatively) higher capital costs' [64, *244*]. These same merchants also possessed marketing and managerial skills that carried over into the conduct of factory industry, thus creating the third link between proto-industry and modern industrialization.

There were two further connections. Within cottage industry there was, according to Mendels, a reservoir of technical knowledge that could be adapted to modern industry: 'many of the machine builders of the industrial revolution in England had been trained in the old handicraft industrial sectors and they were in intimate contact with the scientific advances of the time' [64, *244*]. Finally, with the development of factories and an urbanized labour force, for whom a corn field or a cow were merely objects within a dimming folk memory, the old association between areas of proto-industry and regions of commercial agriculture became more vital than ever.

Proto-industrialization as originally formulated makes no claim that cottage industry prepared workers for the rigours of factory life, although the suggestion appears in Marxist elaborations. There are two reasons for its absence in the original version, one theoretical and one empirical. Modern factory industry produces goods by a combination of fixed capital and labour and, as Mokyr points out, 'it is immaterial whether the workers who become the urban proletariat came originally from the rural-industrial ... sector or were most active in agriculture' [70, *134–5*]. This observation carries with it the important implication that modern factory industry did *not* always grow out of cottage industry.

As far as the empirical evidence is concerned, it is abundantly clear that in England, to take but one example, rural-industrial workers possessed irregular working habits, with a particular predeliction for St Monday as well as the more ecclesiastically recognized holy days; and that they were far from amenable to the regular work discipline of the factories. In the metal-working industries of the West Midlands Monday continued to be observed as a holiday until the third quarter of the nineteenth century despite the attempts of employers to end the practice [see 4, *78*]. This is not to deny that one-time cottage workers were recruited into the factories in the late eighteenth and early nineteenth centuries, but it was economic circumstances, not prior experience of industrial work, that led them there.

Of the five suggested links between proto-industry and factory industry the greatest difficulties of verification are raised by the first. Again using the example of England, there are several reasons for believing that labour became more expensive over the course of much of the eighteenth century. The estimates of Wrigley and Schofield show that until the 1770s population generally grew at less than 0.6 per cent per annum, which, given the level of demand for labour, meant that real wages were either constant or were rising. Only when the rate of growth of population accelerated in the last three decades of the century do real wages, nationally, appear to have fallen [57]. Even then it is probable that real wages continued to increase in the most rapidly industrializing parts of the country where there was a large demand for labour; in these regions there were many complaints from manufacturers about the shortage and expense of labour [see 4; 5; 31]. The organizational changes and technical innovations taking place in English industry in the later eighteenth century therefore did so against a background of rising labour costs in some industries; but this is some way from proving that particular entrepreneurs reacted to mounting wage bills by changing their methods of production.

The most systematic investigation of the operation of labour markets during the period of industrialization is Mokyr's study of the Low Countries. He draws a distinction between the northern provinces that eventually formed the Netherlands, and the southern provinces that eventually became Belgium. The economy of the former was characterized by a concentration on trade and maritime activities; it possessed a highly commercialized agricultural sector and the general level of wages was high. The industrial sector was small and stagnating in the late eighteenth and early nineteenth centuries. Belgium, by contrast, possessed extensive rural industries producing woollens, linens and metal-wares, a rapidly growing population and low wages; and during the early decades of the nineteenth century it successfully made the transition from proto-industry to modern factory industry. In the Low Countries, therefore, the association between high wages and industrial innovation was the reverse of the relationship in England. Mokyr's explanation is that in the Netherlands high wages cut into profits; and since profits were the main source of capital, entrepreneurs could not afford to introduce capital-intensive methods of production. In Belgium there was no such problem. English textile machinery was introduced because its productivity gains, compared with traditional labour-intensive methods, were great, and it was financed by the profits that the cheap labour had made possible [70].

This analysis compels a reassessment of the English experience. If high wages inhibited industrial development in the Netherlands, why did they not also act as a barrier to development in England? Perhaps the most plausible answer to this question is that industrialization occurred earlier in England; the first generation of machines was relatively cheap in capital terms and to some extent the initial costs of development could be offset by savings in working capital and distribution costs. Once installed, new machines yielded to their innovators a quasi-rent that financed the next round of development; that is to say, the earnings of one machine, over and above its operating costs, could be transferred to meet the costs of a new and technically superior machine. In practical terms, we may envisage cotton spinners moving through a hierarchy of machinery from spinning wheels to jennies, to water-frames, to steam-powered mules, each more expensive but more productive than the last. A similar argument applies to centralized workshops initially housing traditional machinery. Their cost savings, compared with dispersed cottage production, could be used to finance the introduction of labour-saving machinery. Hence, in England, high wages were a stimulus to innovation, and the capital costs of new machinery were not a hindrance because they rose only gradually. In the Low Countries, on the other hand, industrialization came later and was based on imported English machinery; investment was more 'lumpy' and needed the prior accumulation of capital which low wages made possible in Belgium but not in the Netherlands.

The lesson to be learnt from these comparisons is that there was no pre-determined path from labour-intensive to capital-intensive forms of industrial organization in the eighteenth and nineteenth centuries. Whatever the state of their labour markets, entrepreneurs had to possess the ability as well as the desire to change production methods. In particular, they needed a command of capital which, in the absence of well-developed capital markets, came principally from profits. Here we come to the second of the connections between proto-industry and factory industry stressed by Mendels. Empirical studies, on the whole, confirm the view that the capital for the building and equipping of factories often came from domestic industry. In the English woollen industry for example:

in both Yorkshire and the West of England the majority of the new factory entrepreneurs had had previous connections with the industry, generally through involvement in its domestic organisation. Many of them were able to bring with them financial resources previously gained in the industry. The scale and methods of organisation of domestic manufacture were undoubtedly an influence on the scale and sources of supply of capital for factory development. [49, *39*]

Similarly, a recent study of approximately 150 Arkwright-type cotton mills operating in England in 1787 emphasizes the 'essential continuity of investment' that existed between traditional forms of manufacture and factory production [44, *81*]. The majority of the new mill owners had backgrounds in the textile industry, either as merchants or manufacturers. Nevertheless, there was no inevitability about the flow of capital from one stage of industry to the next. The same study shows that a quarter of the mill owners in the cotton industry in 1787 did *not* emerge from the textile industry but had been bankers, brewers, landowners and the like. This type of investor was exemplified by a clergyman, the Rev. Dr Benson, who was approached by Jedediah Strutt in 1757, on the strength of a prior acquaintance, for a loan to finance a new type of knitting frame. Benson was willing to lend to Strutt, except that his money was tied up in government stock and the proffered rate of return was not high enough to persuade him to switch [4, *28–9*].

Capital therefore sometimes flowed into factory industry from non-industrial sources. It also, on occasions, moved out of cottage industry into other areas of activity, particularly in zones where proto-industry failed to evolve into factory industry. Thus, in East Anglia and the West of England capital shifted into farming, brewing, innkeeping and retail trading. The transition was easy because fixed capital was rarely specific; buildings and sometimes machinery could fairly readily be turned from textile to non-textile uses. Furthermore, liquid capital, which comprised the greater proportion of total capital requirements, could by its very nature be diverted to other uses according to the state of the market for textiles and other goods [see 14]. Fluidity of capital was an essential feature of proto-industry and it is not surprising to find it flowing into whatever channels its owners judged profitable: machine-based industry was just one of several possibilities.

During the transition from the first to the second stages of industrialization there were few hard and fast divisions between capital raising, management and marketing. As the examples just considered suggest, the backgrounds of the investors and the backgrounds of the entrepreneurs were often very similar. Mendels is right, therefore, to emphasize this link between proto-industry and factory industry. His further suggestion, that the machine builders for the new factories came from the world of the old handicraft industry, is more problematical. It is true that traditional mechanical skills were extremely valuable to the first generation of factory owners. For example, in Lancashire one James Greenwood was taken into a cotton-factory partnership in 1784 although 'not having at present any capital to bring into stock' because he has 'a genius well adapted for constructing the machines and other works to be made use of and employed in and about the said intended mill' [quoted 44, *73*]. In the textile industry, generally, 'it was from the ranks of the master wheelwrights that many of the early specialist engineers emerged' [86, *80*]. Their particular expertise was the calculation of gear ratios and the construction of drive wheels used in milling. However, milling – whether corn, paper or fulling – does not fit into the normal categories of proto-industrial activities for it was centralized and relatively capital-intensive from early times. Furthermore, millwrights were practical, empirical men unlikely, as claimed by Mendels, to be 'in intimate contact with the scientific advances of the time' [64, *244*]. The later machine builders in the tradition of Boulton and Watt were more in the scientific mould, but their links with earlier forms of industry were tenuous.

It is unnecessary to labour the point that as the proportion of a country's workforce engaged in industry increased so agricultural productivity needed to be raised. But if improvements in agricultural productivity took place in zones of proto-industry the effect might be to retard rather than to stimulate industrialization since with rising agricultural productivity come rising agricultural earnings which push up the opportunity costs of manufacturing. In England, for example, East Anglia became one of the most advanced agricultural regions of the country during the industrial revolution and its traditional woollen industry declined. In the Low Countries, as Mokyr points out, industrial expansion occurred in Belgium where agricultural productivity was low, but not in the Netherlands where it was high. What was required was that there should be complementary areas of commercializing agriculture and expanding industry, and an intensification of inter-regional and international trade in agricultural and industrial goods. In short, the emergence of modern industry was accompanied by the development of regional specialization.

Proto-industry, then, contained within itself the seeds of further industrial development. But what of those areas that were subject to deindustrialization? Did the seed fall upon stony ground or was it inherently defective? Before attempting to answer these questions a brief checklist of regions of proto-industry that failed to move to the second stage of industrialization is in order. In England two major textile districts, the West of England and East Anglia, failed to develop as centres of factory industry during the eighteenth and early nineteenth centuries. Some lesser centres, including the Weald of Sussex and Kent, had already fallen by the wayside during the seventeenth century. But the most decisive example of industrial failure in the British Isles occurred in Ireland. The woollen industry, which had been moderately prosperous until the 1770s, succumbed to the weight of English competition. More important, by the early decades of the nineteenth century the Ulster linen industry was in difficulties as the result of competition from English cottons. It contracted in the outlying regions and became concentrated near to Belfast. There it became a factory-based industry in the 1820s – a case of a successful transition from proto-industry to modern industry – but at the expense of deindustrialization in north-west and central Ulster [see 21]. On the Continent there were many examples of deindustrialization: 'for instance much of the west of France which had previously developed export-orientated textile industries ... Silesia, Brittany, and Flanders could similarly be ranked on a continuum of relative failure in achieving the transition' [64, *246*].

A slightly puzzling feature of the model of proto-industrialization is the way that the high cost of labour has been invoked to explain not only the process of industrialization (the English case), but also the lack of industrialization (the Netherlands case). Conversely, an abundant supply of cheap labour can be used to account for the transition from cottage industry to the factory system (as in Belgium), and also as a reason for the failure of some regions of proto-industry to industrialize. A plentiful supply of cheap labour could be a hindrance to industrialization if it postponed the point at which centralized workshops and labour-saving machinery were introduced into production.

The late starters then had the problems of competing with the products of those regions that had industrialized earlier and some never succeeded in getting back into the race.

There are plenty of examples of traditional forms of industrial organization lingering in districts where labour was cheap. Years ago, for example, Sir John Clapham described in graphic terms how handicraft methods persisted in the textile and hosiery trades in England until the 1840s and 1850s – and even later – sustained by cheap labour recruited from the agricultural districts and from Ireland; and also by the 'weaver's passionate clinging to his loom and his independence; by the consequent automatic turning of weavers' children into weavers' in order to keep up total family income [15, *I*, 552]. Similarly, the domestic spinning of linen hung on precariously in the most densely populated districts of the west of Ireland until the 1840s, despite the introduction of machine-spinning in the Belfast region two decades earlier which had resulted in a general geographical contraction of the industry [1].

Nevertheless, cheap labour cannot, by itself, be blamed for deindustrialization. In Belgium, as we have noted, it was a positive advantage. Furthermore the persistence of labour-intensive methods of production could reflect, not a perverse attachment to old ways, but an efficient use of factor endowments. France, for example, 'was poorly endowed with coal but had an abundant supply of labour ... The existence of a large reservoir of cheap labour in both urban and rural areas meant that mechanization in industry was considerably less urgent in France than across the channel' [39, *364*]. Eventually, of course, the increased productivity of all factors of production that the new machinery made possible compelled entrepreneurs - if they wished to remain in business - to change their ways. A late start on the road to modern industrialization certainly carried with it the problems of catching up but, as the industrial history of Britain and her competitors in the later nineteenth century shows, the difficulties were not insurmountable. If some regions failed to develop modern forms of industry it was for reasons other than an abundance of labour.

The reasons for deindustrialization in a region can be established only by an examination of the facts of the case. Take Ireland as a case in point. With the exception of a factory-based linen industry in eastern Ulster, and the partial exception of a short-lived cotton industry that grew quickly from the 1780s and declined with almost equal speed from about 1815 to the 1830s, Ireland's traditional industries decayed during the nineteenth century. No totally satisfactory explanation for this decay has yet been supplied, although the problem has often been discussed, most recently by O'Malley and Mokyr [73; 71]. There are, broadly, three inter-related sets of reasons offered. The first is socio-political, stressing the political relationship between Ireland and Britain, especially after the Act of Union in 1801 which exposed Irish industry to competition from technologically superior English industries, unfettered by tariff protection. The limited success of industry in Ulster is attributed to the unique social structure of the province. A weakness of this argument is that it does not explain why Irish industry needed protection in the first place. Thus a second line of reasoning suggests that markets for Irish industrial goods were generally small, so restricting the opportunity for using best-practice methods. The success of the linen industry in Ulster underlines the point since production was largely geared to export markets. Once more, the argument dodges the question why industry, with the exception of linen, was not competitive overseas. We are thus forced into a third set of explanations focusing on supply conditions. Here the crucial problem was that Irish industry lacked capital. But this raises a question. If labour was cheap in Ireland then, on the analogy with Belgium, the accumulation of capital from profit should have been facilitated. Mokyr offers a possible answer by suggesting that low labour costs in Ireland were matched by low productivity [71].

If the Irish example suggests that deindustrialization was a complex process, the case of Silesia seems more straightforward. There, a once prosperous linen trade decayed in the later eighteenth century and factory-based industrialization made only limited progress. The critical influence was political. Linen production had been in the hands of a 'serf-weaver' who paid his landlord a fee for the privilege of weaving as well as other feudal dues and rent. As long as industry flourished these payments, though heavy, were not crippling but in the late eighteenth century Silesian linen producers were suffering from competition from English cottons and Irish linens. At the same time the cost of living was rising. To make matters worse the incorporation of Silesia into Prussia and the Napoleonic wars disrupted markets. Peasant revolts became frequent, but more important for the development of industry, serf-weavers could not afford to invest in their businesses and their landlords were unwilling to do so [53].

But if the decline of Silesia can be attributed to political events how do we account for the failure of some of the old textile regions of England? The gradual decay of the Norfolk worsted industry is perhaps the easiest to explain. From the mid-eighteenth century the region became relatively less important with the rise of Yorkshire but there was no absolute decline until the 1820s. Norfolk may have suffered from Yorkshire competition to some extent, but the two regions tended to specialize in different kinds of cloth. However, the demand for the higher quality Norfolk goods was depressed by changes in fashion, by disruptions of foreign markets caused by war, and – after 1826 following the removal of tariff duties – by competition in England from woollens, worsteds and silks imported from France [see 49]. Norfolk - and East Anglia more widely – might of course have responded to market changes by following the West Riding in manufacturing cheap textiles using the new technologies, but the region lacked coal. It was, however, well endowed to become one of the most efficient agricultural regions of England, a specialism that developed to an increasing extent during the eighteenth and nineteenth centuries.

The decline of the woollen industry in the West of England was also a long drawn out affair spanning over a century from the 1720s to the 1870s. Initially the loss of some foreign markets caused difficulties, but the development of new products and a greater concentration on the home market carried the region successfully through the eighteenth century. There was, in fact, a good deal of investment in machinery and in water- and steam-powered factories. The real decline of the woollen industry in Gloucestershire, Somerset and Wiltshire occurred after the end of the Napoleonic war and even then decay was more relative than absolute until the 1830s when competition from the West Riding factories became severe. Even so, it is not clear why the West of England industry failed to respond sucessfully to Yorkshire competition [61].

The inability of proto-industrialization to explain industrial decline satisfactorily is a major weakness. One feature that all the examples of deindustrialization share in common is that they experienced competition from rival manufacturing regions, causing them to lose markets. However, competition is not in itself an explanation of deindustrialization; we have to look further for reasons why producers in declining regions did not respond dynamically to competition. Political developments, social structures, inappropriate resource endowments: all may go some way to explain why some one-time manufacturing zones suffered industrial failure. But these reasons do not add up to a general explanation of deindustrialization.

Indeed, it may be that there is none, and that the theory of proto-industrialization is causing us to look at the process of industrial development in the wrong light. Many economic writers in eighteenth-century Britain associated economic development with specialization in agriculture or in industry and not with a growth in dual occupations [see 7]. From this perspective the concentration of, say, Ireland in meat or dairy production in the nineteenth century or East Anglia in cereal farming, was not so much deindustrialization as – at the risk of coining yet another polysyllabic noun – a process of 'agriculturization'. The emergence of modern factory industry in some areas from the first stage of proto-industry was necessarily accompanied by a concentration on non-industrial activities in others. The decay of rural industry in regions best suited to agriculture was an inevitable part of the process of economic development.

4 The Social Dimension

The economic rationale of proto-industry was cheap labour. In the previous chapter we identified a number of conditions producing cheap labour in the countryside. The first was where the growth of population had created a supply of labour surplus to the requirements of agriculture. Farms were too small to provide a livelihood for the whole family, there was much underemployment and manufacturers, consequently, were able to recruit labour at very low wages (alternatively, farming families could diversify their activities into part-time industry with little or no loss of agricultural earnings). Second, there was often a good deal of underemployed labour in areas of barren soils. Third, by the eighteenth century there were tillage regions in Europe possessing large numbers of landless labourers who were eager to supplement agricultural earnings by industrial work. The immediate link between proto-industry and social conditions, therefore, was a passive one: where labour was abundant rural industries were likely to develop – as long, of course, as entrepreneurship, capital and markets were also available.

According to the model of proto-industrialization, however, the connexions between rural industry and population growth were more positive than this, with the former actually stimulating the latter. The demographic aspects have been elaborated by Hans Medick [62; 63]. His starting point is the peasant household devoted to agriculture, which was a unit of production, consumption and reproduction. Land was the household's most valued possession for it was the basis of all its wealth. Inheritance customs therefore were directed towards preventing property from passing out of the family's possession. The father determined the choice of his children's marriage partners and the timing of their marriages, which were delayed until the father died or was willing to give up running the farm. The effect of parental control was to keep households simple, composed of parents and unmarried children. Except for the eldest, who inherited the farm, married children were expected to move out of the parental home and set up establishments of their own. In this way the consumption demands on the household were minimized. Even more important, as far as society as a whole was concerned, the mean age at first marriage was kept relatively high, and a substantial minority of people did not marry at all. Thus fertility in the community was low and population grew only slowly.

Members of peasant households, according to Medick, worked together to produce enough food to satisfy their consumption needs. Some output might be sold at the market in order to raise money to pay rents, feudal dues, taxes or tithes, but the primary purpose of family labour was not to produce marketable surpluses but to feed the household. The amount of effort devoted to this task was determined by the size of the family: the more mouths to feed the greater the effort. The cycle of reproduction was important here. A newly married couple with only themselves to feed would do less work than a family with young children. As the older children moved into adolescence there was even more work to be done, although there were then more hands to share it. At the later stages of the life cycle when the family became smaller again, the level of production diminished. If subsistence needs could be met (and rents and taxes paid) by a smaller expenditure of labour – because, for example, a good summer had brought an abundant harvest – then less work was done. In other words, peasants were 'target workers' producing only enough to satisfy conventional wants.

The intrusion of proto-industry altered the operation of peasant households in several ways. Most obviously, manufactured as well as agricultural goods were now the objection of production. More important, though, a proportion of the output of the household was now intended for the market. The family was no longer a closed unit of production and consumption but became enmeshed in the complex network of commerce. It was the influence of these commercial ties on the process of family formation that Medick calls the 'demo-economic system of proto-industrialization' [63, 74].

According to Medick industrial development eroded traditional constraints on early marriage. As they grew into adulthood, children no longer needed to delay marrying until they inherited the farm, for they could now work at least part-time in industry and earn enough money to support themselves. Children became a positive economic asset. Admittedly new-born babies and infants imposed a burden on the household, not least by impairing the mother's ability to work. There was also a high risk that some would die in infancy, in which case the family gained no economic advantage from them. A young mother, though, was likely to give birth to several children, some of whom would survive to an age at which they contributed to the family income. Once the reproductive cycle was in full swing the earnings of the older children offset the costs of the younger ones and the marginal cost of an extra child was small. Proto-industry also enabled married children to remain in the parental home because their labour was now valued. In a large family, a simple division of labour was possible – father weaving, mother spinning, sons assisting at the loom, daughters sewing or embroidering. A large family also ensured that some children would still be at home to support the parents when they became too old or too ill to work.

There was, nevertheless, a perversity in the link between proto-industry and population growth since, in the Medick version of events, a fall in the demand for labour did not lead to a fall in its supply. On the contrary, if the demand for labour declined and wages fell, the family offered more labour, not less, in an attempt to maintain total household income.

Far from promoting prosperity, therefore, proto-industrialization is often seen as bringing poverty to peasant workers and a growing dependence on capitalist merchants. There were several reasons for this unhappy state of affairs. In the first place, as we have observed, the reaction of peasant-manufacturers to falling wages or declining product prices was to work harder in order to maintain total income. Peasants had been forced into manufacturing in the first place because the subsistence they gained from agriculture was inadequate. Nevertheless, their farms supplied them with some of their food and so they were prepared to accept very low prices for their industrial products, or very low wages if they worked for a putting-out merchant. The wages paid to proto-industrial workers were lower than those required by a landless labourer who had to purchase all his food. The tribulations of peasant-manufacturers, though, did not end here. They were propelled even further into poverty by the unstable nature of markets for industrial products. Whenever trade slumped proto-industrial workers were unable to sell their goods or, if they were wage-earners, they were laid off by their employers. Finally, even when they were earning money from industry beyond the needs of immediate consumption, peasant-manufacturers used much of it to acquire additional land for its status value and as an insurance against the uncertainties of the future; but when trade became bad they were left with rents or mortgages which they could not afford. For the peasant, proto-industrialization was the path to immiseration.

In recent years economic and social historians have devoted greater attention to the study of the arcane complexities of family formation than to the more concrete problems of capital formation and have accumulated a good deal of evidence against which the generalizations of proto-industrialization can be tested. We need not spend too much time with Medick's belief that pre-industrial farmers were concerned chiefly with conventional levels of subsistence and were therefore little involved with the market. There is ample evidence to the contrary. The economic history of western Europe from at least the sixteenth century is in large part the story of the growth of commercial farming; and as far as England is concerned Alan MacFarlane has argued powerfully that 'the majority of ordinary people in England from at least the thirteenth century were ... economically "rational", market-orientated and acquisitive, ego-centred in kinship and social life' [60, *163*]. The development of industries in the countryside was far from being the first experience of commercial capitalism in rural areas.

On the other hand, much recent research broadly confirms the view that marriage took place at a relatively late age in western Europe before the industrial revolution. From at least the sixteenth century the mean age at marriage for men seems to have been in the mid to late twenties; and for women it was only a little lower [2; 35]. It also seems clear that general economic expansion – including the development of rural industry – was accompanied by some slight fall in the age at first marriage and by an increase in nuptiality (see below). The position regarding household size is rather more complex. Laslett has argued that in England and western Europe mean household size was under five until the late nineteenth century and that at least 70 per cent of households were two-generational – i.e. they contained only parents and unmarried children [56]. These claims have been strongly challenged but as yet they have not been refuted [see 2]. In some respects, indeed, the small size of households is not surprising if we accept (i) that marriage occurred at a relatively late age, (ii) that mortality – particularly infant mortality – was high, and (iii) that newly married couples set up independent households of their own. In such circumstances, the majority of households were likely to be small and simple.

It is when we come to a consideration of inheritance practices and their influence on family formation and farm size, and of the relationship between them and the development of rural industry, that we find the greatest differences between the generalizations of the model and reality. There was a great variety in the way that land passed from generation to generation, arising, as Joan Thirsk has pointed out, from differences between *law* and *custom*, from the practices followed by property owners and those followed by tenants, and from an abundance of land in some regions and a scarcity in others. There were also, to complicate matters further, changes in law and custom over time [88]. To make matters even more involved, the existence of a vigorous market in land could cut across the effects of any inheritance customs. In these circumstances generalizations are likely to be misleading. England, for example, is usually regarded as a country where primogeniture (i.e. the bequeathing of property to the first-born child, or more usually to the first-born son) was general, and France as a region of partible inheritance (i.e. the bequeathing of property to all the children or, more commonly, to the sons). In reality, a variety of conditions existed in all countries.

The practical consequences of primogeniture and partible inheritance might be quite similar. Even when the former was practised it was unusual for no provision at all to be made for younger sons or for daughters, and so as property was transmitted from generation to generation there was a slight tendency for it to become divided. On the other hand, partible inheritance by its very nature produced a subdivision of property, but unless population was growing rapidly the fragmentation was unlikely to be excessive [9].

The relevance of this discussion for proto-industrialization is that it is impossible to predict that any one type of inheritance practice will be associated with purely agrarian economies and a different type with rural-industrial economies. Wherever land was scarce and farms were small the community might well move from a system of partible inheritance to one of primogeniture in order to prevent further subdivision. The growth of rural industry might make the need less pressing by providing an income to supplement that derived from the land. To this extent, therefore, proto-industry might be associated with partible inheritance. However, the development of intensive tillage cultivation in the place of extensive pastoral farming or the introduction of new high-yielding crops –

the potato, for example – could have the same effect. Conversely, primogeniture, by preventing the subdivision of farms, tended to create a class of landless labourers, and, as we have seen in the case of the Pays de Caux, such people were sometimes recruited into rural industry.

Just as we cannot assume that a particular pattern of inheritance was associated with rural industry, so we cannot assume that agrarian households were small and simple and proto-industrial households were large and complex. Indeed, the connexion might be the other way round. In agrarian societies shortages of land, patriarchal control of marriage, and impartible inheritance might produce households composed of parents, the eldest married son and his wife, and adult unmarried siblings unable to marry or acquire a farm of their own (the so-called 'stem' family); whereas rural industry with its opportunities for additional earning might enable the children to marry at an early age and set up a home independently of their parents.

Some specific examples will illustrate the complexities of the connexions between economic conditions and demographic structures. The Leicestershire village of Shepshed was a community composed of freehold cultivators; their holdings were small and their incomes low. From the late seventeenth century the villagers became increasingly involved with framework knitting organized by London-based capitalists; by the end of the eighteenth century the village had become one of the most industrialized in the county. The demographic effects seem quite clear. During the course of the eighteenth century the mean age at first marriage for both men and women fell by about five years, from the high to the low twenties. The reduction in marriage ages had a direct effect on marital fertility which rose significantly through the century. The lowering of the age at marriage and the increase in fertility further reinforced the rate of population growth by changing the age structure of the population and progressively enlarging the size of the child-bearing age cohort.

These developments may be contrasted with the demographic history of the nearby but purely agricultural village of Bottesford. This was a landlord-dominated community of tenant farmers which from the later seventeenth century was increasingly turning away from growing corn to fattening and grazing. Employment opportunities in agriculture contracted, there was no rural industry to provide alternative employment, and during the eighteenth century the age at first marriage rose, fertility fell and the rate of population growth declined. Shepshed and Bottesford represent two very different demographic histories in the eighteenth century [58].

In Ireland, the influence of linen spinning and weaving on demographic behaviour has been investigated by Almquist, making use of information contained in the 1841 census. He found that spinners and weavers were most numerous in regions with the greatest population densities, that nuptiality was high and marriage ages were low among spinners and weavers; and that areas containing relatively large numbers of spinners were also areas with relatively high proportions of children in the population. He concluded that the opportunity for employment in textiles increased female nuptiality, but so too did the availability of waste land. Although Almquist's data relate to a period when many parts of Ireland were already deindustrializing, they give support to the view that rural industry and rapid population growth were positively correlated [1].

Studies of regions in continental Europe point in the same direction. In eighteenth-century Flanders, for example, farms in the maritime zone (the Polders) were large and undivided and devoted to commercial agriculture. In the inland districts, however, the land had been divided into many tiny family farms whose occupants were engaged in labour-intensive agriculture and in linen manufacture:

> The population of the Flemish interior grew twice as fast as the population of the Polders ... In the interior the annual number of marriages increased with the prosperity of the linen industry while in the Polders it did not. On the other hand, in the Polders, marriages increased with the prosperity of the commercial agriculture. In both areas, therefore, marriages were noticeably responsive to changes in the market economy. [9, *218*]

In neither area, incidentally, did the system of inheritance have much effect on the size of farms.

A final example is provided by the Swiss canton of Zurich. By the end of the eighteenth century about one-third of the population was employed in various branches of the textile industry. This semi-industrial population, however, was concentrated in the mountainous region of the canton and not in the lowland zone which was purely agrarian. This latter region was composed of closed village communities where farming practices, land use, house building and settlement were strictly regulated. Rural industry had little opportunity to develop. The population grew only slowly and population surpluses emigrated. Some of them moved to the highland zone which at the beginning of the eighteenth century was sparsely populated. Soils were poor and, in contrast to the lowland region, there were few community controls on economic activities, building and settlement. The settler population combined farming and manufacturing, working with materials put out to them by capitalist-merchants. Marriages were numerous and were contracted at an early age, and the population of the highland zone grew rapidly [11].

It seems reasonably clear from these examples that rural industry encouraged the growth of population by lowering the mean age at first marriage, thereby contributing to an increase in fertility – though it should be noted that much of the discussion is based on the marriage behaviour of males, whereas it is the age of females that is important. Proto-industry could also contribute to an increase in population by reducing mortality. This could happen if the extra earnings provided by manufacturing enabled the family to live at a higher standard than was provided by farming alone. We will return to a consideration of living standards in proto-industrial families later. For the moment, though, it should be noted that recent demographic studies stress the fertility rather than the mortality link.

We must not assume that proto-industry was the only cause of the acceleration of population growth during the eighteenth and early nineteenth centuries. Wrigley and Schofield have shown that the increase in England's population from the 1730s was associated with a general economic expansion leading to a rise in nuptiality (but not to any dramatic decline in marriage ages) [96]. At a more local level, Levine demonstrates that between 1775 and 1851 the population of the agricultural village of Terling in Essex grew even faster than the population of the framework-knitting village of Shepshed. Terling was affected, not by industrial expansion but by the growth of commercial agriculture. Levine concluded that 'undermining a traditional economy and replacing it with one where capitalist agriculture or proto-industry held sway had identifiable demographic implications' [58, *147*]. Ireland offers an even more striking case of rapid population growth resting on agricultural rather than on industrial expansion.

In Medick's demographic model population grows as industry expands but growth does not cease when industry goes into decline. The reality was more complex. Levine's study of Shepshed shows that in times of depression the mean age at marriage of men rose although this was not the case with women. Since of course it was the age at which women married that was crucial to fertility a change in the behaviour of men had little effect on population growth. However, there was another strategy open to married couples when times were bad: they could resort to contraception (using *coitus interuptus*) to restrict the size of their families. Family limitation was apparently adopted by framework knitters in Leicestershire during the chronically depressed years after 1825 [58].

Yet another reaction to a fall in the demand for labour was emigration. This process has been studied, for example, in Ulster by Collins. As the Ulster linen industry suffered competition from the English cotton industry, and also from coarse machine-spun English linen yarns, depression hit the northern and western counties, and whole families migrated. Later, in the 1840s, the industry contracted also in north-central Ireland with a consequential outflow of people from that part of the province. Before the Famine emigration from Ireland was greatest from those regions most affected by the decay of the linen industry [21]. Finally, of course, the most basic demographic consequence of deteriorating conditions was a rise in infant mortality, such as occurred in Shepshed in the second quarter of the nineteenth century.

Lying behind these discussions of the response of population to industrialization is an assumption in much of the literature that families were economically rational in their demographic behaviour. That is to say, peasants and proto-industrial workers are believed to have made their decisions about marrying according to whether land or employment were available. This assumed rationality also extends to couples calculating the numbers of children they could afford, which depended on the amount of work that was available. As Collins puts it, 'patterns of family formation are affected by the differential availability of employment for family members ...' [21, *133*]. Farmer-weavers needed the labour of their sons and so endeavoured to keep them at home when they reached maturity. They also needed their wives and daughters to perform those tasks traditionally regarded as female occupations. Households lacking the appropriate age and sex mix were obliged to hire journeymen and apprentices, or perhaps to buy in materials they could not produce themselves. It was quite common in Ulster, for example, for linen weavers to purchase yarn spun by widows and unmarried women. Households composed of widows and unmarried daughters earning their living by spinning were common, and they were often very small – thus running counter to the predictions of proto-industrialization. They were economically viable because of the unbalanced demographic structure of some of the weaving households [16].

The problem with making assumptions about the attitudes of peasant workers is that they can rarely be proved. Contemporary observers sometimes commented on attitudes, or they may be deduced by social historians from sources which, as Louise Tilly puts it, 'tell *about* people rather than ... [were] created *by* people' [90, *137*]. It was not in the nature of peasant-manufacturers to make explicit their motives on such intimate matters as marriage and procreation. Tilly's solution to the absence of personal records is to adopt the 'concept of family strategies' which 'tries to uncover the principles which lead to observable regularities or patterns of behaviour among households'. In other words. by studying groups of families and observing regularities in their behaviour she believes it is possible to make statements about motives. Thus an investigation of large numbers of proto-industrial workers in Zurich has led Braun to argue that:

> putting-out industry gave girls and boys the material prerequisites for marriage, and this possibility did away with any hesitation or fears that the young might have about knowing and getting to love each other. With no material considerations to stand in the way, one could yield to the attractions of the other sex. [11, *315*]

It is difficult to see that Braun's judgement is any less an assumption of motives for the behaviour of an inarticulate mass of individuals by being based on a large sample of households than it would have been for resting on the study of only a few. The 'family strategy' concept does not really get over the problem of explaining as opposed to describing behaviour.

We come, finally, to an assessment of the belief contained in much of the literature of proto-industrialization that rural industry caused the immiseration of peasant manufacturers. If by immiseration is meant lower earnings than could be obtained in alternative employments, then the proposition is not firmly established either logically or empirically. It may be true that the earnings of workers in cottage industry were very low, but even on the assumptions of the model they were higher than could be earned from agriculture alone [see 70]. Whether earnings of proto-industrial workers were lower than those accruing to purely industrial workers with no land to fall back on is a moot point. Rural linen workers in late eighteenth-century Flanders earned slightly less than other unskilled rural workers and considerably less than urban craftsmen, but the alternative before them was underemployment and totally inadequate agricultural earnings [65]. In England, to take another example, framework knitters in Shepshed in the 1830s and 1840s were certainly impoverished, they lived in overcrowded conditions and their mortality was higher than that of their agricultural neighbours [58]. But this was at the end of three-quarters of a century of rapid population growth when the industry was suffering from the competition of technologically superior processes; the picture at an earlier stage may have been different.

Empirical investigations elsewhere suggest that rural industry actually raised levels of living. In the English metal-working districts of the West Midlands and South Yorkshire in the seventeenth and eighteenth centuries, the levels of comfort enjoyed by metal craftsmen were as high or higher than those of the neighbouring farmers and labourers [38; 82]. In Ulster an observer noted in 1812 that in linen households, because the weaver 'supplies work to everyone under his roof, he is enabled by their earnings to consume oatmeal instead of potatoes and to allow his wife and children to wear cotton or linen gowns' [quoted 21, *135*]; almost half a century earlier Arthur Young and others had remarked on a similar relative prosperity among linen workers. Admittedly proto-industrial workers often were extremely poor. As Mendels points out, poverty and unemployment co-existed with proto-industrialization [65]; but this is not the same as saying that proto-industry created more poverty than existed in purely agrarian societies.

It seems, however, that when writers such as Medick refer to immiseration they have in mind, not so much earnings or living conditions, as the changing relationship between peasant-manufacturers and the merchants who linked them to the market. It is undeniable that proto-industrialization accelerated, although it did not initiate, the growth of a wage-earning class dependent on capitalist employers for their livelihoods. This loss of independence undermined what Medick and others have called the 'plebeian culture' of the proto-industrial family economy: the right to work when it chose; to engage in 'traditional leisure time rituals'; to be part of a local village community; to enjoy traditional patterns of consumption. From this perspective even the extra consumption that industrial wages made possible is evidence of worsening living and working conditions: 'coffee, tea, and alcohol became necessary stimulants as the conditions of production deteriorated and work became more degrading' [63, 69].

As with discussions of the attitudes of proto-industrial workers towards marriage and children, it is very difficult to show that the wage nexus was, in fact, regarded by the workers themselves in the dismal manner that some historians assume. If the yoke of industrial capitalism did indeed weigh so heavily on the once-independent peasant, then it must be remembered that it burdened him also with the additional purchasing power with which to buy an ever widening range of consumption goods. It also conferred on him the opportunity of marrying early and to a wife of his own choosing.

5 Conclusion: The Model Assessed

We stated in the introduction that models in history are intended, first, to provide a generalized description of events that occurred, or seem to have occurred, with some regularity in the past; and, second, to offer explanations of how events changed over time. Proto-industrialization is concerned with the widespread presence of industries in the European countryside in the century or so before the industrial revolution and the way in which these cottage industries evolved into modern factory industrialization. There is also a third and more ambitious purpose of models: to discover in the past policy prescriptions for the present and future. How far does the particular model under discussion meet these objectives?

The proto-industrialization thesis has two parts: the economic and the social. As far as the former is concerned, proto-industry was a phase of industrial development found in many parts of Europe between the later seventeenth century and the industrial revolution in which manufacturing was carried out in rural cottages by men, women and children who divided their time between agriculture and industry. The goods they produced were destined, not for local consumption, but for world-wide markets. Peasant-manufacturers lived in regions where, for a variety of reasons, agricultural incomes were low and cultivators therefore had a strong incentive to turn to manufacturing to supplement them. The link between peasant-producers and the wider world was provided by merchants who visited the market towns in the regions of cottage industry to buy manufactured goods. Towns were not primarily centres of industrial production but places where proto-industrial workers disposed of their goods, obtained supplies of raw materials and bought such food as they were unable to grow themselves. This food came from areas of commercial agriculture where farmers devoted themselves to growing crops for sale and did not engage in manufacturing to any great extent.

This description has the merit of capturing many features of the industrial life of western Europe before the industrial revolution. It has the additional merit of being applicable also to non-European societies and so facilitating comparisons across regions and continents [see 75]. But the concept has many limitations. The most obvious is chronology. Taking the manufacture of woollen textiles as an example of what is now fashionable to call proto-industry, the production of goods for distant markets by workers who combined farming with spinning and weaving had been a characteristic feature of European economic life long before the seventeenth century. Furthermore, there had been a considerable growth of rural textile production during the later middle ages in England, the Netherlands and elsewhere, for the very reasons offered by proponents of proto-industrialization to explain the growth of rural industry in the late seventeenth and eighteenth centuries: i.e. growing competition in international markets which induced manufacturers to seek ways of reducing costs by employing country labour [see 20; 69; 92]. In the light of these earlier developments it is difficult to see why the years after 1650 should be picked out as the critical phase of proto-industrialization. The reason must be that in western Europe the period from the mid-seventeenth century culminated with the industrial revolution; in the language of the model, proto-industrialization was followed by a second phase of factory industrialization. An assumption has been made that the chronological sequence of years was matched by a logical progression from one form of industrial organization to another. Closer attention to the 'proto-industries' of the later middle ages, however, would demonstrate the fallacy of such an assumption.

Even if the ignoring of the earlier presence of rural industries and the concentrating on their later manifestations could be justified, this would not dispose of the problem of dating. As a phase in industrial development proto-industrialization is as untidy at its ending as at its beginning. There is no need to labour the point that the timing of the onset of modern industrialization is extremely difficult to determine. As late as 1851 the majority of people employed in Britain – the most advanced of the industrial nations – still worked in the unmechanized sectors. Cottage industry did not disappear with the development of factories, even in those branches of production most affected by the innovation of new machinery.

A central feature of the concept of proto-industrialization is the emphasis it places on the combination of agricultural and industrial occupations. However, any student even superficially acquainted with the nature of pre-industrialized economies will know that there was a low level of occupational specialization throughout society, reflecting the limited opportunities provided by the market. Proto-industrialization, notwithstanding, associates dual occupations with particular types of agrarian systems; it also postulates that they actually became more common as market opportunities opened up for peasant-manufacturers. Such an interpretation would have puzzled Adam Smith, who argued that widening markets created greater opportunities for occupational specialization. So it is worth emphasizing that as the demand for industrial products increased during the eighteenth century, the amount of time that peasant-manufacturers devoted to farming seems to have diminished. In places as far apart as the linen-producing areas of County Armagh in Ireland, and the framework-knitting villages of Leicestershire in England, industry had almost displaced agriculture as a source of income by the end of the eighteenth century.

We also need to remember that the geography of proto-industry was not always of the kind suggested by the model. Once again using the textile industries as an illustration, there were indeed many areas of Europe where the manufacture of textiles was combined with the cultivation of poor soils and tiny farms. But there were also rural industrial zones that did not fit into this pattern. In eighteenth-century Ulster the finest linen manufacturing was undertaken in the northern part of County Armagh which was a fertile region capable of producing food surpluses. In eighteenth-century Normandy the manufacture of cotton textiles, using cottage labour, developed in a tillage zone. In England, both the Suffolk and the Wiltshire woollen industries were found in association with pastoral farming, a connexion that the model explains by arguing that caring for animals left farmers time to spare for spinning and weaving. Yet, as pastoral farming developed in the Leicestershire village of Bottesford during the eighteenth century, the manufacture of hosiery did *not* become important in the parish, although it did so in villages nearby [58]. The conclusion to be drawn is that cheap rural labour, attractive to industrial producers and merchants, could develop in a variety of agrarian systems which cannot be neatly embraced in a generalized model.

Before leaving the geography of proto-industry we should recall that the model stresses the importance of towns as marketing centres and neglects their importance as centres of manufacture. This arises from the fact that the archetypal proto-industrial worker is seen as one who combined farming with manufacturing and almost by definition such people were not common in towns.

Nevertheless, industry organized on a domestic or putting-out basis was an important part of the economies of many towns in England and western Europe. Many urban workers followed more than one occupation for the same reason as their rural counterparts: to maximize total income. From the point of view of the employer or the merchant it did not matter a jot whether labourers lived in towns or in the countryside as long as their cost was cheap. For high-quality products, indeed, towns were better locations, for skills were likely to be available and employers could more readily supervise manufacturing processes.

We now come to what is perhaps the most serious weakness of proto-industrialization as a description of 'industrialization before industrialization': it is very restricted in the range of occupations that it encompasses. Practically all the examples are drawn from the woollen, linen and cotton industries. There are glancing references to other activies such as the manufacture of metal or leather goods, but little else. Also excluded are the great multitude of manufacturing occupations found in pre-industrial towns and villages, such as woodworking, thatching, glazing, building, tailoring, dressmaking, brewing, shoemaking, in fact all those activities catering for local demands for essential consumer goods but not geared to distant and overseas markets. Neither are the more capital-intensive enterprises such as iron-smelting, mining, milling and paper-making embraced by the notion of proto-industrialization. The reason for their neglect, of course, is that such forms of manufacturing do not fit into the dynamic aspects of the model.

How good, in fact, is proto-industrialization in explaining the development of modern factory-based industry? If the industrial revolution were merely a matter of the textile industries, the model might be regarded as a useful though incomplete explanation of how cottage workshops came to be replaced by centralized factories. It does not capture all the complexities of reality – such as the simultaneous existence of dispersed cottage workers, centralized workshops using hand-operated machines, and factories operated by water or steam power – but then models are always simplified versions of the truth. However, modern industrialization comprised much more than the textile industries, although, admittedly, these were central to the early stages of industrialization in Europe; an explanation of industrialization that has almost nothing to say about, for example, the metal-smelting and mining industries is clearly incomplete. These industries did not, in their early development, display the characteristics of the first stage of industrialization as identified by the model and they are therefore ignored. This brings us back to an earlier criticism, that as a description of the first or 'proto' stage of industry the model is concerned only with those branches of manufacture that evolved in a particular way.

Even as an explanation of the growth of the textile and similarly organized industries, the internal dynamics of the model lack precision. Thus, it is argued that rising labour costs eventually made rural workshops uneconomic and so promoted the growth of modern factory industrialization. But it is also argued that increased labour costs inhibited the development of the second stage of industry by cutting into profits and therefore preventing the necessary accumulation of capital. This uncertainty as to the effects of shifting factor costs is related to a still greater difficulty. According to the model, proto-industry might be followed either by modern industrialization or by deindustrialization. It is not possible to discover from general principles why a particular course of development occurred. Particular case-studies indicate that political and social structures existing within a region were important in determining whether or not there would be further industrial development, but the operation of these influences has to be established by empirical research.

What of the social aspects of proto-industrialization? According to the model marriages were contracted at a younger age in areas of rural industry than elsewhere, families were larger, and households more complex. The model also suggests that the motivation for marriage was different among peasant-manufacturers, with young couples marrying because of romantic attachments and not as a business arrangement organized by their parents. A good deal of empirical evidence has been assembled to demonstrate that the age at first marriage was indeed relatively low among peasant-manufacturing households; but as the case of Ireland shows, other influences, such as easy access to land or cheap food, could also facilitate young marriages in farming communities. The evidence concerning the size and structure of households reveals a more complicated picture. A family's need for cheap labour provided an incentive to keep children at home and to accommodate other relatives; on the other hand the income derived from rural industry made it possible for young men and women to set up households of their own, thus creating smaller family units. Similarly, widows living by themselves or with adolescent children could survive as small independent households by spinning yarn, embroidering or carrying out other ancillary tasks in the textile industry [see 16]. As to the reasons why marriages were entered into by cottage workers, we remarked in Chapter 4 that historians are largely guessing at motives from behaviour, the individuals themselves being almost totally silent on the matter.

Another social feature of proto-industrialization is the assertion that as peasant households became enmeshed in the commercial production of industrial goods individuals suffered a decline in their social and economic condition, with once independent producers being turned into wage-earners and suffering 'immiseration'. We noted, though, in Chapter 2 that the model does not provide convincing reasons why cottage workers sometimes were self-employed producers and at other times were wage-earners. Nor is it clear from the model why wage-earning should have become more prevalent as time went by. On the matter of immiseration, both the logic of the model and empirical studies suggest that proto-industrial workers were wealthier than they would have been in the absence of industry; and the increased purchasing power they enjoyed permitted them to buy commodities which, even if they were bad for their health and morals, were the goods that they desired.

The model is probably most useful in drawing attention to the changes that could take place in peasant households as industrialization got under way, although, as we have noted, those changes could be complex. It is the relationship between early industrialization and peasant labour that has led development economists to look to the past and has persuaded some historians that their researches are relevant to the problems of the developing world. According to historians who have formulated the model, industry expanded in western Europe in the century and a half before the industrial revolution on the basis of cheap labour in the countryside. For countries in the underdeveloped world today possessing abundant supplies of cheap labour the European experience seems, superficially, to point to a possible path of development.

However, any testing of the model of proto-industrialization against the realities of the European past reveals its limitations. It is doubtful, therefore, whether the development economist will really gain much guidance for the future from the European experience, except for the important but frequently forgotten lesson that economic and social changes are always very complex events. As for the historian, he will find the concept of proto-industrialization more helpful in prompting him to look afresh at the process of industrial development than in providing him with explanations of his findings.

Bibliography

As an introduction to the subject for English-speaking readers, this bibliography concentrates on works in English. References to publications in other languages, chiefly French and German, may be found in [28], [54] and [79]. Recent issues of journals such as *Annales, Journal of European Economic History, Journal of Family History* and *Social History* contain much relevant material. Because proto-industrialization is part of a long debate in history on the origins of modern industrial society I have included works which are not part of the proto-industrial canon, and also those that are critical of it. Broadly speaking, anything published before 1970 is uncoloured by the concept, and not everything published since is in agreement wth it.

[1] E.L. Almquist, 'Pre-Famine Ireland and the Theory of European Proto-industrialization: the Evidence from the 1841 Census', *Journal of Economic History*, XXXIX (1979). Uses the 1841 census to test the relationship between population density and rural industry.

[2] M. Anderson, *Approaches to the History of the Western Family 1500–1914* (1980). A valuable introduction to the subject.

[3] T.S. Ashton, *The Industrial Revolution, 1760–1830* (1948). Remains the best short introduction to the subject by far.

[4] T.S. Ashton, *An Economic History of England: the 18th Century* (1955). Chapter VII is an excellent analysis of the eighteenth-century labour market and the whole book is a perceptive account of economic development on the eve of the industrial revolution.

[5] T.S. Ashton, *Economic Fluctuations in England, 1700–1800* (1959). Should be read together with [4].

[6] M. Barkhausen, 'Government Control and Free Enterprise in Western Germany and the Low Countries in the Eighteenth Century', in P. Earle (ed.), *Essays in European Economic History, 1500–1800* (1974). A wide-ranging and detailed regional study. Should be read together with [53].

[7] M. Berg, 'Political Economy and the Principles of

Manufacture 1700–1800', in [8]. A survey of contemporary perceptions of industrialization.

[8] M. Berg, P. Hudson and M. Sonenscher, *Manufacture in Town and Country before the Factory* (1983). Seven essays critical of proto-industrialization.

[9] L.K. Berkner and F.F. Mendels, 'Inheritance Systems, Family Structure, and Demographic Patterns in Western Europe, 1700–1900', in C. Tilly (ed.), *Historical Studies of Changing Fertility* (1978). A study of the relationship between access to land, family formation and economic activity.

[10] R. Braun, 'The Impact of Cottage Industry on an Agricultural Population', in D.S. Landes (ed.), *The Rise of Capitalism* (1966). Studies the effect of rural industry on family formation in Switzerland. Extract from a longer study published in German.

[11] R. Braun, 'Early Industrialization and Demographic Change in the Canton of Zurich', in C. Tilly (ed.), *Historical Studies of Changing Fertility* (1978). A much elaborated and fully documented statement of the argument in [10].

[12] R. Brenner, 'Agrarian Class Structure and Economic Development in Pre-industrial Europe', *Past & Present*, 70 (1976). A restatement of the Marxist view of long-run economic development. Has provoked a lively debate. See *Past & Present*, 78 (1978), 79 (1978), 80 (1978) and 85 (1979).

[13] J.D. Chambers, *Nottinghamshire in the Eighteenth Century* (1932). A classic regional study.

[14] S.D. Chapman, 'Industrial Capital before the Industrial Revolution: An Analysis of the Assets of a Thousand Textile Entrepreneurs c. 1730–50', in [36]. A useful empirical study. See also [44].

[15] J.H. Clapham, *An Economic History of Modern Britain:* I *The Early Railway Age, 1820–1850* (1926); II *Free Trade and Steel, 1850–1886* (1932); III *Machines and National Rivalries, 1887–1914, with an Epilogue, 1914–1929* (1938). A masterly account of industrialization in Britain emphasizing the gradual nature of the process.

[16] L.A. Clarkson and B. Collins, 'Proto-industrialization in an Irish Town: Lisburn, 1821', in [28]. A study of an urban linen and cotton industry in domestic workshops.

[17] D.C. Coleman, 'Industrial Growth and Industrial Revolutions', *Economica* (1956); reprinted in E.M.

Carus-Wilson (ed.), *Essays in Economic History*, III (1962). A powerful plea for not calling every industrial spurt before the late eighteenth century a revolution.
[18] D.C. Coleman, 'An Innovation and its Diffusion: the "New Draperies"', *Economic History Review*, 2nd ser., XXII (1969). Analyses the way in which peasant manufacture becomes linked to international markets.
[19] D.C. Coleman, *Industry in Tudor and Stuart England* (1975). A succinct survey of industry in pre-industrialized England.
[20] D.C. Coleman, 'Proto-industrialization: A Concept Too Many', *Economic History Review*, 2nd ser., XXXVI (1983). A highly sceptical critique of the concept. Essential reading.
[21] B. Collins, 'Proto-industrialization and Pre-famine Emigration', *Social History*, 7(1982). A study of decline in the Ulster linen industry in the early nineteenth century and its effects on the family economy.
[22] P. Corfield, 'A provincial Capital in the late Seventeenth Century: the Case of Norwich', in P. Clark and P. Slack (eds), *Crisis and Order in English Towns, 1500–1700* (1972). Demonstrates the importance of textile manufacture to the economy of an English city.
[23] W.H.B. Court, *The Rise of the Midland Industries, 1600–1838* (1938). A classic study of early industrialization, concentrating on mining and metallurgy.
[24] W.H. Crawford, 'The Origins of the Linen Industry in North Armagh and the Lagan Valley', *Ulster Folklife*, 17 (1971). With [25] an important qualification of the arguments contained in [32].
[25] W.H. Crawford, 'Economy and Society in South Ulster in the Eighteenth Century', *Clogher Record* (1975).
[26] W. Cunningham, *The Growth of English Industry and Commerce* (1882). The first general textbook on English economic history containing many examples of rural industries before the eighteenth century. Strongly influenced by the stage theories of economic development discussed in [45].
[27] J. De Vries, *The Economy of Europe in an Age of Crisis 1600–1750* (1976). A general textbook incorporating the theory of proto-industrialization into its analysis.
[28] P. Deyon and F.F. Mendels (eds), *La Protoindustrialisation: Théorie et Réalité*, 2 vols (1982). Proceedings of the Eighth

International Conference on Economic History held in Budapest containing forty-eight essays in three languages and dealing with three continents. At present in mimeographed form, but publication is threatened.

[29] M. Dobb, *Studies in the Development of Capitalism* (1946). An important Marxist statement.

[30] M.W. Flinn, *Origins of the Industrial Revolution* (1966). A useful survey of interpretations of industrialization before the proto-industrialization literature appeared.

[31] E.W. Gilboy, *Wages in Eighteenth Century England* (1934). An old but still useful empirical study.

[32] C. Gill, *The Rise of the Irish Linen Industry* (1925). Still the standard work, but needs to be read in conjunction with [24] and [25].

[33] J. Goody, J. Thirsk and E.P. Thompson, *Family and Inheritance: Rural Society in Western Europe 1200–1800* (1976). A useful collection of essays.

[34] G.L. Gullickson, 'Agriculture and Cottage Industry: Redefining the Causes of Proto-industrialization', *Journal of Economic History*, XLIII (1983). Challenges the view that proto-industry was associated only with subsistence or pastoral agriculture. Based on a study of the Pays de Caux in Normandy.

[35] J. Hajnal, 'European Marriage Patterns in Perspective', in D.V. Glass and D.E.C. Eversley (eds), *Population in History: Essays in Historical Demography* (1965). An important essay arguing for a relatively late age of marriage in western Europe.

[36] N.B. Harte and K.G. Ponting (eds), *Textile History and Economic History: Essays in Honour of Miss Julia de Lacy Mann* (1973). Fifteen essays on aspects of the English textile industry.

[37] H. Heaton, *The Yorkshire Woollen and Worsted Industries from Earliest Times up to the Industrial Revolution* (1920). An old but still important study.

[38] D. Hey, *The Rural Metalworkers of the Sheffield Region: A Study of Rural Industry before the Industrial Revolution* (1972). A useful empirical study.

[39] C. Heywood, 'The Role of the Peasantry in French Industrialization, 1815–80', *Economic History Review*, XXXIV (1981). Critical of the view that the structure of agrarian society inhibited industrialization in France.

[40] R.H. Hilton et al., *The Transition from Feudalism to Capitalism* (1978). Contributions to the Marxist debate on industrialization.
[41] R.H. Hilton, 'Capitalism: What's in a Name?', in [40].
[42] E.J. Hobswawm, 'The Crisis of the Seventeenth Century', *Past & Present*, 5 and 6 (1954); reprinted in T. Aston (ed.), *Crisis in Europe, 1560–1660* (1965). Argues that seventeenth-century Europe suffered an economic 'crisis' that was eventually overcome by 'the triumph of capitalism'.
[43] E.J. Hobsbawm, 'From Feudalism to Capitalism', in [40].
[44] K. Honeyman, *Origins of Enterprise: Business Leadership in the Industrial Revolution* (1982). A study of entrepreneurship in lead mining, cotton spinning and lace manufacture. See also [14].
[45] B.F. Hoselitz, 'Theories of Stages of Economic Growth', in B.F. Hoselitz (ed.), *Theories of Economic Growth* (1960). A review of the work of the German school of historical economists.
[46] R. Houston and K. Snell, 'Proto-industrialization? Cottage Industry, Social Change, and Industrial Revolution', *Historical Journal*, 27 (1984). An extended review of [54]. Highly critical, with excellent references.
[47] P. Hudson, 'Proto-industrialization: the Case of the West Riding Wool Textile Industry in the 18th and early 19th Centuries', *History Workshop Journal*, 12 (1981). An important critical article. See also her essay in [8].
[48] S. Hymer and S. Resnick, 'A Model of an Agrarian Economy with Nonagricultural Activities', *American Economic Review*, 59 (1969). A theoretical discussion of rural industry. See also [59].
[49] D.T. Jenkins and K.G. Ponting, *The British Wool Textile Industry 1770–1914* (1982). A very useful survey.
[50] E.L. Jones, 'Agricultural Origins of Industry', *Past & Present*, 40 (1968); reprinted in E.L. Jones, *Agriculture and the Industrial Revolution* (1974). Argues that rural industry developed in Europe from the later seventeenth century in farming regions not well suited to cereal production.
[51] L. Jorberg (ed.), 'Proto-industrialization in Scandinavia', *Scandinavian Economic History Review*, XXX (1982). Issue devoted to a discussion of the concept as applied to the textile, wood-working and metal-working industries in Denmark, Finland, Norway and Sweden. Highly sceptical.

[52] H. Kellenbenz, 'Rural Industries in the West from the End of the Middle Ages to the Eighteenth Century', in P. Earle (ed.), *Essays in European Economic History, 1500–1800* (1974). A comprehensive regional survey.

[53] H. Kisch, 'The Textile Industries in Silesia and the Rhineland: A Comparative Study in Industrialization', *Journal of Economic History*, XIX (1959); reprinted in [54]. An important empirical study pre-dating the proto-industrial literature.

[54] P. Kriedte, H. Medick and J. Schlumbohm, *Industrialization before Industrialization* (1981). First published in German in 1979. Translation is only partly to blame for the proliferation of polysyllabic nouns and almost endless sentences. Eight important essays on all aspects of proto-industrialization. Excellent bibliography.

[55] P. Kriedte, 'Proto-industrialization between Industrialization and De-industrialization', in [54].

[56] P. Laslett and R. Wall (eds), *Household and Family in Past Time* (1972). A pioneering collection of essays on family size and structure, sometimes displaying premature generalization. See also [94].

[57] R.D. Lee and R.S. Schofield, 'British Population in the Eighteenth Century', in R. Floud and D. McCloskey (eds), *The History of Britain since 1700*, I (1981). Succinct survey of eighteenth-century demography. See also [96].

[58] D. Levine, *Family Formation in an Age of Nascent Capitalism* (1977). Probably the most detailed local study in England of the relationship between family formation and early industrialization.

[59] W.A. Lewis, 'Economic Development with Unlimited Supplies of Labour', in A.N. Agarwala and S.P. Singh (eds), *The Economics of Underdevelopment* (1958). With [48] supplies much of the theoretical underpinning for the model of proto-industrialization.

[60] A. Macfarlane, *The Origins of English Individualism: The Family, Property and Social Transition* (1978). Iconoclastic and stimulating. Should be contrasted with [62] and [63].

[61] J. de L. Mann, *The Cloth Industry in the West of England from 1640 to 1880* (1971). A study of the final era of a once-important textile region.

[62] H. Medick, 'The Proto-industrial Family Economy: The Structural Function of Household and Family during the

Transition from Peasant to Industrial Capitalism', *Social History*, I (1976); reprinted, with elaborations, in [54]. The seminal statement on the relationship between industrialization and family formation.

[63] H. Medick, 'The Structures and Function of Population development under the Proto-industrial System', in [54]. A further elaboration of the argument in [62].

[64] F.F. Mendels, 'Proto-industrialization: The First Phase of the Industrialization Process', *Journal of Economic History*, XXXII (1972). The seminal article on the subject.

[65] F.F. Mendels, 'Agriculture and Peasant Industry in Eighteenth-Century Flanders', in [74]; reprinted in [54]. Contains much of the empirical evidence on which the generalizations contained in [64] are based.

[66] F.F. Mendels, 'Seasons and Regions in Agriculture and Industry During the Process of Industrialization', in S. Pollard (ed.), *Region und Industrialisierung* (1980). Argues that cottage industry was located in regions of subsistence agriculture.

[67] D.R. Mills, 'Proto-industrialization and Social Structure: The Case of the Hosiery Industry in Leicestershire, England', in [28].

[68] R. Millward, 'The Emergence of Wage Labor in Early Modern England', *Explorations in Economic History*, 8 (1981). An ingenious if not entirely convincing analysis.

[69] H.A. Miskimin, *The Economy of Early Renaissance Europe, 1300–1460* (1969). Contains a useful survey of late-medieval developments in the European textile industry.

[70] J. Mokyr, *Industrialization in the Low Countries, 1795–1850* (1976). A theoretical and empirical study of Belgium and the Netherlands.

[71] J. Mokyr, *Why Ireland Starved: A Quantitative and Analytical History of the Irish Economy, 1800–1850* (1983). Concerned with deindustrialization only as part of a larger study of the Irish economy. Stresses shortages of capital and low labour productivity.

[72] J.U. Nef, *The Rise of the British Coal Industry*, 2 vols (1932). Stresses the importance of industrial development in the sixteenth and seventeenth centuries. Responsible for the notion of industrial progress in Britain as a series of revolutions.

[73] E. O'Malley, 'The decline of Irish Industry in the Nineteenth Century', *The Economic and Social Review*, 13 (1981). Re-

views explanations of deindustrialization and concludes that it was the result of the tendency of industries to centralize.
[74] W.N. Parker and E.L. Jones (eds), *European Peasants and their Markets* (1975). Contains eight essays on various aspects of agriculture and European economic development.
[75] F. Perlin, 'Proto-industrialization and Pre-colonial South Asia', *Past & Present*, 98 (1983). An application of the concept to non-European societies.
[76] S. Pollard, *Peaceful Conquest: The Industrialization of Europe 1760–1970* (1981). Part I is a comprehensive survey of European industrialization to the 1870s and includes a discussion of proto-industrialization.
[77] G.D. Ramsay, *The English Woollen Industry, 1500–1750* (1982). An excellent, up-to-date introduction.
[78] D.A. Reid, 'The Decline of Saint Monday, 1776–1876', *Past & Present*, 71 (1976). A review of working practices in the Birmingham metal trades.
[79] *Revue Du Nord*, LXI (1979). Special issue 'Aux origines de la révolution industrielle. Industrie rurale et fabriques'. Twelve articles on aspects of industrialization in continental Europe.
[80] W.W. Rostow, 'The Stages of Economic Growth', *Economic History Review*, 2nd ser., XII (1959). A succinct summary of [81].
[81] W.W. Rostow, *The Stages of Economic Growth* (1960). A modern version of nineteenth-century stage theories. Has greatly influenced thinking on the nature of economic development.
[82] M.B. Rowlands, *Masters and Men in the West Midland Metalware Trades before the Industrial Revolution* (1975). A detailed local study concentrating on industrial organization and social relations.
[83] W. Seccombe, 'Marxism and Demography', *New Left Review*, 137 (1983). Attempts to incorporate long-term demographic change into Marxist interpretations of capitalist development.
[84] J. Stuart, *Historical Memoirs of the City of Armagh (1819)*.
[85] P. Sweezy, 'A Critique [of Maurice Dobb]', in [40]. Part of the Marxist debate on the origins of capitalism. See [29].
[86] J. Tann, 'The Textile Millwright in the Early Industrial Revolution', *Textile History*, 5 (1974). A useful empirical study.

[87] J. Thirsk, 'Industries in the Countryside', in F.J. Fisher (ed.), *Essays in the Economic History of Tudor and Stuart England in Honour of R.H. Tawney* (1961); reprinted in J. Thirsk, *The Rural Economy of England: Collected Essays* (1984). An important statement of the association between farming regions and rural industry in England.

[88] J. Thirsk, 'The European Debate on Customs of Inheritance', in [33]; reprinted in J. Thirsk, *The Rural Economy of England: Collected Essays* (1984). A survey of contemporary thought on inheritance customs.

[89] C. Tilly and R. Tilly, 'Agenda for European Economic History in the 1970s', *Journal of Economic History,* XXXI (1971). Responsible for the first use of the word 'proto-industrialization' in print and anticipates ideas developed in [64].

[90] L.A. Tilly, 'Individual Lives and Family Strategies in the French Proletariat', *Journal of Family History,* 4 (1979). Develops the concept of 'family strategies' as a way of explaining individual behaviour during industrialization.

[91] A. Toynbee, *Lectures on the Industrial Revolution in England* (1884). Introduced the idea of the industrial revolution into English historiography a century ago and still worth reading.

[92] H. Van Der Wee, 'Structural Changes and Specialization in the Industry of the South Netherlands, 1100–1600', *Economic History Review,* 2nd ser., XXVIII (1975). An example of late-medieval adaptation in the textile industry, including the development of rural manufacturing, in response to market changes.

[93] G. Unwin, *Industrial Organization in the Sixteenth and Seventeenth Centuries* (1904). An early and still important discussion of the evolution of industrial organization. Influenced by the stage theories discussed in [45].

[94] R. Wall, J. Robin and P. Laslett (eds), *Family Forms in Historic Europe* (1983). Seventeen essays discussing the household in its economic and social context. See also [56].

[95] R.G. Wilson, 'The Supremacy of the Yorkshire Cloth Industry in the Eighteenth Century', in [36]. Stresses the importance of superior organization rather than labour costs in explaining Yorkshire's supremacy.

[96] E.A. Wrigley and R.S. Schofield, *The Population History of England 1541–1871: A Reconstruction* (1981). A masterpiece.

Chapters 10 and 11 relate long-term population and economic trends.

[97] A. Young, *Tour in Ireland: with General Observations on the General State of that Kingdom* (1780).

Enclosures in Britain 1750–1830

Prepared for
The Economic History Society by

MICHAEL TURNER
Lecturer in Economic History
University of Hull

Acknowledgements

MY thanks to Brenda Buchanan, Dr R. C. Allen and Dr J. Chapman for the opportunity to see their work in advance of publication. Jan Crowther and Colin Munro respectively gave me an item of information and a reference which perfectly illustrated important points in the script and for which I am grateful. Professor T. C. Smout and Dr I. D. Whyte gave me valuable advice in constructing the Scottish bibliography, and Professor Smout also gave me instruction about Scottish rural tenurial relationships. Derek Waite drew the maps and diagrams. I am particularly indebted to Professor Smout for his editorial guidance which transformed an excessively long first draft into a script of pamphlet size.

MICHAEL TURNER

Note on References

References in the text within square brackets refer to the numbered items in the bibliography. Colons separate italicised page numbers from their appropriate references and semicolons separate different references.

1 Introduction

(i) DEFINITION

THE term enclosure mainly refers to that land reform which transformed a traditional method of agriculture under systems of co-operation and communality in communally administered holdings, usually in large fields which were devoid of physical territorial boundaries, into a system of agricultural holding in severalty by separating with physical boundaries one person's land from that of his neighbours. This was, then, the disintegration and reformation of the open fields into individual ownership. Inter alia enclosure registered specific ownership, adjudicated on shared ownership (for example by identifying and separating common rights), and declared void for all time communal obligations, privileges and rights. Enclosure also meant the subdivision of areas of commons, heaths, moors, fens and wastes into separate landholdings and again involved the abandonment of obligations, privileges and rights.

There was enormous regional variability in enclosure. For example, there were different ways of raising a boundary, from the quickset hedges of the Midlands, in vivid contrast to the heavy stone walls of the Pennines, and the combination of enclosure and drainage schemes in the fens of Lincolnshire, Norfolk, Cambridgeshire and Somerset often producing ditches rather than fences. In some highland areas physical boundaries were not constructed at all but instead there was reassessment of stinting rights (for example a reassessment of the number of sheep that could be depastured on a given area of land). In Scotland, as we shall see, enclosure could mean something entirely different again.

This pamphlet is concerned mainly with parliamentary enclosure, that is enclosure conducted by the instrument of an Act of Parliament. Men known as commissioners were employed to divide the communal interests of the parish, township, etc., among the claimants of those interests, and to lay out the courses of new roads, footpaths, bridlepaths and tracks. These men were nominated by the major interests in the parish, by the church in its position as a major owner of the tithes, by the lord of the manor as the owner of the rights of the soil, and by the majority in value of the freeholders. The commissioners employed a battery of administrators, surveyors, clerks, bankers, and so on. The parliamentary proceedings and the subsequent administration of enclosure are well explained elsewhere [98]. The procedures were complicated to the extent that enclosure could be privately and locally sponsored, and publicly and locally applied, or generally applied. Thus private acts, public acts, and general acts resulted. In the cases of the first two methods active application was made to Parliament, but the third was most frequently a case of creating a set of conditions or regulations which encouraged local applications to be made [see 10: *esp. 28–34*].

We must emphasise early on that enclosure, involving as it did the shift from communal ownership and husbandry into individual ownership and husbandry, was far more complicated than this brief introduction suggests. In addition, the open fields and commons and wastes that were enclosed were by no means a static, unchanging method of ownership and husbandry but should be viewed in terms of an evolving system in which enclosure was the final item of change. Chapter 2 will explore the geographical and temporal variations in parliamentary enclosure, and the important exception of enclosure by non-legislative means. Chapter 3 will question the necessity for enclosure, whether it was stimulated by the promise of economic gains in prevailing economic conditions. Chapter 4 will look at the cost of enclosure and Chapter 5 will discuss the social consequences of enclosure.

(ii) Historiographical note

Long-held popular beliefs related to the economic, social and political background and consequences of enclosure have relatively recently been overturned. Historiographically there are three uneven periods: a pre-1914 phase of cataloguing and interpreting, often with a pessimistic note in regard to the social consequences; a phase of revisionism and much local history enthusiasm beginning in the 1930s and continuing well into the post-Second World War era, sounding a more optimistic note; and lastly a phase still in motion, which in many ways is counter-revisionist because it is confronting the broadest issues thrown up by research with greater clarity and more secure data. This note is concerned with the first period while the arguments in later chapters bring the historiography up to date.

To begin at the beginning, or in our case the beginning of the end, the first decade or so of the twentieth century marked both the end of enclosure in Britain, practically speaking, and the beginning of great speculation as to its impact. To some extent enclosure is not yet complete and within the framework of existing law it never will be. The 1965 Commons Registration Act called for the local registration of commons over the period 1967–72 and fossilised the last vestiges of what was once a more extensively 'open' Britain [13 and 14 Eliz.II, c.64, 1965]. From 1972 onwards over one million acres of common in England was recorded and its status safeguarded for the foreseeable future, though there is a move by some landowners to have these commons deregistered and enclosed behind fences [*Sunday Times*, 26 July 1981: *4*].

The enclosure of the Gloucestershire parish of Elmstone Hardwicke in 1914 effectively marked the end of British enclosing activity, though more realistically we should consider the enclosure movement complete by about 1870. Our first phase of writing on enclosures therefore came in the wake of the enclosure movement, but sufficiently detached from its principal thrusts a hundred or more years earlier for a relatively unromantic, disinterested view to be obtained. The spatial impact of enclosure was first quantified by Slater in his *The English Peasantry and the Enclosure of Common Fields* (1907). It remained for long the standard reference though we now accept that it underestimated the enclosure of common and waste by a large margin. A more accurate statement was Gonner's *Common Land and Inclosure* (1912). He mapped his evidence at the level of the registration district and rightly those maps have become standard interpretations of the distribution of enclosure. This was a wider history of enclosure than Slater with almost as much emphasis on the origins and operation of British agrarian systems as on their periods of dissolution from medieval times onwards.

Accompanying these two classics of cataloguing and description were a number of other studies which were more concerned with interpretation. Johnson's *The Disappearance of the Small Landowner* (1909) was a particularly inspired piece of interpretation because it approached a particular problem involving a special socio-economic group. It also involved an otherwise forgotten primary source which was contemporary with the dominant period of parliamentary enclosure, the land tax of 1780–1832 [see also 21].

Of these early twentieth-century agricultural histories the greatest impact was left by the Hammonds' *The Village Labourer* (1911). Their message was set in overt political terms as part of a trilogy of work on the process of proletarianisation in Britain. Part of their popularity was born out of a contemporary political awareness of the ambiguity of property rights and the intractable process of inheritance. When it came to the peasant inheritance of something so essential as common rights it was seemingly subject to such cursory consideration by squire, church, and parliament at enclosure as to make a mockery of any concept of equity. This was the tone of the Hammonds' argument, reinforced by persuasive if biased evidence of injustices. This evidence has been re-examined periodically and the Hammonds' views tempered considerably, though the latest researches have partially rehabilitated much of their message.

The Hammonds were not alone in their discourse on property rights. Marx also chose the British experience in outlining a theory of capitalism and contemporaries of the Hammonds also spoke in terms of the inequity of capitalist revolutions, whether agrarian or industrial.

The basic tools of research of early investigators were the digests of statistics found in the parliamentary Blue Books, particularly the 1914 *Return in Chronological Order of all Acts passed for the Inclosure of Commons and Wastes* [9; see also 8]. In spite of its misleading title the Commons refers to common fields. It was the best of the official digests though it contains a number of errors and omissions. The productivity of scholarship during the first decade or so of the twentieth century gave successive scholars a valuable reference library. It is only in relatively recent times that some of the basic facts and information have been found incomplete, unreliable or misleading. Curtler's *The Enclosure and Redistribution of our Land* (1920) was about the only new major work to deal with enclosures nationally until Tate made new acreage estimates for 27 of the 42 English counties between 1935–51 [listed in 2: *27–9*; and 10: *4–5*]. Tate also produced a large number of enclosure-related studies [listed in 10: *4*]. From 1951 until his death in 1968 he tried to complete the county handlists to bring them together in a single volume of revised English statistics. The work was completed posthumously, the summary statistics setting out the broad spatial and temporal features of English parliamentary enclosure as we now understand them [10; 107].

As an aid to the most recent historiography the reader should note the relatively recent appearance of a bibliography on enclosures and the open fields; two review essays, one with an appended bibliography; and a bibliography of theses and dissertations on British agrarian history [2; 1; 4; 3].

2 Enclosure in Time and Space

(i) ENGLAND

IT is unclear why parliamentary enclosure became the dominant method of enclosure by the mid-eighteenth century in preference to existing methods. The first act was for the enclosure of Radipole in Dorset in 1604, but acts do not become common until well into Georgian times. Perhaps the success of enclosure by local agreement among interested parties in the century or so up to the eighteenth gave way quite naturally to a firmer instrument. Perhaps the subdivision of rights became more complicated and perhaps there were more interested parties which necessitated the decision of a referee to separate claims of ownership. Perhaps there was opposition to enclosure or squabbling over the spoils, making an instrument of parliament necessary and inevitable. Whatever the reason, parliamentary enclosure dominated after c.1750. But we must emphasise that enclosure *per se* was not new; it had been the method of dividing the open fields for centuries. In some counties mere vestiges of the open fields remained to be enclosed by the mid-eighteenth century and in other areas agriculture had not been pursued in open fields, and so a cross-section across Britain would reveal the whole evolutionary history of agriculture from complete open field arrangements to enclosed farms and fields sometimes of long or ancient origin.

Parliamentary enclosure was important in England and Wales but Scotland must be treated separately with much enclosure in that country enacted under laws which antedated the Union with England in 1707, though in fact most of the enclosure occurred after Union. Additionally we must attempt an estimate (qualitative rather than quantitative) of non-parliamentary enclosure.

In England there were over 5250 private or public acts of enclosure or individual enclosures under the umbrella of the nineteenth-century general acts. The parliamentary enclosure of open fields, commons, wastes, etc., was predominantly by private local acts and can be more narrowly placed between 1750–1850 or even 1750–1830. Over 85 per cent of all parliamentary enclosure was complete or on the statute book by 1830, but to stop in 1830 excludes all of the mid- and late-nineteenth-century enclosure under the authority of the General Acts of 1836, 1840 and 1845. In some areas such enclosure was very important, though only in Cambridgeshire and Oxfordshire did post-1830 parliamentary enclosure amount to more than 10 per cent of county area [107: *186–95*].

Figure 1 captures the chronology of the main thrusts of English parliamentary enclosure. Quite clearly it was not one but two movements, each of which in a number of ways was quite distinctive. They were different in a spatial sense, in a chronological sense, and also in an economic sense because we can identify different motivating forces behind the enclosures. In the spatial sense there were parts of East Anglia where parliamentary enclosure had barely begun by 1790 [see 27: *197*], as was also the case in much of West Sussex [49: *75–7*], but in other parts of the country (Northamptonshire, Warwickshire, and Leicestershire) most parliamentary enclosure was over by this date [107: *72–6*]. Such a chronological dispersion increases the difficulty of debating the social and economic record of parliamentary enclosure.

Of all acts 38 per cent were concentrated in the first wave of activity between c.1755–80. The peak year of activity was 1777 when 92 acts were passed and the busiest half decade was the late 1770s when 321 acts were passed. The second peak of activity occurred between 1790 and the mid-1830s, though more importantly it was concentrated during the period of the French Revolutionary and Napoleonic wars. Nine of the ten busiest years in parliamentary enclosure history occur in this period, and the first half of the 1810s was the busiest half decade of all when 547 acts were passed. The war years accounted for 43 per cent of all parliamentary enclosures. It was also a period when marginal land was increasingly brought into regular or regulated cultivation [56; 139]. With subsequent nineteenth-century incursions into marginal lands the commons and wastes of England and Wales were reduced to trivial proportions [112].

Thus two movements of roughly equal duration and size can be recognised. The first movement embraced mainly, though not exclusively, the heavier soiled counties of the Midland clay belts in Northamptonshire, Warwickshire, Leicestershire and the east and south-east Midlands in general. It also included the lighter clays of

Figure 1

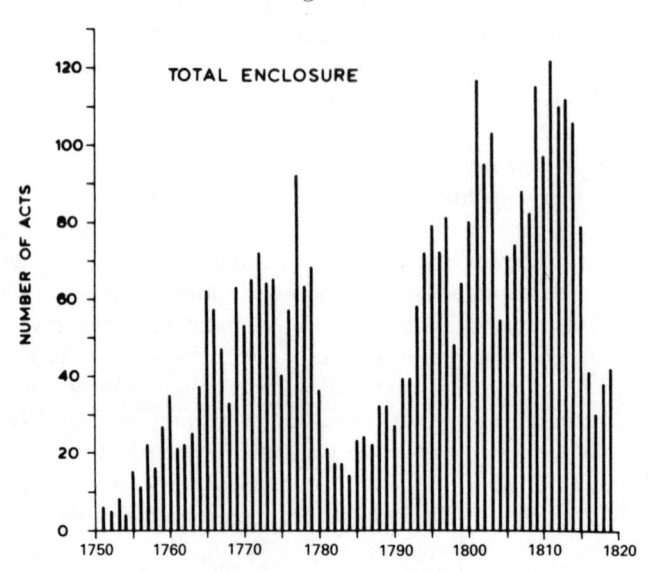

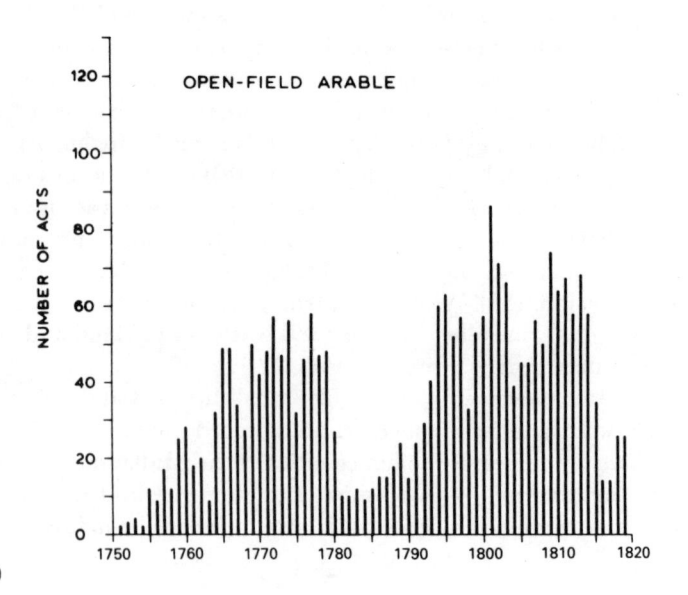

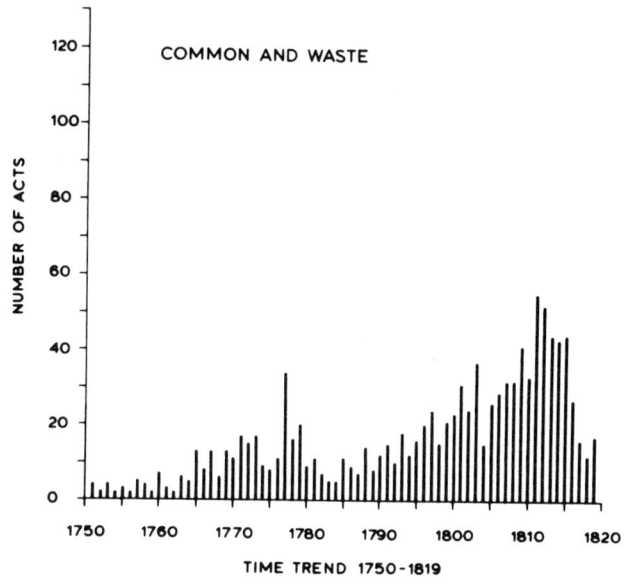

Figure 1   Chronology of Parliamentary Enclosure in England 1750–1819
Source: M. E. Turner, *English Parliamentary Enclosure* (1980), p. 70

much of Lincolnshire and over 60 per cent of East Riding acts. The second movement completed the enclosure of these heavier soils and also included the lighter soils of East Anglia, Lincolnshire, and the East Riding, the marginal soils of the Pennine uplands in West Yorkshire, the Lake District of Cumbria, and the heaths of the southern counties (Surrey, Berkshire, Middlesex).

This division into the arable and the marginal soils, or more correctly into open fields and commons and wastes, can be given greater quantitative expression, as was Tate's intention, but in baldly separating the open fields from the commons and wastes he may have created more problems than he solved because so often the enclosures were composite land reforms involving many land use types (arable, regulated pasture, open pasture, uncultivated commons, genuine wastes and others) [in general see 50; see also 48; 49]. The fact that enclosures were often composite land reforms produces an overestimation of the arable and an underestimation of the common and waste [50]. Another problem is highlighted from a Wiltshire study showing

221

Table I

The Supply of Parliamentary Enclosure 1730–1844

(a) Half Decade	Number of acts	(b) The ten busiest years	Number of acts
1730–4	24	1811	122
1735–9	15	1801	117
1740–4	26	1809	115
1745–9	13	1813	112
1750–4	26	1812	110
1755–9	91	1814	106
1760–4	130	1803	103
1765–9	263	1810	97
1770–4	319	1802	95
1775–9	321	1777	92
1780–4	105		
1785–9	132		
1790–4	235		
1795–9	344		
1800–4	450		
1805–9	430		
1810–14	547		
1815–19	232		
1820–4	115		
1825–9	101		
1830–4	66		
1835–9	59		
1840–4	62		

Source: M. E. Turner, *English Parliamentary Enclosure* (1980), pp. 67–8.

that Tate overstated the arable by including pasture in the arable acreage, either in the form of commons and wastes or as meadow and regulated pasture [152; *7–8*]. Following from this is the problem of whether fallows, either temporary or semi-permanent, should be considered as commons and wastes in the sense of unused land, or as pastures however temporary, or as arable because they were potentially arable or involved in what was essentially an arable régime.

Notwithstanding these problems, until the next major revision of statistics is undertaken, Table II is the current summary of enclosure statistics which is available.

Table II

Chronology and Summary of English Parliamentary Enclosure

	Total	Open field arable	Common and waste
Acts	5,265	3,093	2,172
Acres (millions)	6.8	4.5	2.3
Percentage of England	20.9	13.8	7.1

	Acres (millions)	Acres (millions)	Acres (millions)
Pre-1793	2.6	1.9	0.7
1793-1815	2.9	2.0	0.9
1816-1829	0.4	0.2	0.1
Pre-1830	5.8	4.1	1.8

	Percentage of England enclosed in the following periods:		
Pre-1793	7.9	5.7	2.2
1793-1815	8.9	6.1	2.8
1816-1829	1.2	0.7	0.4
Pre-1830	18.0	12.6	5.4

Source: M. E. Turner, *English Parliamentary Enclosure* (1980), pp. 62, 71.
Note: The figures are subject to rounding errors.

Williams has focused attention on the eighteenth- and nineteenth-century wastelands of England and Wales and revised upwards the estimation of the amount of land which was reclaimed and brought under regulated cultivation, whether by enclosure, drainage or whatever [112–14]. In 1800 perhaps 21 per cent of England and Wales was wasteland. Locationally it was simply related to physical geography with a heavy concentration in highland Britain where soils

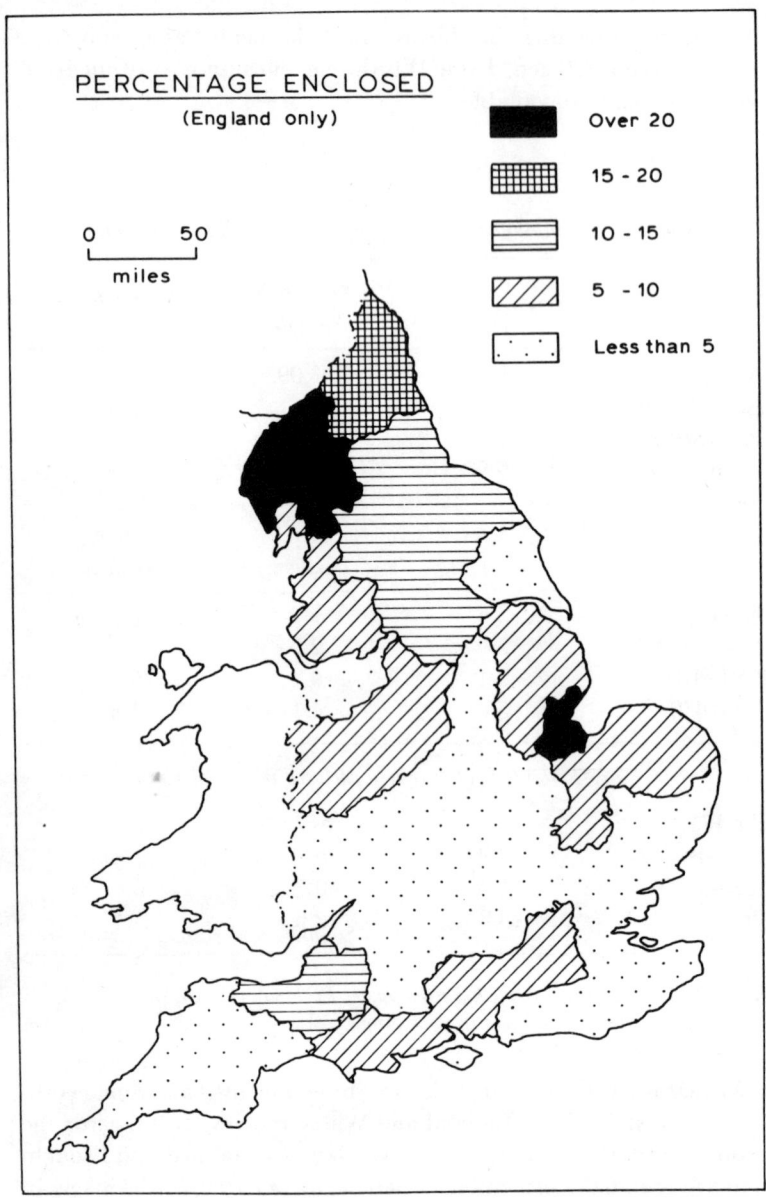

Figure 2 Common and Waste Enclosed as a Percentage of County Area (England only), c.1750–1870
Source: M. E. Turner, *English Parliamentary Enclosure* (1980), p. 61

were poor and thin, and where there was broken relief and high rainfall. The greatest concentration of waste was in the six northern counties (related to the Lakes and the Pennines), in Wales, and in the south-west of England (the moors). In fact in central Wales in 1800 waste represented 40 per cent and more of land area. Elsewhere the main areas of waste occurred in the fenlands of eastern England and on the heaths and sands of the southern counties [112: 58–9]. Figure 2 shows the amount of common and waste enclosed as a percentage of county area, c.1750–1870. By the 1870s these wastes had largely been eliminated from the lowlands of eastern and southern England and had been reduced by half in the uplands and in Wales [ibid.: 60]. By 1873 perhaps only 6–7 per cent of England and Wales was still wasteland.

When was the main attack on the wastes conducted? 'It was the wars with France. . . , that brought about an increased awareness of the value of the waste, and the conquest of the waste and the conquest of France became synonymous in some minds' [ibid.: 57]. Sir John Sinclair, the President of the Board of Agriculture, said in 1803: 'Let us not be satisfied with the liberation of Egypt, or the subjugation of Malta, but let us subdue Finchley Common; let us conquer Hounslow Heath, let us compel Epping Forest to submit to the yoke of improvement' [quoted in ibid.: 57]. The wastes were reduced from something like one-fifth to one-fifteenth of the land area of England and Wales in the first three-quarters of the nineteenth century [for examples from Somerset see 113–14; and for Durham see 63]. Enclosure was not the only agent of reclamation, but it was clearly one of the most important.

Enclosure of commons and wastes should not be regarded as a once and for all process which once identified can be catalogued and locked away in a chronological time capsule. The commons and wastes should be seen as a tidal margin which retreated up the hillside, on to the heath and moor, and into the fen, during times of relative land shortage (perhaps in response to population change), or rising prices; to advance again during times of depression or static or falling population. Evidence of the plough quite high up the Peak is indicative of arable cultivation as far back as medieval times on soil and topography that ordinarily was better suited to grazing in rough or permanent pastures. The steep slopes of the uplands remained as rough pasture until between the sixteenth and eighteenth centuries when 'improvements in farm implements and a desire to improve the quality of the stock made the enclosure of some of these steeper commons desirable' [56: *61–74* but esp. *72*]. Similar processes were at play in Scotland, in Wales during the Napoleonic wars, in Somerset and in the reclamation of the Durham Pennines [139; 99: *130–41*; 114: *108–9*; 63: *95–6*]. The reclamation of the Devonian wastes in the two and half centuries before 1800 was evidence of an economic margin related to population change, though more importantly and indirectly to the good fortunes of the local woollen industry [65: *91*]. Much of the advance into and enclosure of the marginal lands was inspired by the inflationary profits of the Napoleonic wars.

Figure 3 maps the density of distribution of open field arable enclosure for the English counties. It is the complement of Figure 2, though for reasons explained earlier it is likely that some common and waste has been mistakenly classified as arable. The map shows the intensive enclosure of open fields within a distorted triangular-shaped area with Gloucestershire at the peak and the East Riding, Lincolnshire and Norfolk at the base, mainly after 1750 and before 1870.

There were considerable county and regional variations. In Suffolk most enclosure was concentrated in the west on the Cambridgeshire border and close to the heartland of the Midlands open fields [107: *46–50*]. In West Sussex enclosure was also limited in extent. The south-western end of the Sussex coastal plain was enclosed in two periods either side of the Napoleonic wars while the eastern end with the neighbouring lowlands and the land to the north of the Downs was enclosed during the war. The Weald and the Downs were enclosed later in the nineteenth century, mainly after 1845 [49: *73–88*, esp. *75*]. In Somerset most enclosure occurred before the eighteenth century and what remained was the great commons and wastes of the low-lying Somerset fenland Levels, the Mendip Hills, and the southern and western hills [113; 114]. Exceptionally, an early enclosure of these commons was in train in the 1770s, before the Napoleonic period. In the western hills there was a second wave of enclosing activity in the period 1830–70 [114: *103*]. Over 40 per cent of Somerset enclosures involved the Levels and were drainage schemes as much as they were enclosures [see also *39*].

In Northumberland and Durham the common arable fields were concentrated in the eastern third of these counties, on the coastal plain at altitudes below 400 feet, with some western penetration along the major valleys of the Tyne and Tees. The Pennines were virtually devoid of common arable fields. Most of the 70–80,000 acres enclosed

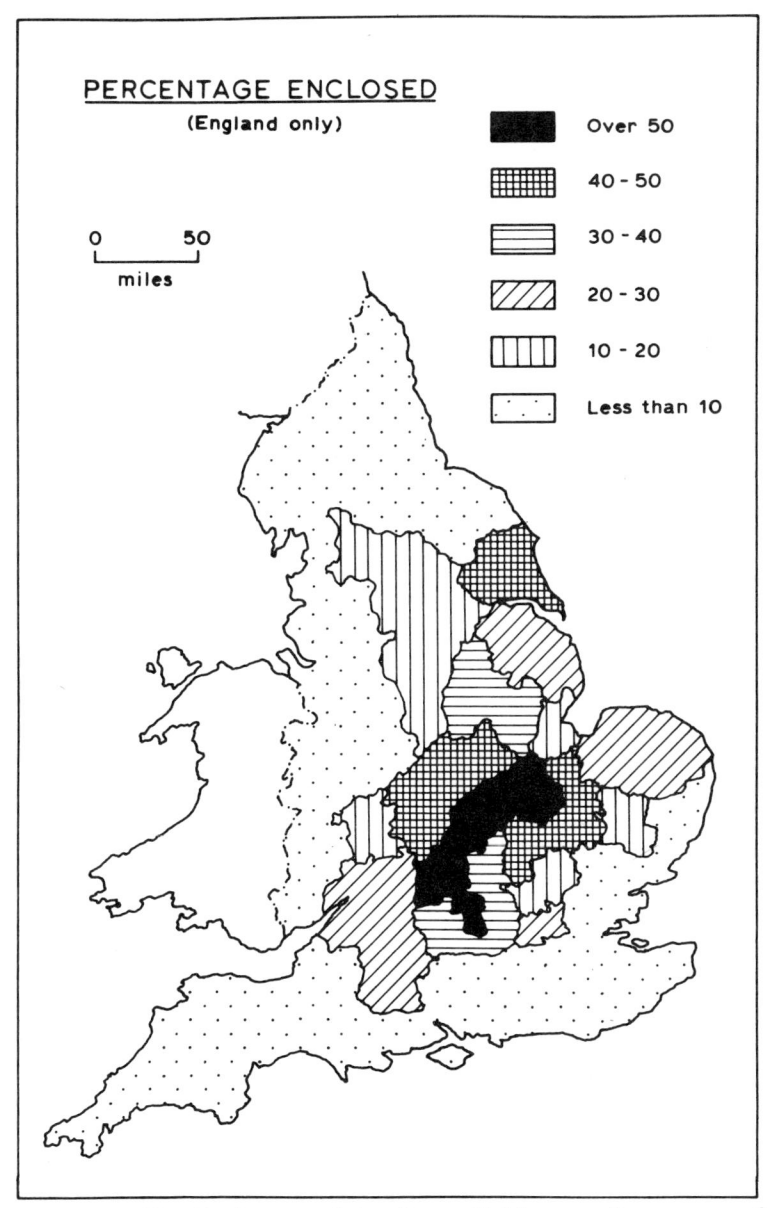

Figure 3 The Enclosure of the Open Fields as a Percentage of County Area (England only), c.1750–1870
Source: M. E. Turner, *English Parliamentary Enclosure* (1980), p. 59

in Durham between 1550–1750 was open field arable and located in the east, and nearly all of the 107,000 acres enclosed by eighteenth- and nineteenth-century statutes was common and waste located in the Pennines. A similar pattern emerges for Northumberland [63: *84–5, 87–8* for Durham; 40 for Northumberland; 41 for both]. Similarly in Wensleydale in the West Riding, open fields had disappeared by the end of the seventeenth century, and the subsequent enclosures concerned various descriptions of common and waste [57: esp. *172*]. In Lincolnshire, variations in soil and drainage influenced soil fertility, which in turn accounted for quite widely separated chronology of enclosure even for neighbouring or near neighbour parishes [82; 61; 68].

The Felden in south Warwickshire was different from the pastoral Arden Forest in the north, and within the Felden the fertile Avon valley was different from the intractable clays of the south-east towards the Northamptonshire border [77: *19*]. This variation in Warwickshire can also be traced into Staffordshire and Worcestershire [88: *191–4*]. In the champion country of south Worcestershire there were extensive open fields with a density of parliamentary enclosure as high as 43 per cent, whereas in the woodland country in the north and west it was as low as 4 per cent [116: *157–8*]. If Staffordshire can be regarded as a northern extension of the woodlands of Worcestershire and Warwickshire then there was a reasonably uniform enclosure history for the region. Early enclosure had practically denuded the Staffordshire open fields before the eighteenth century so that only about 3 per cent of the county was enclosed by act [88: *204, 209*; see also 115].

This exercise of dissecting the countryside within the counties or within broad agricultural regions could be repeated for many other areas in many other chronologies, but the point is well made without further detail.

(ii) A NOTE ON WALES

While a similar analysis of Welsh enclosures is possible [for example at the local level as in 100–1] it remains unsatisfactory as long as the basic statistics remain unrevised. At the moment the best available are Bowen's of 1914 with additions made by Jones in 1959 [6; 7]. There were about 250 enclosure acts for the Principality of which only 12 were enacted before the 1790s. There was a Napoleonic wars' peak of activity when 93 acts were passed and a second peak under the powers of the 1845 General Act resulting in extensive enclosure in the 1850s and 1860s when 89 acts were passed [107: *216*]. There is some ambiguity over the amount of land that was enclosed. Some evidence suggests nearly one million acres of mainly common and waste was involved. This sounds high and would have meant the enclosure of 20 per cent of the land area. A second estimate of 385,000 acres is more reasonable [6: *11–13*]. The enclosures of the war period accounted for 200,000 acres or one-eighth of the land then lying in common and waste [99: *32–3*]. We must remember, however, that much of Wales remains commons or wastes as regulated or unregulated pastures.

One of the crucial differences between Welsh and English enclosures was the nature of the terrain and the accompanying land uses. There was a dominance of commons and wastes in Wales. Thomas's point is well taken; in the uplands,

> where pastoral farming had always been predominant, the economy itself was not fundamentally modified, although the detail of its practice was considerably changed . . . what the enclosure movement did for these regions was to abolish the usage of common grazing, and to divide the old commons into blocks of land, which were then allotted according to the claims of those landowners who had previously exercised grazing rights. [100: *27*]

The emphasis was on improving existing animal husbandry rather than changing to arable production, even during the Napoleonic wars when much of pastoral England became arable. To categorise Welsh enclosures as the enclosure of commons and waste therefore is in some ways misleading, they were always an essential part of a pastoral economy supplying the low-lying farms with much needed grazing [101: *27*]. This is a point to bear in mind with respect to other so-called 'wasteland enclosures' elsewhere in Britain, such as the commons above Wensleydale [57: *173*].

In general, during the peak of activity at the time of the Napoleonic wars, the moorland edge was developed irregularly by enclosure and encroachment, though there was not necessarily a great improvement in the economy of the uplands as a result [99: *160*]. There was a similar enclosure of the coastal wastes and the low-lying marshes and valleys. Even when common fields were enclosed it is evident they were often in pasture or used in a system of pastoral husbandry, rather than in arable farming [ibid.: *130–41*].

(iii) SCOTLAND

Late seventeenth-century Scotland was a vastly different place from the Scotland we know today:

> In place of a chequerboard of separate fields one must imagine the ground everywhere lying as open as moorland . . . seldom divided in any way by hedge, wall or dyke . . . The pastoral land . . . was all more or less rough brown waste: there was no question of grass being cultivated as a crop. The ploughed land within was a series of undulating strips or rigs. [141: *120*]

This general scene stands in contrast to England during the same period, with different topography and land use: even the commonality of open field farming, dear to English agrarian history, was present in Scotland but in a fundamentally distinct form. The Scottish enclosure movement, when it came, was a major transformation of the agricultural economy and society and apparently was a very rapid one. It was also very late by English standards. Enclosures of any sort were scarcely known until late in the seventeenth century, though by then much of England had already been enclosed.

A recent lively debate has discussed the 'evolutionary' as distinct from the 'revolutionary' changes in Scotland after the mid-seventeenth century [147; 136; 138; 121; 149]. In the debate enclosure could not be properly separated from other aspects of agrarian reform. Certainly the popularised picture of Scotland in c.1750 as a backward agricultural country is under intense scrutiny, but whether the identification of new crops, new techniques, enclosures, etc., from the mid-seventeenth century onwards is sufficient to establish chronological turning points is open to doubt. It is an issue which has taxed historians of the English agricultural revolution and remains inconclusive on certain issues. In Scotland similar problems occur. Adams, in contrast to Whittington's argument for evolution over a long period, emphasises the narrow chronology of the Scottish agricultural revolution, including enclosure, and in particular the post-Jacobite concentration of the revolution [120: *15*; 121]. Caird establishes that a new rural landscape was deliberately created by revolution rather than evolution, mainly in the eighteenth and nineteenth centuries, in which enclosure was only a part of more expansive agricultural changes [123: *72–3*]. Lebon's study of Ayrshire and Renfrewshire emphasised the rapid revolutionary transformation of the agrarian landscape in the eighteenth century, even though important evolutionary processes were traced well back into the seventeenth century [135: *100–1*]. Gray's wider survey similarly recognised the early origin of individual elements of agrarian reform, but nevertheless focused attention on the drama of change, not simply in the late eighteenth century but in many instances well into the nineteenth century [131; see also 130].

It is not clear from the debate how far the evolutionists wish to overturn the revolutionist school, or whether they simply wish to establish that c.1750 Scottish agriculture was far from backward. In any event, a brief review of enclosure may help to resolve some of the chronology and untangle some of the processes.

There seems little doubt that Scottish enclosures were primarily an eighteenth-century phenomenon by which infield-outfield was replaced by a geometrical field pattern within which the system of runrig was obliterated [119: *252*]. The general enclosure of the lowland estates began in earnest in many areas in the 1760s and 1770s and that of the uplands at the end of the eighteenth century [124: *205*]. It is tempting to draw a parallel with the open field enclosures of the English Midlands after the mid-eighteenth century and the increasing enclosure activity of wastes and commons during the Napoleonic wars, but, as we shall see, what was undergoing enclosure and the meaning of enclosure in Scotland was quite different.

The origin of Scottish enclosure certainly lay before 1750 however, in a late-seventeenth-century process which followed the fashion and interest of the wealthier landowners and was related to the evolution of country houses, hardly touching the tenantry directly. Whyte contrasts the utilitarian English enclosure agreements with the fashion-inspired Scottish counterparts; profit was not completely ignored by Scottish landowners but it has been suggested that conspicuous consumption was more important. This early enclosure in any case was not on a large scale and each project rarely exceeded 250–350 acres, creating 'islands of improvement in a sea of open-field, infield-outfield cultivation, and unenclosed rough pasture' [151: *130*]. It can be seen as a modest but vital achievement before the main thrust of enclosure in the eighteenth century [150: *100–10, 113–33*; 151].

The legal process involved in Scottish enclosures was different from that in England and Wales, and what was enclosed was also different [see 130: *90–1*; on Scottish field systems see 128; 148]. In both cases a statutory process was formed with the Scottish one in some ways a precursor of the Westminster General Acts of the mid-nineteenth century [150: *100–10*; 144: *454–5*; 146]. From 1661 to the end of the century a series of acts was passed to promote agrarian reforms and innovations. The first, in 1661, was a general enclosure act obliging, in principle at least, every proprietor whose lands were worth at least £1000 Scots in annual rent to enclose a minimum of 4 acres per annum for ten years. Smaller landowners were obliged to enclose proportionately smaller areas. The wording of the act is sufficiently ambiguous to raise doubts over its effectiveness. Was it a device which helped reafforestation as much as it improved animal and crop husbandry? In 1669 two further acts built upon the 1661 legislation, and in 1685 the 1661 enclosure act was renewed [150: *100–6*]. These acts have been associated with promoting tree plantations and the expansion of the cattle trade because they were largely used for facilitating, encouraging and protecting enclosures for young trees and grazings. The association of planting timber with enclosure continued in some areas until the late eighteenth century [142: *xix–xx*]. Scottish enclosures well into the eighteenth century were mostly for these purposes of creating *physical boundaries*, for whatever reason, as distinct from the *division* of holdings or the introduction of individual farming over collective husbandry [132: *56*; on grazing aspects see 143].

However, two acts passed in 1695 were quite different. The first, an Act anent Lands lying Runrig, empowered the division of proprietary runrig [126: *127–34*]. The second, the Division of the Commonties Act, empowered the Court of Session to divide waste or uncultivated land which was used as pasture among those proprietors who held commonable rights over them, on the application of a single heritor with interest in the common [133: *191*; 150: *106*]. The origin and evolution of runrig is complicated [146: esp. *69*; see also 127; 128: esp. *70–6*], but for simplicity perhaps it can be likened to the relationship between strip scattering and ownership and tenantry units in the English open fields. But it would be wrong to assume that the act for the division and removal of runrig was the same as the English enclosure act because no provisions were made in the Scottish case for the construction of boundaries for the newly divided holdings. In this sense the 1695 act removed runrig as an impediment to enclosure, and opened up the possibility of enclosure [126: *129*; 132: *57*]. Perhaps the desire for enclosure hastened the end of runrig [146: *71*], because the disappearance of runrig and subsequent enclosure often went together. This seems to have been the case in the eighteenth century in the Lowlands, and it continued into the nineteenth century in the Highlands [133: *192–3*].

The minimum effects of the 1695 acts have been described as a prerequisite to improvement, which 'had been widely though not universally, taken advantage of in the Lowlands by 1770' [134: *17*]. But these late seventeenth-century acts have been seriously questioned as great enclosing devices. They may have had little effect until economic circumstances became favourable, and that may not have been until after 1750 [121: *199*]. Besides, it should be noted that both these acts affected estates only where ownership was intermingled whereas in Scotland the most normal pattern was for ownership to be concentrated in the hands of a single landowner, in which the termination of runrig and the enclosure of commons and open fields could proceed by fiat, without any regard to the position of the tenantry, both before and after the legislation of 1695 [on the abuse of tenantry rights see 133: *191–2*].

Can we measure the extent of enclosure in Scotland? In the mid-eighteenth century a land survey was established, the Military Survey of 1747–55. The resulting work is popularly known as 'Roy's Map', and from its disparate sections O'Dell has reconstructed mainland Scotland. In 1754 there was much farmland apparently enclosed along the eastern coastal belt, along and either side of the Forth–Clyde axis, in the eastern borders [for which see 126: *132–3* and the mid-eighteenth-century concentration of the removal of proprietary runrig] and along the Solway Firth towards Stranraer [137: *61*]. In the Lothians and Berwickshire the system of runrig and commonality of property had already been widely replaced by compact holdings and exclusive possession by 1760 [134: *17–18*]. In spite of these widespread 'enclosures', the composite distribution of open field with enclosed farmland for the same period and even in the same areas shows that in a wider spatial sense the enclosure of mainland Scotland was still awaited in the mid-eighteenth century. 'Roy's Map' perfectly identified the pioneering areas of agrarian reform, but the greatest enclosure movement was yet to come [137: *60*; 134: *19–28*]. In Perthshire in the 1790s at least three-fifths of the arable was unenclosed, a third of Dunbartonshire was open and by 1810 Kincardinshire in general remained open [134: *22–3*; for Argyllshire see 129]. The Montgomery Act of 1770 (10 Geo.III, c.51) encouraged the improvement of land in Scotland held under settlement of strict entail (about one-third of the country was so entailed) [134: *37 et seq*; 133: *202–3*]. It was another example, comparable to the enactments of the second half of the seventeenth century, where the law intervened in a general way to assist and encourage Scottish agricultural improvement, but not necessarily a great enclosing device, which was the hallmark of the English local private act [see also 145: *89*].

The chronology has also been measured, in so far as this is possible. The measuring rod is the registration of commonty divisions from the summons issued in the Court of Session under the aegis of the second 1695 act. The commonties were the lands 'possessed in common by different proprietors' [5: *vii*; 120: *esp. 16*]. There was a peak of activity from 1750–80, especially in the 1760s, and lesser peaks in the 1810s and 1830s. Some authorities emphasise the prices and profit inflation of the Napoleonic wars as the focal point of the general enclosure movement in Scotland, but even by the end of the war much remained open and unenclosed (in the sense of unfenced or unwalled) whilst in fact divided or appropriated in severalty [133: *200*]. Here again the Scottish distinction between *enclosures* and *division* is well made.

Over 650,000 acres of commonty were divided by the Court of Session between 1720–1850, an area equivalent to the size of Warwickshire [119: *252*; 5: *vii*; revised in 121: *199, 203*]. Such an area does not compare with English enclosures but it must be remembered both that some commons lying within the domain of a single landowner will have been enclosed without the intervention of the Court of Sessions, and the amount of land available to agriculture, or at least to enclosed farms, was and is relatively small in Scotland.

Enclosure was often the final deed in a long-drawn-out process of change. The development of large compact farms sometimes preceded the formal enclosure created by rigid boundaries in much the same way as consolidation took place in the English open fields [in general see 133: *190–8*; on the division of runrig without enclosure see 145: esp. *83–9*]. Even in an advanced area like Fife there was land still unenclosed in 1830 that had been in a relatively compact state for 50 years [131: *114*]. In Aberdeenshire, while enclosure of the open fields was over by the 1840s [125: *22*], reclamation of wastes, which in England would often be referred to as enclosure, was still taking place into the 1850s [ibid.: *56–7, 195–6*].

(iv) A NOTE ON NON-PARLIAMENTARY ENCLOSURE

Though this pamphlet is mainly concerned with parliamentary enclosure it is necessary to mention other forms of enclosure in order to put the scale of what we are considering into perspective. Kerridge believes that historians have overestimated the importance of parliamentary enclosure. By about 1700 he suggests that only 'one-quarter of the enclosure of England and Wales remained to be undertaken' thus relegating to limbo 'the hoary fable of the supreme importance of parliamentary enclosure' [69: *24*]. It is not merely that parliamentary enclosure diverts attention from his own views of the origin and progress of agricultural revolution but also he wishes to reduce the importance of all enclosures, seeking other changes as the heart of agrarian reform. Earlier summaries in this chapter suggest that 21 per cent of England was enclosed by act, which, if Kerridge is correct in his own appraisal of the survival of open fields and commons, does not leave much margin for enclosure by private agreement during the eighteenth and nineteenth centuries. Either Kerridge's estimate of the amount of land available for future enclosure in 1700 is too low or other authorities have overstated the case of non-parliamentary enclosure after 1700. McCloskey, for example, says that in 1700 an open field system of some sort or other existed in a 'broad swath' across England but that 150 years later '5,000 odd acts of Parliament *and at least an equal number of voluntary agreements* had swept it away' [72: *15*, my emphasis; see also 73: *123–5*]. He also states that one-half of the agricultural land of England was enclosed during the eighteenth and nineteenth centuries. The evidence is taken from Ernle and Slater, giving a guess by Slater of about 8 million acres enclosed by private agreement against 6 million acres by parliamentary act. The 6 million acres is not seriously disputed though it should be reckoned nearer to 7 million. The 8 million acres is now completely unsupportable. Chambers and Mingay are more cautious: 'It is impossible to say how much land was enclosed by agreement rather than by Act, but it must have been very large, perhaps half as great as the open field area enclosed by Act' [46: *78*], which would give a total area enclosed of something like 9–10 million acres. This is more plausible simply in terms of the finite area of land available.

Kerridge and McCloskey have therefore identified the two areas of debate: was parliamentary enclosure so important when compared with pre-eighteenth-century enclosure, and was parliamentary enclosure so important when set against the volume of private enclosure in the eighteenth and nineteenth centuries?

Historians of post-Tudor England have suggested that evidence of anti-enclosure committees, pamphleteers and depopulation enquiries, as well as known enclosure agreements, undermine the scale and importance of the later parliamentary enclosures. But was the weight of words in public outcry and public enquiry inversely proportional to the number of acres affected? As Darby points out

> it may seem strange to find that, after all, the Midlands were the main area of Parliamentary enclosure. The counties which had produced such a volume of complaint in Tudor times were the very ones in which open fields flourished triumphantly right on into the eighteenth and even into the nineteenth century. How is the paradox to be explained? [55: *322*]

Much of England outside the Midlands was already enclosed before the fifteenth or sixteenth centuries or had never been 'open'. The political message that was broadcast may have distorted the magnitude of the events.

A recent survey of the period 1600–1750 suggests that perhaps Kerridge had a valid point in emphasising pre-parliamentary enclosure [42: *66*]. Renewed authority has now been given to the 1607 Depopulation Inquisition as a source for sixteenth-century enclosures, a source incidentally in which Kerridge had little faith; and if that inquiry is more acceptable, then perhaps so are those of the sixteenth century [81]. The enclosures evidence from the Decree Rolls adds weight to the argument. Beresford's use of this source confirms our impressions about Leicestershire, Warwickshire, Lincolnshire and Northamptonshire as counties affected by seventeenth-century anti-enclosure action and which we know had a history of enclosure immediately prior to mass enclosure by act after c.1750 [38]. For example, at least 25 per cent of Leicestershire was enclosed before 1607. By 1710 the proportion was 47 per cent [42: *69*]. With the new evidence we might consider raising this figure. But we also know that 47 per cent of Leicestershire was enclosed by act of parliament after 1730, so if we revise pre-parliamentary enclosure estimates upwards we are virtually dismissing any possibility of enclosures by agreement in any significant numbers in the eighteenth and nineteenth centuries [107: *180*]. Very few other attempts have been made to estimate the chronological history of enclosure for any large areas like counties, but in so far as it has been done it reveals considerable gaps in information. For example, in Durham, Hodgson can account for 29 per cent of the county enclosed in two phases c.1550–1730 (peaking in the 1630s) and 1750–1870 (peaking during the two classic phases of parliamentary enclosure in the 1760s and the 1810s); 15 per cent was never enclosed at all; leaving 56 per cent to be accounted for by medieval enclosure or by private agreement that has left no documentary trace [63].

To summarise, perhaps the best that we can say with current information is that enclosures in the 200 years before 1700 were probably more important than was once believed, but if that is so then enclosure by agreement was probably rather limited after that date. Parliamentary enclosure, if not the most dominant form of enclosure ever known in England was, nevertheless, the most important after 1700.

3 Enclosure and Investment: The Decision to Enclose

(i) GENERAL FACTORS

IT would be easy to catalogue the types of economic factors which may have motivated capital investment in agriculture. We could analyse changes in aggregate demand by investigating population growth, by investigating relative price movements, by looking at the supply of funds to finance capital projects, by looking at technical changes and the relationships with soil and topography, and so on. Such a catalogue might be more baffling than revealing. What is really required is to distinguish the causes from the favourable conditions, in which case it might be a question of conjunction of factors rather than prime causes [66: *272*].

In Warwickshire, Martin identified a conversion of arable to pasture after 1750 resulting from enclosure, perhaps in response to the long period of depressed prices in arable farming in the preceding three decades. Then up to 1780 enclosure was encouraged by a reversal of the price trend and the long upward movement of food prices. In this case enclosure perhaps was followed by improvements in arable production rather than a land use change. The phase after 1780 can be related to the influence from a growing food market and sharply rising land prices [77: *24–9*]. In the Scottish Lowlands 'enclosure was *normally* accompanied by an expansion of arable and mixed farming, not by the laying down of plough to grass and houses to cattlesheds: land was also reclaimed in many areas from the waste and the moor' [141: *328*, my emphasis]. The enclosure of common and waste in the north Somerset uplands in the 1770s may have been the response to the upward trend of wheat prices after 1750 because the lighter soils were more easily adapted to tillage under conditions of enhanced revenue. The richer but heavier soils of the wet grasslands in the county were not enclosed until the war years, perhaps a response to the rise in meat prices. In this second case it was the organisation of existing grazing lands which changed rather than the land use [39]. In the one case relative price movements may have hastened enclosure and in the other the overstocking of commons was alleviated by upgrading the productivity of the wastes [114: *101*].

These few examples indicate the approaches that have been made to answer the broad question of why there was so much parliamentary enclosure. The problem is that we may confuse observable outcomes with investment motives. If the two are the same then enclosure might be heralded as an unqualified entrepreneurial success, but we must remain cautious at this early stage in the investigation.

(ii) THE OPEN FIELDS: INFLEXIBLE OR ADAPTABLE?

McCloskey reminds us that the antithesis of 'why' enclosure after 1750 is why were conditions, catalysts or motives not right before 1750: 'So plain has the inefficiency [of the open fields] seemed that the question has been not why enclosure occurred when it did, by why it did not occur earlier' [72: *17*; see also 32: *64*]. His later work on the open fields, on strip division and scattering of strips in the open fields which he hypothesised as an insurance against the risks of agricultural failure, suggests there were considerable reasons why the open fields persisted [73–5]. There is a protracted debate, that has reached no consensus, over the organisation and dynamic of the English open fields, involving discussion of the scattering and dispersion of holdings for the purposes of risk aversion within the theoretical framework of property rights analysis. It is tangential to the substance of this pamphlet and though the protagonists involved are not all itemised in the bibliography the reader is advised nevertheless to consult the pages of *The Journal of Economic History, Explorations in Economic History, The Journal of European Economic History* and *The Journal of Development Economics*, among others, for the late 1970s [see also 54].

The disjunction of factors before 1750 is just as important as their conjunction after, but the inefficiency of the open fields is by no means as plain and obvious as once it seemed. The retarding qualities historically attributed to them have been refuted in varying degrees in a number of studies. Kerridge suggested that an outstanding feature of common-field husbandry was the liberty the cultivator had to choose what crops he liked in the various parts of the particular open field, though within a set field course. He also suggested that this was nothing new and not necessarily indicative of progress or adaptability [69: *94–5*]. Havinden demonstrated from parish agreements the way the open fields were regulated to meet changing economic circumstances, in which case enclosure was perhaps rendered unnecessary [62]. A counter-argument has been developed from similar parish agreements, using them to indicate the constraints and retarding qualities of open field practice [107: *ch.6*; and on the general debate see also 77: *21–2*; 29; 118: *163–70*].

The inefficiencies of the open fields, though not satisfactorily refuted or vindicated in these counter-arguments, are nevertheless subject to irrefutable qualifications. The open fields were not completely backward or obstructive but neither did they permit complete autonomy in decision-making [on a general theory of rigidity in the open fields see 74: *151–2*]. A case in point might have been a leading landowner in the Derbyshire village of Mapleton whose lands in the six open fields in the 1720s were scattered in 75 separate pieces. The enclosure of 1731 consolidated his ownership into one field by exchanging his lands in the other five with like-minded neighbours [58].

It is, however, by no means certain that enclosure automatically reduced the technical inefficiencies of all agriculturalists. In parts of Durham, for example, agriculture remained technically backward after enclosure and made more widespread the orthodox technique of two crops and a fallow [63: esp. *96–8*]. As Thomas Davis recognised in 1811, 'severalty makes a good farmer better' but it makes 'a bad one worse' [12: *46*].

Even if crop choice within the open fields is evidence of flexibility, it has yet to be demonstrated as a widespread practice. Furthermore, inflexibility was most evident in some areas by the frustrated desire to adjust cropping to withstand a heavier animal population. The inflexibility was not so much within arable farming as in limiting choice between arable and pastoral or mixed farming. The pressures upon common grazing in Buckinghamshire, for example, created by the undesirable but unavoidable practice of overstocking animals, resulted in bottlenecks in the local economy once the desire to increase pastoral farming at the expense of arable farming gained momentum. Adjustments in local field and stinting rules inhibited this desire and halted the expansion of animal activities, or even reduced existing ones. Shortage of land for pastoral activities seems to have developed as a result, protracted for a century or more before 1750 [107: *ch.6*; and for sixteenth- and seventeenth-century evidence of pasture shortages in Kesteven see 82: *93*]. The problem may have come to a head in the two or three decades before 1750 during a depression of arable prices when real incomes improved and increased the demand for animal products [for a summary and fresh interpretation of the agricultural depression of 1730–50 see 35]. There is considerable evidence in this period to suggest conversion to grass, with enclosure as one of the agents of change. The early acts before 1750 may have been an alternative to the traditional Chancery instruments of the seventeenth century, an extension of enclosure activity stretching back to the fifteenth century in which conversion to grass was usual. This was the case for much of Warwickshire, Leicestershire and the Midland heartland generally [77: *27*; 66: *266*]. It is not difficult to see a connection with long-run economic trends because these counties of early parliamentary enclosure are the same counties involved in the 1607 and earlier depopulation enquiries. Throughout the seventeenth century and well on into the third quarter of the eighteenth, central England came to look greener than ever [55: *326*]. Even Durham, a county not usually associated with the heavier soils of the Midlands, also experienced a wave of early enclosures (pre-1750) and these were related to the development or extension of the pastoral economy [63: *93*].

In Lindsey it appears that pre-eighteenth-century enclosure took place on water-retentive soils and marshlands associated with reclamation, and this enclosure arose from the desire to increase or improve pastoral activity. But such a move did not act as a spur to dissolve the open arable fields or other features of communal life; instead the general concentration on grass farming served to keep arable farming in a backward state, the open fields surviving well into the eighteenth and on into the nineteenth centuries. In this case pastoralism caused the enclosure of the arable to be delayed [68: esp. *139*].

(iii) PRODUCTIVITY GAINS AND ENCLOSURE

Contemporaries were generally certain about the productivity gains achieved by enclosure. In the Vale of Aylesbury, for example, Arthur Young reported that 'the tenants reap bushels, where they ought to have quarters'. After enclosure the productivity gains for landlords were just as impressive, 'the rents before were fourteen shillings but now arable lands let to twenty eight shillings per acre; none under a guinea; and grass from forty shillings to three pounds, all tithe free. This rise of rents on enclosing justifies by observation on the expediency of inclosing' [16: *24–5*]. It is interesting that Young linked productivity effects for both farmers and landlords together (improved output and improved rent) [on productivity effects see 86: *102–12*; 17: *91*; and on the problems of relating landlords' profit through rental changes and farmers' profit through productivity gains see 118: *211*]. It may also be the case that farmers' profits were enhanced after enclosure not necessarily through a simple improvement in output, but also, or instead, by a reduction in expenses, in spite of increased rents [for an illustration of this see ibid.: *212–13*].

Enclosure petitions, bills and acts complained of the unimprovable nature of the soil while husbandry remained in open fields, dispersed in small pieces, with intermixed ownership and tenancy, adding that open fields were capable of considerable improvement if divided and allotted among the proprietors in severalty. A preamble to this effect headed most major enclosure documents, though it might have meant little more than the country solicitor using existing petitions, bills and acts to frame succeeding ones. There is, though, a good deal of evidence from modern scholarship to support the idea of productivity gains at enclosure, though not always on a dramatic scale. In some Oxfordshire parishes there was a 10 per cent improvement in the yields of the basic grains when enclosed fields were compared with open ones [158: *479*], and in both Northamptonshire and Warwickshire there were similar improvements [107: *95–7*]. For a large number of widely scattered places both Yelling and Turner have demonstrated considerable improvements in grain yields when comparing enclosed villages with open field ones, improvements of the order of 25 per cent [110: *497–500*; 118: *171–2, 203–4*].

The main problem with productivity studies of this kind is that they are not necessarily comparisons of the same parishes before and after enclosure, but rather of open field parishes and enclosed ones co-existing at the same time. The ones with inherently more fertile soils may be already enclosed, or the gains may not be from enclosure alone but from better practice techniques, including the freedom of crop choice which was so problematic in the open fields. So at Barton upon Humber in Lincolnshire in 1801 there was 'a decrease in the number of acres under the plough since the inclosure of 1793, *yet from a superior mode* of cultivation' there was 'an increase upon the whole', a view which was echoed in other Lincolnshire parishes. But enclosure by itself could produce gains by eliminating losses through trespass and too frequent fallows. In Standish in Gloucestershire two crops and a fallow held back the productivity of the open fields whereas if enclosed 'they would not require a fallow oftener than once in six or seven years'; in Bosbury in Herefordshire the common fields were 'highly injurious to agriculture, as they invariably lie fallow every third year'; and in Latton in Wiltshire the open fields lay fallow every fourth year: 'The course of common field husbandry allows not of turnipping nor of any other late and valuable improvements in agriculture' [110: vol. 190: *102*; vol. 189: *193*, *225*; vol. 195: *85* respectively]. Enclosure was the vehicle for improvement but in itself was not inherently an improvement.

Enclosure often brought about land use changes. In the Midland clays there was a move out of arable into pasture up to the late eighteenth century. In Worcestershire there was an increase in wheat cultivation at the expense of the other grains and a general improvement in the variety of crop combinations and rotations [117: esp. *24–34*]. How do we measure productivity changes which arise from land use alterations? The answer might be through farm revenues, and in the absence of data on farmers' incomes these can perhaps be inferred from rental changes.

(iv) RENT AND PRODUCTIVITY GAINS

It has been suggested that from a landlord's point of view enclosure was an investment, the profit from which was a higher rent. If rents doubled after enclosure, which was not unusual, net profit could be of the order of 15–20 per cent, making enclosure one of the best investments of the age. On the Fitzwilliam estates there was a 16 per cent return in original outlay after enclosure; on certain Lincolnshire estates in the 1760s there was a 32 per cent per annum improvement on the rent roll attributable to enclosure [cited in 108: *245–7*]. There is some confusion over gross and net measurements of return, nevertheless the pattern is clear enough, with considerable supporting evidence of higher rents in enclosed situations compared with open ones [for examples from Lincolnshire, Oxfordshire, Buckinghamshire and Warwickshire see 34: *90–3*; 17: *91–4;* 157: *359–60*; 77: *29*].

No doubt rental revaluation was important in the decision to enclose but unfortunately it has been treated as an automatic economic gain rather than as one element leading to considered economic or entrepreneurial decisions. Purdum, however, has set up a descriptive model of the responsiveness of landlords to monetary benefits [87]. If the efficiency gain of enclosed over open fields is measured by rental changes then enclosure was easily financed by these rental improvements. There is the hint of cost benefit when Purdum introduces the idea of discovering what factors influencing gains from enclosure 'were known prior to enclosure', because such factors may have influenced the timing of enclosure. For the owner of a single estate such prior knowledge was probably only guesswork or based on information from neighbours, but for the owner of more than one estate the potential to predict future rates of return based on existing experience may have been crucial in the timing of enclosure. The main finding to emerge is that rent as the monetary return from enclosure must be measured for efficiency gain against the rates of return on alternative investments. The model is therefore couched in terms of opportunity costs [see also 72]. For example, if rent returns were less than the prevailing rate of usury of 5 per cent then rental gains as a motive for parting with investment funds cannot be accepted as a working hypothesis and enclosure therefore was an inefficient use of capital. Purdum's rates on five manors out of five investigated in Nottinghamshire exceeded 5 per cent.

But what about changes in interest rates and what about alternative investments? Ashton and McCloskey regarded interest rate movements as the prime economic indicator which at times encouraged enclosures and at others held them in abeyance [31; 72]. But Purdum considers that if enclosures were as profitable as was popularly believed then movements in interest rates would have had only a minimal effect on the decision to enclose. Certainly his rates of return support that view, but this was at an opportunity cost of only 5 per cent. In the mid-eighteenth-century Levant trade one merchant considered that the risks were not worth while unless an annual return of 8 per cent could be assured, meaning a gross profit of 30 to 40 per cent over four years, which was the gestation period of the original outlay [R. Davis, *Aleppo and Devonshire Square: English Traders in the Levant in the Eighteenth Century* (1967), *222, 226*]. While trade and enclosures are not comparable, a gestation period is also appropriate in other forms of investment. This is a significant gap in our literature of the eighteenth century.

Rental improvements have been related to the theory of property rights. A spectrum of property rights existed with common ownership at one end and private ownership at the other. The former was the ultimate in shared or non-exclusive rights and the latter was an exclusive right in property. Between the two existed a combination of rights: some were temporary common rights in force during periods of fallow; some were full common rights operating for long periods on commons and open fields; and some were partial common rights where partial or piecemeal enclosures existed. Furthermore, these rights could vary through the course of the harvest year. The more exclusive the right the greater the opportunity for rent maximisation, the less exclusive the right the more dissipated the rent because more people had to share it. The ability to gain exclusivity of property ownership may have been reflected in the extent of improved post-enclosure rents [32: esp. *64–5*; see also 33; 54: *ch.3*]. Thus it has been argued that Tudor enclosures, in so far as they were primarily for extending pastoral husbandry, had the most to gain from renegotiated rents at enclosure because grazing rights were the least exclusive property rights available. The argument then follows that parliamentary enclosure, which was essentially in arable areas the ownership of which was already more exclusive, therefore commanded a lower level of rent gain. Consequently these enclosures occurred later because the gains were smaller. The proposition, while interesting, is far too simplistic, misunderstands Tudor enclosures which were not simply to separate grazing rights but rather to enclose arable fields and convert to pasture, and does not accommodate the great variability that there was in enclosures, many of which were composite land reforms or involved changes of land use.

Allen offers two explanations for the rise of rents after enclosure. Firstly, farmers of enclosed farms could pay more because of post-enclosure efficiency gains, though alternatively enclosure could have led to a redistribution of income from farmers to landlords if open field farms were underrented in the first place. This second explanation rests on the outcome of clauses in enclosure acts which terminated existing leases. The opportunity was given, effectively, to abandon these leases in the mid-term and allow landlords and tenants to renegotiate them, though if necessary with compensation for those leases with less than 21 years to run [10: *37*]. Yelling asks the question, what happened when enclosures took place in times of inflation? 'There is some reason to believe that rent levels tended to freeze in the immediate pre-enclosure period, and to be released in the renegotiation of rents and leases on enclosure' [118: *211*]. This is precisely the issue which Allen has tried to unscramble. The period from the mid-eighteenth century to the end of the Napoleonic wars was one of rising prices and thus any Ricardian rent surpluses arising from this rise in prices of agricultural produce on open field estates would have accrued to the tenants because their rents were fixed, and not to the landlords who thus would have fixed money incomes. Enclosure, it is supposed, allowed landlords to recoup these surpluses by exacting new rents now corrected for inflation. Allen's research supports this proposition to the extent that he calculates that only about one-half of the open field surpluses accrued to the landlords as rent or to the church and state in tithes and taxes. While it is plausible that rents lagged behind inflation, especially the inflation of the Napoleonic war years, the rate of inflation before 1790, a period which encompassed the entire first phase of parliamentary enclosure, was not very pronounced. But crucially, Allen's theory is based on data from Arthur Young from the 1760s, a period of only modest price inflation. In addition, it is hard to maintain confidence in Young when we learn from Allen that grain yields were actually smaller, on average by 9, 18 and 12 per cent respectively for wheat, barley and oats when comparing enclosed fields with open ones [29: *949*, my percentage differences based on Allen's mean yields figures], a conclusion which goes against the findings of most modern scholarship, including my own, which supports the idea of productivity gains [as in 109: *497–500*; 118: *171–2, 203–4*; 158: *479*]. At the moment therefore the evidence favours the alternative explanation to Allen's, namely productivity gains at enclosure, part of which accrued to the landlord in terms of higher rents. The exact nature of the division of productivity gains between landlords and tenants is clearly debatable at the present state of research, perhaps Yelling has summarised the nearest to a consensus in saying that the farmers are believed to have benefited, though to a lesser extent [118: *211*].

(v) COST-BENEFIT

Let us return to a point raised in the previous section. We cannot discuss profitability and productivity without establishing what the enclosers expected to gain from their investments. Were accountancy procedures, however crude, employed? As historians we are wont to analyse the outcome of enclosure in terms of cost-benefit, but did the encloser also view his investment in this way?

Purdum's rental analysis rests heavily on an interpretation of opportunity costs, as do those arguments which seek a relationship between chronology of enclosure and movements in the rate of interest, in which the rate of usury is the assumed opportunity cost [eg. 72; 74: *136–7*]. This question of opportunity costs must be taken further and must not be ignored in examples where enclosure was *not* financed out of borrowed capital. As McCloskey points out, those who ignore interest rates on the grounds that much enclosure was financed out of current income and not by mortgage miss the significance of opportunity costs. To expend current income on enclosures certainly avoided future interest repayments on loans, but incurred the penalty of the foregone income by not investing in alternative projects whose rate of return exceeded the rate of usury, usually measured as the yield on consols. Self-financing therefore also carried an element of opportunity cost [74: *137*]. Some evidence suggests that enclosers were sensitive to opportunity costs, invoking the capital cost of enclosure only in terms of the foregone income from investing the same money elsewhere. At Hessle in the East Riding in the 1790s, for example, it was calculated that the opportunity cost of the enclosure was 2 shillings per acre. The expected improvement in rent from 20 to 30 shillings per acre greatly exceeded the foregone income from alternative investment. The principal landowner in the Buckinghamshire hamlet of Sedrup in 1775 calculated the expected improvement on his estate in the event of an enclosure. Current rents were £404–15–0 and improved rents would be £689–5–6 (including some old enclosures and orchards); but the net improvement would not be £284–10–6 (i.e. new minus old rents), but rather £232–0–6, which allowed for a deduction of £30 for the improvement of the tithes, and a second deduction of £22–10–0, the foregone income from laying out £560 on enclosure costs at $4\frac{1}{2}$ per cent interest [Buckinghamshire County Record Office, D/LE/8/100]. Enclosure costs were considered only in terms of an opportunity cost. The projected rent improvement would have repaid the capital cost after three years.

Such an example of cost-benefit, while not commonplace, was also not so unusual. For example, it was not unusual for recognised enclosure commissioners and land surveyors to make this kind of estimate as a preliminary to framing a bill [104: esp. *41*]. Perhaps the importance of opportunity costs was greater and more widespread than scholarship has allowed. Sir William Lee of Hartwell in Buckinghamshire valued an estate in nearby Bishopstone at a little over £1554 (date unknown but probably in the 1770s). Bearing in mind the interest such a sum would earn if invested, Sir William was advised not to offer more than £1400, thus allowing for the foregone income in such investment [Buckinghamshire County Record Office, D/LE/8/4]. In this case, on a one-year basis, he was allowing for a 10 per cent return for foregone income, though this is not stated in the document.

(vi) OTHER ECONOMIC CONSIDERATIONS

Before discussing obvious economic factors, we should bear in mind that relatively irrational factors may have influenced the timing of enclosure. For example, lack of entrepreneurship coupled with agricultural conservatism is sometimes alleged to have produced late enclosures. In Kesteven 'poor farmers and a conservative tradition failed to help, if they did not positively hold back, parliamentary enclosure' [82: *94*]. In neighbouring Lindsey the backwardness of the arable farmer, tenurial bottlenecks, and local conservatism, rather than fundamental physical environmental factors, are said to have partly determined the late arrival of enclosure on the lighter soils of the region [68: *147*]. Thomas Stone in 1787 pointed to the conservatism of the open field farmer who through centuries of inheritance believed that he already farmed by best practice methods and who, given a village and farms newly enclosed, might have looked for another open field situation 'rather than subject himself to deviate in the least from the beaten track of his ancestors for the means of subsistence' [15: *25*]. Who is to say that the landlords through their own perceptions of custom and change may not have been conservative as well, and held enclosure in abeyance?

But there are more concrete economic reasons why enclosure may have been delayed and why the whole movement was protracted over time. The cost of enclosure for most owners was a serious issue, a dividing line between financial independence and a lesser position in the social and agricultural hierarchy. A consideration of costs could hold enclosure in abeyance, whether by the individual or by the collective decision of those in the same socio-economic niche. We must also consider more general factors about the economy and society at large in which enclosures were situated. It becomes a question not merely why enclosure was not completed by 1750 but also why it was concentrated in two relatively restricted peaks of activity within the broader chronology of 1750–1830.

Whether or not a landowner could afford to enclose depended on the availability of funds and their cost, that is the rate of interest. Whether he wanted to enclose also depended on his judgement of the tenants' ability to pay higher rents after enclosure, in which case he needed to be sensitive to tenants' income, and the price trends which affected that income.

Were interest rates or prices the more potent factor? Considering prices first, the first graph on Figure 4 shows a money or current wheat price index for the period 1731–1819, with a rise in prices up to the early 1790s [see 107: *112–13*]. When the peaks and troughs are smoothed this increase settled down gently at 1–2 per cent per annum. Thereafter the price rise was dramatic with wild fluctuations and also a much steeper rate of inflation which when smoothed advanced annually by up to 10 per cent and more, and in outstanding years by 100 per cent or more. The 'Agricultural Depression' of 1730–50 is evident, when though prices may not have actually fallen they did remain relatively static. The beginning of the rise in wheat prices therefore came a little after the mid-century. The coincidence of this price history with the rate of enclosure activity is clear; the permanent turning point in prices coinciding with the emergence of significant numbers of parliamentary enclosures, and the major peak of enclosure during the Napoleonic wars coinciding with a 300–500 per cent increase in money prices when compared with the 1730s. Hunt, working on Leicestershire, advanced an explanation of enclosure based on this price trend at least up to 1795. Thereafter there was little enclosure in that county though he suggested a relationship between the high wartime prices and the enclosure of common and waste in other Midland counties [66; esp. *266–7*]. Williams similarly explains the incidence of wartime enclosures in Somerset where for him the lower prices in the post-war depression account for the subsequent fall-off in enclosure activity [114: *101*]. Yelling refers to the 'greatest amount of enclosure' which 'of course coincided with the great upsurge in the price of agricultural products which occurred during the French wars', and for marginal lands 'it needed the high prices of the Napoleonic war period to encourage conversion' [118: *16, 34*]. Chambers and Mingay also champion a prices approach to explain the chronology of enclosure [46: *84*]. A matter which may have confused the reader is that the identifiable turning point in prices around 1750 precedes the main thrust of the first enclosure movement in the 1760s and 70s by 10 years or more. Contemporaries, of course, could not conceivably recognise a permanent point until

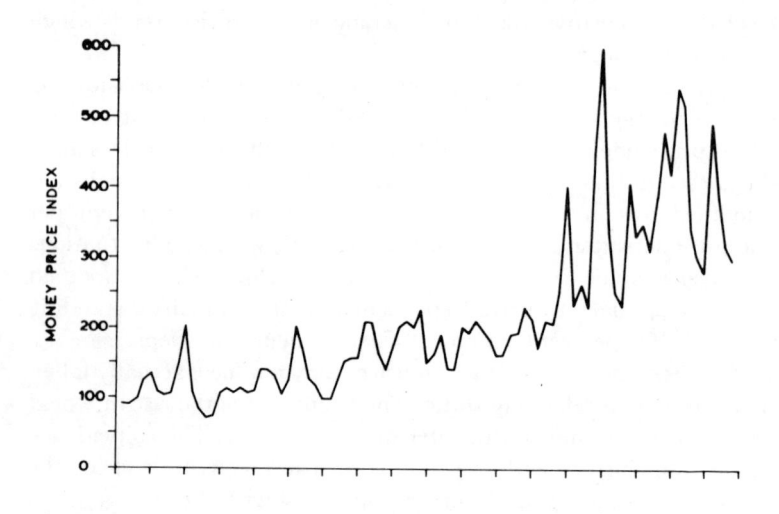

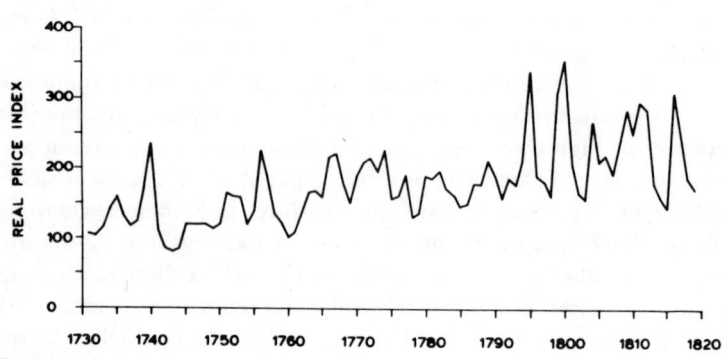

Figure 4   Trends in Wheat Prices and Interest Rates 1731–1819

Sources: Taken from M. E. Turner, *English Parliamentary Enclosure* (1980), *107, 112–13*.

The *Money Price Index* is taken from B. R. Mitchell, *Abstract of British Historical Statistics* (1962), *486–7*, who reports in shillings per bushel the price of *wheat* at Exeter, Eton and Winchester. The price series used here is the Winchester one recalculated as an index with base 100 in 1701. This date is chosen to fit in with the base dates used in other indexes itemised below.

The *Real Price Index* is the money index above deflated by the Schumpeter–Gilboy price index of consumer goods other than cereals as printed in Mitchell, *468–9*, thus

[*continued*]

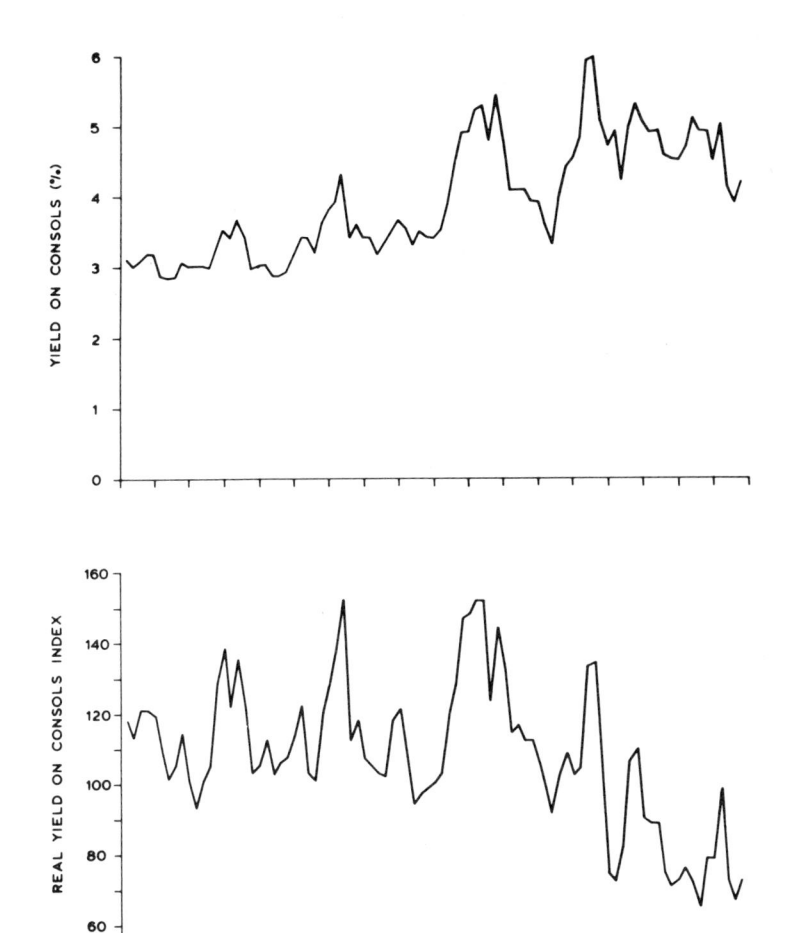

Real Prices = $\dfrac{\text{Money Price of Wheat}}{\substack{\text{Consumer Goods Price} \\ \text{Index other than Cereals}}} \times 100$.

The *Yield on Consols* is taken from S. Homer, *A History of Interest Rates* (1963), *161*, *195*.

The *Real Yield on Consols* is the ordinary yield itemised above, indexed on the same base date as the other indexes employed, and then deflated by the Schumpeter–Gilboy consumer goods index as printed in Mitchell, *468–9*, thus

Real Yield on Consols = $\dfrac{\text{Yield on Consols Index}}{\substack{\text{Consumer Goods Price} \\ \text{Index}}} \times 100$.

years after it had happened. What we see therefore is a lagged response [on the diffusion of enclosure through time see 51: *242–3*].

The attractiveness of the price theory is clear in at least one respect. The war inflation, after 1793, does appear to provide a strong reason for the additional enclosure of common and waste. Though such land was poor in quality, giving low arable yields, the rise in arable prices may have been an incentive to enclose and reclaim, and possibly to convert from grazing into arable. The higher prices, even at low yields, may have given returns in excess of what they would have been if left as common or rough pasture, and these returns may have been enough to warrant the costs involved in enclosing and reclaiming. Again a lagged response is evident with the peak of activity occurring in the decade or so after 1800. This was also the time of vigorous appeal for the improvement of wastes, particularly from parliamentarians and parliamentary select committees [for which see 112].

A criticism of the prices theory by McCloskey is that the rise in wheat prices was less impressive when compared with the rise in other prices. 'Other prices are meant here to stand as a rough proxy for the costs of enclosure' [72: *31*; 74: *151*]. In general it is true to say that the cost of enclosure increased more than the increase in general prices, including the price of wheat [107: *131–4*]. But in real terms, compared with a general price index, though the great inflation of money wheat prices is reduced it is still quite clearly an inflationary price movement [as in Figure 4, real price index].

If the prices theory helps to explain the wartime enclosures it less obviously accounts for the first wave of activity which peaked in the 1770s. One suggestion is that these enclosures came about because enclosers wished to change land use from arable into pasture, and hence to increase the stock of animals and the flow of animal products [107: *ch.6*]. This is directly related to price movements in the sense that it was a response to the agricultural depression of the first half of the eighteenth century and the stability of prices in the long run dating back to the late seventeenth century. The peak of enclosure activity occurred in the wake of this price stability rather than during it. A learning process took place producing a diffusion of enclosure activity from the pre-1750 modest beginnings (which included the adjustment of field rules explained in section ii above) to a peak of enclosing in the 1770s. While adjustments provoked by economic stimuli occur instantaneously in some places, the complete adjustment is lagged over some considerable time as the learning process breaks down local custom and conservatism [on diffusion processes see 51: *242–3*]. These early parliamentary enclosures were not necessarily to lay all arable crops down to grass, but allowed more freedom to mix crops with animals. In this respect we should look for relative increases in animal and animal product prices before 1780 rather than the modest rise in grain prices which actually occurred. Unfortunately a series of animal prices is not available, or at least not one to compare with the series of grain prices.

Ashton focused attention on money supply as a determinant of enclosure investment. The yield on consols was the indication of money demand and supply chosen (as in Figure 4). An observable relationship between the fluctuations in the yield and enclosure activity was identified. Though interest rates rose gently over the course of much of the eighteenth century they were relatively stable or declining in the 1760s and 1770s. Conversely, high interest rates during the American war of the late 1770s and early 1780s coincided with a decline in enclosure activity [31: *40–1*]. So, before 1790 enclosure could apparently be related to the ease or difficulty of borrowing money, falling or stable interest rates encouraging investment in enclosure and rising ones taking funds away from agriculture and other private investment by attracting them into government financing of the American war. At first sight the explanation seems to fall down after 1790 when interest rates reached record eighteenth-century heights and so also did enclosure activity. But as Figure 4 shows, the trend in interest rates failed to keep pace with inflation, and the real rate was generally stable or even falling from about 1750 onwards. The wartime peaks are still evident (Austrian Succession, Seven Years' War, American war), but the 'dearness' of the French war seems to evaporate into a period of 'cheap' or cheapening money [74: *137–8*; see also 51; 72; 107: *ch.5*].

We are still left with the choice between interest rates and prices. The former explanation has its champions [72; 107], as does the latter [46; 51], but neither is convincing as a full explanation of enclosure activity. At the same time we should not expect either of them to be exclusive explanations. The opportunity cost of investment in enclosure can be compared with other forms of investment, as in consols, but the income from investment in enclosure for the landlords came from rents, and these must have reflected price changes in order to maximise income without bankrupting the tenants, and the income from enclosure for the owner-occupiers was a delicate balance between costs (the cost of borrowing for example) and revenue gains which necessarily reflected price movements.

4 Investment and Cost: Part 1, The Economic Cost

(i) THE TOTAL COST

IN the last section we isolated the motivating forces which may have encouraged landlords and owner-occupiers to invest heavily in enclosures in the eighteenth and nineteenth centuries, particularly the economic factors which may have triggered off such investment and sustained it. The suggestion was that there were economic gains through higher output and revenues on the one hand and enhanced rents on the other. This is a petitioners' or landlords' view of investment which gives little consideration to the perspective of those who did not petition for enclosures and may indeed have counter-petitioned against. To the extent that counter-petitions were often couched in terms of the high costs of enclosure a fairer assessment of costs all round is essential before we proceed to discuss the social consequences of enclosure.

Recent research has suggested that the cost of enclosure was greater than scholars believed even as recently as two or three decades ago [97; 78; 104]. This reassessment has shed new light on the social consequences of enclosures [105; 80], and also found that the financing of enclosure was more problematic than was once assumed [108].

We can distinguish two types of costs involved, the public and the personal costs. The former included the costs involved in local negotiations in preparing and presenting the bill to parliament, the cost of soliciting that bill, the parliamentary fees of obtaining the act, fees and expenses paid to the commissioners, their clerks, surveyors and bankers, and the physical costs of enclosure. These last included the cost of fencing the lands allotted to the tithe owners, the cost of making the new roads, bridlepaths and other rights of way, and the costs incurred for husbandry expenses. To elaborate, the tithe owner was not expected to share any of the costs of commuting tithes from a money payment or payment in kind to a land settlement in lieu thereof. This tithe commutation could be equivalent to one-fifth or one-sixth of all open field land and one-seventh or less of the commons and wastes which were enclosed. The cost of doing this would be redistributed as a burden on all the other landowners and quite clearly could be a sizable extra cost. Not only would the tithe owner not contribute to the general expenses of the enclosure but also his subdivision fences which separated his new land from that of his neighbours would be constructed at public expense. The cost of making the roads and other physical items like drains, but predominantly the roads, was usually the result of the commissioners inviting tenders and contracting the work out. As we shall discover, the roads were very costly. The cost of husbandry evidently mainly involved the grass seed which the commissioners purchased and applied to those fields which came out of crops and were laid down to grass in the normal course of husbandry. An enclosure usually took one or more harvests' seasons to complete and the commissioners were vested with the power to administrate local husbandry, including ploughing, seeding and so forth. The fear was that if left to themselves the farmers would not be efficient in attending to their lands in the open fields because they might be allotted (as owner-occupiers) or succeed (as tenants) to land elsewhere in the parish and therefore not gain the full benefit of their own industry. The commissioners as neutral parties ensured the proper upkeep of the village lands.

The commissioners' fees ranged from one guinea per day in the mid-eighteenth century up to two or more by the nineteenth. The clerical fees (often the clerk was a representative of the same firm of solicitors who carried the bill to parliament) likewise were usually daily assessed, though the surveyors' fees were on a per acre basis. In general therefore the longer the enclosure took to administer the greater was the cost, and the larger the surviving open fields or commons in a parish the greater was the cost of surveying.

The public costs were calculated ostensibly to reflect the size *and* quality of lands which were awarded. The commissioners employed the 'quantity' surveyors to make this calculation and so generally we may be assured that it was done on a unit acre basis. 'Quality' surveyors were also employed to ensure fairness over the different qualities of land in the parish [see 106]. There is a lot of suspicion that acre for acre the smaller owners were treated less than fairly in these calculations [78: *138–9*], though some contemporary opinion and some modern scholarship emphasise the impartiality of the commissioners and their staff in the fulfilment of their duties [see particularly 37].

The commissioners began collecting fees to cover public costs before the completion of their work. The fees therefore reflected expected costs rather than actual ones. Sometimes the fees were overestimated, in which case a refund was given, and sometimes they were underestimated, resulting in second or even third supplementary demands for money. The important point was that the money or 'rate' was payable by the landowners during the course of the enclosure or by a specified time after the commissioners had completed their work. Evidence of the commissioners having difficulties in exacting the fees and threatening to call in the bailiff to distrain for unpaid fees suggests considerable hardship by some landowners in finding the large sums of money required, and more particularly in finding this money before the economic benefits from enclosure could be translated into higher incomes [see particularly 104]. Raising a rate was the most common method the commissioners used to pay for enclosures. In the nineteenth century, however, especially for the enclosure of common and waste, they increasingly allowed the sale of communal land to cover costs, or deducted land from individual owners before allotting; such land, in either case, was sold by private treaty or auction and the proceeds from the sales paid for the public costs of enclosure [in Somerset this was common even in the eighteenth century, for which see 39; see also 47; 108: esp. *240–2*]. The pure financial burden of enclosure was therefore easier to bear, but the amount of land deducted and sold could be as much as half the land available for allotment [39: *122–4*], reducing the final allotments to some owners to uneconomic units or mere gardens.

Such were the public costs and the two methods the commissioners used to collect the appropriate money. The personal costs principally involved the fencing of allotments, but would also include any additional buildings, drains and other general agricultural improvements. Each landowner had to fence, by outward or ring fences as they were known, his allotment from his neighbours. This fencing had to be completed within a time limit prescribed by the commissioners, usually three, six or less frequently nine or more months after the commissioners had finished the administration of the enclosure. As we shall see, the fencing was a very expensive item. These fences, which defined the boundaries of each person's territory, completed the minimum personal expenditure. But to gain the fullest benefit from farming in severalty the landowners would give serious consideration to subdividing their allotments with subdivision fences to create fields of manageable and economic proportions. They would also consider new drains, buildings, etc. But subdivision fences and other improvements were personal choice decisions and not obligatory under the provisions of the individual acts. It is evident that such internal improvements took many years to complete on many estates and were a continuous long-term call on the finances of those estates.

Three types of fencing have therefore been defined: the tithe owners' fencing at public cost; ring or outward fencing at personal but mandatory cost; and subdivision fencing, an optional personal cost.

Scholarship once held the view that 'the average total costs [of enclosure] for the small proprietors amounted to about £3 [per acre]' [85: *23-4*, but my brackets]. Though such costs 'might be a heavy burden' they 'were not insuperable' [ibid.], especially when set against the benefits of farming in severalty. Tate concluded similarly, if the small proprietor was driven out of business in the eighteenth century it was not due to the unreasonable expense of enclosure: 'In this, as in several other matters, it appears then that parliamentary enclosure has been saddled with a responsibility which does not properly belong to it' [97: *265*]. Two important issues were, however, substantially neglected until the mid-1960s. Up to £3 per acre reflected the public costs of enclosure (as in Table III) but it was a sum net of the costs of fencing and other costs which finally effected the post-enclosure improvement of the land. Secondly, the financing of enclosure has been a neglected issue and only recently has it been seriously researched, with some surprising results [39; 47; 152].

Martin was the first modern scholar to revise our views on the scale and burdens of enclosure costs, suggesting they had been underestimated and also stressing the heavier penalty which fell on smaller and poorer landowners. Generally speaking, unit costs increased the smaller the amount of land awarded, thus defying any notions of equity [78: *114, 138-9*; see also 28: *105*]. There is also Henry Homer's contemporary comment that fencing costs were larger per unit on progressively smaller allotments, amply confirmed by recent research. For example, for an allotment four times the size of another only twice as much ring fencing was required [13: *97-8;* 78: *140*; 74: *144-5, 149-50*].

Table III
Public Cost of Parliamentary Enclosure in England 1730–1844
(in shillings per acre)

Period[a]	Lincs[b] (Lindsey)	Oxon	Leics	Warws	Wilts	Bucks[c]
Pre-1760		18.0[e]	12.0	11.0	10.3[h]	
1760s	13.0 (16.0)	15.1	12.0	13.7	21.6[i]	16.9 (15.8)
1770s	18.7 (28.1)	21.1	16.0	19.6	25.3	21.2 (18.8)
1780s	20.3 (27.3)[d]	21.3[f]	11.0	19.7	17.4	24.1 (23.9)
1790s	20.3 (22.3)	39.1	23.0	34.1	17.0	39.2 (37.5)
1800–14				58.8[g]	52.8	81.9 (90.6)
1815–44				83.9	43.3	71.7 (71.8)

[a] The date of the act determined which period an enclosure would be counted in.
[b] The first figure is derived from Tate and the bracketed figure from Swales. The latter is total cost divided by the net acreage after deducting tithe, glebe, gravel pits and other areas financed at public cost. The former estimation is the one usually used, that is, total cost divided by gross acreage.
[c] The first figure is the average of all the individual average costs of enclosure. That is to say, the 16.9 shillings per acre in the 1760s is the mean of ten separate average costs. This seems to be the usual method of estimation. The bracketed figure is the total acreage enclosed in the decade divided by the total costs for the decade for those enclosures for which details are available. The estimates can be quite strikingly different.
[d] 3 enclosures only: [e] 1 enclosure only: [f] 3 enclosures only.
[g] 3 enclosures only: [h] 2 enclosures only: [i] 1 enclosure only. In all other cases at least 4 cost estimates were available.
Holderness in 1971 used the information from Lindsey, Oxon, Leics and Warws, which were already published, and added information from other odd enclosure accounts to give national averages for the given periods of 10.5, 12.7, 19.3, 19.2, 31.0, 42.8, and 67.3 shillings per acre respectively [64: *163*].
Sources: T. H. Swales, 'The Parliamentary Enclosures of Lindsey', *Reports and Papers of the Architectural and Archaeological Societies of Lincolnshire and Northamptonshire*, in two parts, XLII (1937), New Series 2 (1938); W. E. Tate, 'The Cost of Parliamentary Enclosure in England', *EcHR*, v (1952); H. G. Hunt, 'The Chronology of Parliamentary Enclosure in Leicestershire', *EcHR*, x (1957–8); J. M. Martin, 'The Cost of Parliamentary Enclosure in Warwickshire', in E. L. Jones (ed.), *Agriculture and Economic Growth in England 1650–1815* (1967); J. R. Ellis, *Parliamentary Enclosure in Wiltshire* (Unpublished PhD, University of Bristol, 1971); M. E. Turner, *Some Social and Economic Considerations of Parliamentary Enclosure in Buckinghamshire 1738–1865* (Unpublished PhD, University of Sheffield, 1973).

Table III brings together for comparative purposes estimates of the public costs per acre of enclosure for various counties. In Buckinghamshire they varied in individual parishes from 11 shillings per acre at Westbury in the 1760s to 139 shillings per acre at Monks

Risborough in the 1830s. For the county as a whole there was a 140 per cent increase in costs from the 1760s to the turn of the century and a further 94 per cent increase thereafter. This was more exceptional than the general inflation in other prices over the same period [107: *132–3*]. A similar pattern to a greater or lesser degree emerges for the other counties. For Warwickshire the percentage increase was greater, up to 1800 there was a threefold increase and thereafter costs doubled, giving a sixfold increase over the whole period [78: *131*].

Before the 1790s, in Leicestershire, Oxfordshire, Lindsey, Buckinghamshire and Warwickshire, the unit costs per decade were comparable, but thereafter in Buckinghamshire there was ostensibly a disproportionately large increase in enclosure costs. It has been claimed that probably this was due to the more complete manuscript material which is available for Buckinghamshire after 1790. The nature of this material suggests that unit costs before c.1790 were higher than the general source materials have shown. If this turns out to be the case elsewhere it would have the effect of reducing the general rate of increase of enclosure costs before 1790 but increasing the overall unit costs in this earlier period [full argument in 104].

There is another reason why we should be cautious about attaching too much importance to the rate of increase of enclosure costs. Perhaps these costs were small in earlier enclosures because they were simpler enclosures, with fewer owners and other claimants to satisfy, and costs like commissioners' fees which were calculated on a daily rate would have been smaller if enclosures were expeditious. These earlier enclosures were often completed within one or two harvest cycles. Perhaps the more complex, costly enclosures were delayed until market conditions were more favourable, for example during the profit inflation of the Napoleonic wars. The ideal procedure must be to compare information on enclosures with unchanging specifications so that 'the observed increase in costs is a reflection of the increase in benefits, not of an increase in costs for a given enclosure' [74: *142*]. This approach has yet to be tested.

Recent research has established that much common and waste enclosure was financed by selling-off parts of the communal land. In this case there was no direct out-of-pocket expense to the individual landowner, though the cost in the loss of otherwise communal property was great. In Kent, sales of common, all in the nineteenth century, ranged from 6 to 35 per cent of all the land allotted (with a mean of 21 per cent), and in two Middlesex enclosures such sales represented 16 and 28 per cent respectively of all the land allotted [108; *241–2*]. In 20 out of 68 West Sussex enclosures land sales were used to defray public costs. These varied from 1 to 40 per cent of the total land allotted with a mean of 15 per cent [47: *337–41*]. The mean cost of 21 Wiltshire enclosures where land sales took place was 33 shillings per acre, the 8 open field enclosures all fell below this mean whereas the 13 common and waste ones were all above [90: *passim*]. In over 30 North Somerset wasteland enclosures where land sales occurred the range of public costs was from 37 to 199 shillings per acre. These enclosures involved the sale of from 5 to 58 per cent of all the land allotted in individual cases [39: *122–4*]. In this last example, in most cases, the costs did not include a contribution for the tithe owners' fencing, grass seed and general husbandry expenses, and road construction costs, which were all important items in open field enclosures. Thus even in the absence of such weighty items of public costs nevertheless these few examples reveal the vastly more costly nature of common and waste enclosures.

The financial burden of enclosure did not end when the business was formally completed by the commissioners. There were other items of expenditure which were essential if the final improvement of the land was to be maximised, and many of these became a long-term call on the incomes of estates [108: *247*]. This expenditure was not necessarily officially required by the authority vested in the act of enclosure and collected by the commissioners as a public cost, but rather amounted to costs incurred for those fences and buildings which finally completed the improvement. It has been suggested that the final total cost of enclosure, including fencing and other improvement costs, was double the public costs [e.g. 158: *72–81*]. Even this might be an underestimate when we consider that both Martin and Turner have calculated that boundary fences alone often cost as much, when expressed in unit acre terms, as the public costs [78: *140–1, 151*; 157: *303*]. Add to this the cost of subdivision fences and new buildings and it is clear that the full cost of an enclosure was a considerably underestimated burden. Holderness suggests that by 1800 the total cost of an enclosure, including public charges, fencing, ditching and other capital improvements amounted to about £12 per acre, a far cry, even with caution, from the up to £3 otherwise accepted [64: *167*]. He further estimated that the possible capital cost of English parliamentary enclosure was about £10 million in public costs plus a further £19–25 million in capital investment after enclosure [ibid.: *166–7*, the upper bound includes an estimate for underdrainage, the lower bound does not]. These are estimates which did not have the benefit of data from recent local studies of common and waste enclosures. In view of the fact that such enclosures were more costly than their open field counterparts we might consider them as lower bounds.

Without many separate studies of agricultural and enclosure investment such national estimates appear to be meaningless, yet they may have value in comparative terms. The government made loans of £500 million to finance the French wars, so enclosure investment looks inconsiderable by comparison, but the lower bound estimate of £29 million was 50 per cent greater than the £20 million invested in canals between 1750–1815 [P. Mathias, *The First Industrial Nation* (1969), *14*]. In these terms we can wonder whether the diversion of resources into enclosure, let alone agricultural development in general, was large enough to impede the progress of British industrialisation. Probably not, but on the benefit side it may have been enough to release much needed labour for industrial use, enough to raise surplus incomes through productivity gains to service at least part of the capital requirements of industry. In addition, it was probably not enough to prolong the wars with France but enough to ensure that Britain did not starve, and was not bankrupted by otherwise excessive importation of food. Indeed, possibly the enclosure of common and waste after 1800 secured British independence.

(ii) DISTRIBUTION OF PUBLIC COSTS

How were the public costs distributed between different items? Taken together the charges for the act, fees to solicitors, commissioners and surveyors, the physical costs such as went into laying new roads and ditches, and the tithe fences are familiar to us [e.g. 97; 78; 89; 157], but there has never been sufficient disaggregation of these items of cost. In contemporary accounts the administrators of enclosure rarely emerge with much credit on the issue of their charges. Homer criticised the solicitors for unnecessarily increasing their bills and fees by attending the petitions at Westminister 'even where there has been no opposition' [13: *107*]. It has also been suggested that enclosure costs were inflated by the practice of commissioners taking on too many commissions at one time [e.g. 106]. One witness to a Select

Committee of 1800 reported that in one enclosure 'the bill of the commissioners came to four guineas, besides their expences. The Act directed only two guineas but they stated they worked double days and therefore were entitled to double fees'. He suggested a prohibition on commissioners taking on more than three enclosures at one time [14: *232*].

This last point is very important. Per enclosure, the commissioners' fees were not a large proportion of total costs, considering the responsibility attached to the job, but their delay and neglect in completing enclosures because they were involved in several at the same time was more injurious to the interested parties than the actual sum of money allowed them [ibid.: *232*]. Whether they made exceptional profits from enclosures, as is sometimes stated, is open to doubt, though quite clearly some of them had very successful careers [106].

Table IV compares the distribution of costs in Warwickshire and Buckinghamshire. In the former county the fees for expenses on travel and entertainment have been separated, whereas for the latter they have been apportioned to the particular administrators who incurred them, usually the commissioners. For 17 Wiltshire enclosures (1743–1847) the comparative distribution of costs was 36 per cent on legal fees (of which 22 per cent was incurred in parliament), 37 per cent on commissioners and surveyors and only 9 per cent for tithe fences and roads [152: *207–8*].

In early Warwickshire enclosures the largest item of cost was the legal expense. It remained high, but so too did all administrative fees. Surely the commissioners were not guilty of the absurd extravagance often attributed to them, especially since the recorded fees were divided among three, five or even seven commissioners who were appointed to each enclosure. The commissioners' profession was certainly a rewarding one but they could not or did not extort exaggerated fees. The solicitors who presented the petitions to Westminster very often became the clerks to the commissions (in Buckinghamshire at least), and the combined legal and clerical fees always came to more than 20 per cent of total costs in Buckinghamshire and more than 30 per cent in Warwickshire, and 36 per cent in Wiltshire. Enclosures provided almost continuous employment for solicitors. They were engaged at every stage: during the pre-act negotiations; petitioning the bill; acting as clerks to the commissioners; and conducting normal land conveyancing for any land

Table IV

Distribution of Enclosure Costs in Warwickshire and Buckinghamshire (in percentages)

Period	Legal fees Parliamentary fees & solicitors' fees for soliciting the bill	Administration fees commissioners clerks		Survey	Tithe Owners' fences at public cost	Physical costs (i.e. roads, drains, etc.)	Expenses
			Warwickshire				
Pre-1770	36.2	13.1	12.1	12.7	5.4	Negligible	11.4
1770–89	40.7[a]	11.1	a	12.9	18.3	Negligible	2.0
1790–1810	16.8	14.6	14.6	10.3	9.3	19.3	2.4
			Buckinghamshire				
1770–89	17.9	18.6	13.7	18.3	9.7	9.0	
1790–1809	18.2	14.9	14.5	11.3	9.2	26.2	
1810–29	13.1	12.7	8.3	13.8	8.0	33.5	
Post-1829	18.2	13.5	9.3	11.6	5.8	33.6	

[a] In this case the clerks' fees could not easily be separated from the solicitors' fees. It was not unusual for the solicitor to become the clerk. 'Other' costs have been omitted.

Sources: Adapted from J. M. Martin, 'The Cost of Parliamentary Enclosure in Warwickshire', in E. L. Jones (ed.), *Agriculture and Economic Growth in England 1650–1815* (1967), pp. 148–50; M. E. Turner, *Some Social and Economic Considerations of Parliamentary Enclosure in Buckinghamshire, 1738–1865* (Unpublished PhD, University of Sheffield, 1973), pp. 320–4.

exchange, sale, or mortgage which arose because of enclosure [157: *260–5*].

The main features of Table IV are the relatively inexpensive survey, the requirement to fence the tithe allotment at public expense, and the growing importance of the physical costs of making roads, drains and bridges, but particularly roads. Tate suggested that paying for public fencing could put as much as one-seventh on to the bill of all other landowners [97: *265*]. In Warwickshire and Buckinghamshire public fences averaged one-tenth or one-twelfth of total costs. Road costs rarely entered into normal details in accounts until after c.1790, but then they seemed to overwhelm all other charges, representing 25 per cent and more of total costs in Buckinghamshire.

There is a suspicion from recent research that for the earlier period, before 1780, road costs were not included in the cost schedules appended to the enclosure awards. Much post-enclosure expenditure evidently was for completing the road account [157: *ch.8*]. It seemed to be customary in the early enclosures to allot the land before setting out the roads, in which case it is hardly surprising that the road accounts were not included in the general cost schedules, since the roads had not yet been constructed. Even taking into account that road technology in the early period was somewhat primitive, it must be recognised that the roads and other routeways were an authorised part of enclosures, required labour and were nearly always serviced with an acre or more set aside for the collection of stones and gravel. They were substantial structures, upwards of 40 to 60 feet in width in most cases, at least one-third of which was gravelled. With all the evidence it is inconceivable that road costs were as low as the extant accounts for the earlier period suggest. As Curtler stated: 'It is evident that a considerable portion of the expense of enclosures *came after allotment* and was incurred in the making of roads, drains and fences' [18: *166*, partly my emphasis; see also 64: *164*; 11: *90*; 20: *84*]. The roads became the largest single item of expenditure during the period after 1790 when in general we recognise that the unit acre costs of enclosure were high as well. If the cost of roads has been underestimated for the period before 1790 then our entire appreciation of the burden of enclosure costs heretofore has also been underestimated.

5 Investment and Cost:
Part 2, The Social Cost

(i) SOCIAL CONSEQUENCES: THE BACKGROUND TO THE DEBATE

THE evils and excesses of parliamentary enclosure identified by the Hammonds in the early twentieth century in their denunciation of it as an agent of mass proletarianisation sustained generations of students until challenged in the mid-century by scholars who focused attention more heavily on the earlier origins of both agrarian and industrial capitalism. It was no longer accepted that parliamentary enclosure provided the labour force which was channelled to the factories and it was demonstrated that enclosure was the source of much sustained new employment in the countryside.

The tone of the debate was perfectly set by the Hammonds who said that enclosure was a process in which 'the suffrages were not counted but weighed'. It was landownership strength measured in property rather than numbers which influenced parliament, through the custom that to pass an act for enclosure it was usually necessary to gain the consent of those who owned two-thirds or more of the acres proposed for enclosure, rather than the consent of two-thirds or more of the total number of landowners [22: *25* in 4th edition]. The modern form of this is Thompson's observation that: 'Enclosure (when all the sophistications are allowed for) was a plain enough case of class robbery, played according to fair rules of property and law laid down by a parliament of property-owners and lawyers' [102: *237–8*]. To have recourse to parliament also indicated that local dissent was present. More important, the nature of parliament in responding to a property measure rather than a head count indicated that the dissent was by the many against the few, the small against the big, the defenceless against the powerful authority which elected parliament in the first place.

The examples the Hammonds used to demonstrate their case were, however, clearly biased and a simple empiric refutation by weight of alternative examples would have been easy. But such a refutation did not immediately come, and so the enclosures of Otmoor in Oxfordshire, Haut Huntre in Lincolnshire, King's Sedgemoor in Somerset, and others, passed into legend as the exemplars of enclosure with associated social evils. That they were enclosures mainly of large commons, on which, relatively speaking, vast populations depended for essential services like fuel-gathering, was almost lost in the polemics of the case. Quite clearly the landless and those with tenuously held or tenuously established common rights suffered the loss of those commons greatly. But they were not typical commons enclosures, let alone typical enclosures in general. The Hammonds concentrated on the small farmer, the cottager, and the squatter, and, not surprisingly, concluded that they above all others were severely damaged by enclosure.

Apart from an empirical study by Davies (1927), a challenge to the Hammonds did not emerge until the 1940s, when Tate largely refuted the bad press which parliamentary enclosure had received, touching upon such issues as opposition, the relationship between the enclosers and members of parliament, and dispelling any notions of collusion or conspiracy [93–6; and see also 79]. The Hammonds, however, remained the popular interpretation, reinforced as they were through the researches in the 1930s of the Soviet historian Lavrovsky [24–5; 70]. He established how important the church was in collaborating to bring about enclosures with the vast transfer of land from lay to church hands through tithe commutation. This was the annulment of church tithes, previously paid in money or in kind, by substituting a quantity of land. The net result was that the church became one of the great landowning institutions in many English villages though entirely at the expense in land and costs to the mass of proprietors [24: 71]. This land transfer has been well illustrated for Leicestershire, among other counties [67: *499–500*]. An important aspect which is often neglected, however, is that in many areas lay tithes were more important than clerical ones, and this brought about a land transfer from some lay hands to other lay hands. In Warwickshire over 17 per cent of common field and common was transferred in this way, of which about one-half went to lay impropriators, and in Buckinghamshire the tithe owners received up to 20 per cent of the land allotted at enclosure [77: *37*; 157: *78*]. Tithe commutation was calculated at about one-fifth or one-sixth of the open field land and one-eighth or ninth of the commons in the south Midlands. This level of tithe

267

commutation was almost certainly in excess of the value of the original tithe, and so we might observe that the transfer of commuted lands was effectively a redistribution of income. At the same time it was a once and for all commutation, the easing of the annual burden of tithes was much welcomed by landowners, and it left many clerics with unaccustomed landlords' responsibilities.

In eleven Suffolk parishes enclosed between 1797–1814 Lavrovsky found that there was a numerical predominance of small landowners (owning less than 25 acres), and the emergence of a small group of middle and well-to-do owners (owning up to 150 acres), and richer ones (owning over 150 acres) who were approaching capitalist sizes [25]. In another study he found that for a parish enclosed in 1803 landowners who were not defined as members of the nobility, gentry or church held nearly 40 per cent of the land but that the earlier the enclosure the weaker was their position. Thus in a parish enclosed in 1797 they held nearly 24 per cent but in a parish enclosed in 1780 they held less than 6 per cent [70]. The implication was that for early enclosed parishes the peasantry (as he referred to them) were almost extinct but in later ones they were stronger, and this may have been a reason for delayed enclosure, the recalcitrance of a strong peasant society which was persuaded by the profit inflation of the French wars to enclose. Evidence from Buckinghamshire supports this approach [157: *chs 4, 5*].

Such studies concentrated attention on the dynamic nature of the social and economic countryside, in which enclosure played a part, but not necessarily a dominant part, in landownership adjustments. It followed that the real issue was not necessarily the social upheaval at enclosure but more broadly the social upheaval caused by all elements of agrarian capitalism. Recent understanding of eighteenth-century rural society in England suggests that the fracture of landownership among a large number of small proprietors was a reason for delayed enclosure. In Kesteven resident lords and monastic foundations coincided with early enclosure (i.e. before the eighteenth century) while the stronger the freeholder tradition the later the enclosure [82]. In Warwickshire there was considerable social differentiation according to chronology of enclosure, not unrelated to the difference between 'open' and 'close' parishes [77: *22–7*]. The earliest enclosures in this county (before 1750) were promoted by the squirearchy seeking to consolidate estates, but after 1750 the inspiration came from freeholders trying to improve farming in general. After 1780 the growing food market and sharply rising land values brought about the enclosure of the great overcrowded 'open' parishes, in which, though landownership remained widely dispersed among small owners, big landlords were still a substantial force. And it was in these parishes enclosed after 1780 that the most striking post-enclosure changes took place [for Leicestershire see 67].

Small or medium-sized landowners, as well as large ones, could have held enclosure in abeyance, albeit against a resentful squirearchy, church and parliament, only to relent and give their sanction to enclose when conditions of the moment suited them. This might have occurred during the inflation of the Napoleonic wars [77: *29*; 107: *ch.7*]. Some of these 'peasants', in fact, were behaving like capitalists, and we must recognise that a strong, commercially minded small landownership structure is not incompatible with a Marxist interpretation of the eighteenth century. Yet Lavrovsky also argued that through enclosure the peasantry as a whole was weakened, for example by the expropriation of lands through tithe commutation, and in general that there was a concentration of wealth and influence towards the larger and wealthier landowners and the poorer and smaller ones were either weakened or disappeared altogether. These and other general observations of the social effects of enclosure were not to go unchallenged.

(ii) J. D. CHAMBERS AND REVISION

Leading the revisionists in the period after the Second World War was J. D. Chambers, himself a product of the East Midlands peasantry, and it was from his own neighbourhood that he gathered his evidence [43–5]. In Lindsey, Derbyshire and Nottinghamshire he largely confirmed Davies's earlier (but partly overlooked) findings that from c.1790–1830 there was an increase in the number of owner-occupiers in general. At its most basic the owner-occupier was the symbol of independence, he was the peasant. Subsequently Grigg confirmed these broad trends for south Lincolnshire for the period 1798–1832, but in Wiltshire, one of the first non-Midlands-type open field areas to be studied in depth, there was no significant change in owner-occupancy related to enclosure [61: *87–8*; 60; 152: *ch.7*].

Whether the language used was in terms of peasants, owner-occupiers or independent men, the scene was set for the next major area of debate. Chambers could, if he wished, have suggested that far from a decline in the position of the independent 'peasant', his standing in the community was strengthened. But was it a period during which the large peasants grew at the expense of the small, or was there a general resurgence of small peasant farming? Davies had found that the growth was actually greatest in the group of the smallest owners, those possessing fewer than 20 acres, and the chief decline was in a group of middle-sized owners:

> we are therefore dealing with owners of from 20–100 acres, whose farms were too large to work with family labour alone and too small to permit the accumulation of a reserve against adversity; they were big enough to be dependent on the grain market and to be vitally affected by its fluctuations. [43: *122*]

The smaller owners were better able to cope with the post-Napoleonic wars agricultural depression because their farms were supplementary rather than basic to their subsistence. However, Davies's estimates of acreage size groups were based on calculations which converted the money evidence in the land tax into an acreage equivalent. Chambers questioned this procedure, as did Grigg, Mingay and Martin subsequently [60; 84; 76; 80; see also 105 and the latest land tax debate in *Econ.Hist.Rev.*, 35 (3), Aug.1982]. The most that might be conceded to Davies is that those paying the smallest sums, less than £1 (which at 1 shilling per acre gives up to 20 acres), increased in numbers up to 1830 (though not necessarily continuously nor uniformly over time) and those paying £1–5 declined in numbers.

Chambers next turned specifically to the role of enclosure in producing landownership structural changes. In those parishes where enclosure took place at the time the land tax was available (1780–1832) he found that there were larger numbers of owner-occupiers than in parishes which were already enclosed [43: *123*]. The more ancient the enclosure the weaker was freeholder society and the stronger was the absentee squirearchy in the late eighteenth century. Conversely, those places which in the late eighteenth century were awaiting enclosure had a more broadly based resident freeholder society, a peasant society.

Chambers partly upset his own arguments when he pointed out that much of the increase in the land tax paid by the smallest contributors resulted from the recognition at enclosure of the legal rights of some cottagers and squatters who otherwise were landless. In many respects he was responding to the Edwardian criticism of enclosure as a social evil, as the creator of a labour surplus, and his 1947 study was particularly aimed at Herman Levy's contention that 'the small plots of the cottagers and little farmers, holdings of from one to eight acres or so, on which the occupiers had mostly raised livestock and dairy produce, practically vanished altogether in the course of the Napoleonic Wars' [44: *16*, quoting from H. Levy, *Large and Small Holdings: a Study in English Agricultural Economics* (1911), p. 17]. Chambers contended that the marginal unit of production (i.e. 25–100 acres) was the most vulnerable, was the likely victim of enclosure. This included tenants of comparable size who may have felt the post-enclosure rent increases more severely than both the smaller units where holdings were supplementary rather than basic to needs, and the larger units which had developed accumulated reserves of capital [43: *126*]. What was not pointed out was the economic ramifications of the Napoleonic wars and the subsequent post-war depression. Perhaps owners and tenants of these 'marginal' units had most to gain from the inflation in agricultural prices and incomes during the war, but they also had most to lose in the subsequent downturn. These 'marginal' owners may have promoted enclosures during the war years, they may have held it in abeyance before 1790, but they certainly burnt their fingers in the aftermath of war having overcommitted resources on enclosure at fixed high interest rates when the bulk of their repayments occurred in the post-war deflation.

Hunt's point is worth considering at this stage. In Leicestershire between 1790–1830 there was a decline in the number of small owners, but this decline was observable in parishes quite unconnected with recent or current enclosure as well as in those recently affected by enclosure. This suggests important consequences arising from the profit inflation of the Napoleonic wars followed by deflation in the subsequent depression [67: *503–4*]. Great sums of capital were expended by people during the profitable times of the war, not only on enclosure, and much of the time they borrowed when real interest rates were low (a point made in Chapter 3 above). They found that during the depression their repayments remained unchanged but their incomes were squeezed. A second point is that if small owners were in decline, whether persistently or simply ultimately, the larger owners, over 100–150 acres, were growing in landownership strength. They were engrossing but this was a feature not necessarily confined to parishes of parliamentary enclosure, though perhaps it was more evident in those parishes. Perhaps this was a case of selling out by small absentee owners while land was rising in value, as much as selling by residents because of the cost of enclosure [ibid.: *504–5*]. In Warwickshire though, there was a trend detectable before 1780 which continued to 1825, for the proportion of land held by owners of from 4–100 acres to decline in parishes where enclosure had taken place or was taking place, and it was strongest in those parishes enclosed after 1780 [77: *35*]. The debate had turned full circle, back to a consideration of the small owners [80].

The argument that parliamentary enclosure was a source of English industrial proletarianisation, that it had created a landless agricultural class which marched to the cotton mills, was once again open to discussion. Chambers had conceded that a certain amount of buying out of freeholds and leases for lives was a prelude to enclosure. But, even if those dispossessed owners became tenants, it may have been within a system of larger tenancies. Some of them remained landless or replaced existing tenants. The process is unclear but a rationalisation of tenancies effectively reduced the number of tenant occupiers. The suspicion is that there was a filter which produced some degree of landlessness over and above that which prevailed anyway. The discovery that there was a good deal of differentiation within and between parish landownership structures is not evidence of when or how such differentiation took place. As Hunt found for Leicestershire:

> It would be wrong to say . . . that the engrossing of land by a few large proprietors and the almost complete disappearance of the small landowner generally preceded and facilitated parliamentary enclosure by removing a class who would otherwise have opposed it,

and in Buckinghamshire it is difficult to establish a special land market as a prelude to enclosure [67: *501*; 157: *104–11*]. Much the same can be said for Warwickshire, though there are isolated examples which tend towards a theory of estate engrossment before enclosure [77: *34, 36*]. The beneficiaries of this adjustment in landownership profiles were the large landowners and also large tenant farmers. In particular the proportion of land owned by freeholders in possession of 100–199 acres increased [ibid.: *36–7*], the middle-to-richer peasants of Lavrovsky's model.

(iii) REVISIONISM, COUNTER-REVISED

However, Chambers' findings did not immediately come under detailed attack. That parliamentary enclosure had little effect on small landholders became, for a time, the new conventional wisdom, reinforced by his joint work with G. E. Mingay and restated in Mingay's pamphlet about small farmers [46: *ch.4*; 85; see also 59; 83]. The first reaction was a mild yet clear enough counter-revisionism, pointing out the importance of viewing the history of landownership over a longer time period. As Saville put it 'Nowhere save in Britain was the peasantry virtually eliminated *before* the acceleration of economic growth that is associated with the development of industrial capitalism, and of the many special features of early industrialisation in Britain none is more striking than the presence of a rapidly growing proletariat in the countryside' [91: *250*].

Authors of all political shades have couched their arguments in terms of the 'peasantry'. It is a term which seems to have as many definitions as historians trying to unscramble its origins and demise. Saville tried to clear some of the ground by drawing a sharper distinction between the peasant as a tenant farmer and as an owner farmer. He objected to the confusing use of small farmer, small occupier, and family farmer when the revisionists were really referring to the small tenant farmer: 'what is not acceptable is that this emphasis upon the small *tenant* farmer should be used to blur a fact of change which is more significant, namely the elimination from the English rural economy of an independent peasant class' [ibid.: *253*]. The preoccupation of historians with technical changes in the history of the agricultural revolution ignores more significant long-term structural changes and the decline of an independent, owner-occupying, peasant class. When they did begin to decline or even disappear is a more important question than dating their final decline, because if this process presaged a subsequent development in society then the genesis was crucial. Though the small farm by the end of the eighteenth century and even up to the mid-nineteenth century remained an important feature in rural areas, especially in Wales and Scotland and in west and north-west England, its survival obscured the other important feature of British farming, the emergence of 'the large farm using hired labour and working wholly for the market', that is the emergence of capitalist farming and the existence of a substantial rural proletariat, a feature quite without comparison in most of Continental Europe [ibid.: *258*]. There can be some confusion, however, when such disparate regions are summarised in this way. For example, in Scotland, Saville fails to point out that the small farm was always a tenant farm. Does this mean that in the absence of owner-occupancy there was no Scottish peasantry? Of course not, but it does mean that we must be more sensitive to regional and cultural variations. Nevertheless, Saville's attempt to unscramble the peasant owner and occupier from the wider discussion of farmers, which included tenants, was necessary. In so doing he certainly misjudged the regional differences but more important, he may have underplayed this other important feature of the British rural scene, namely tenant farming [in this context see 56; 83; 85].

Working from Gregory King's base of 1688 and recognising the imperfections in King's estimates Mingay has placed the good or bad fortunes of the tenant farmer into a subsequent chronology of change. In 1688 the 180,000 freeholders exceeded the number of tenants estimated at 150,000. These figures include large as well as small tenants. Mingay suggests that two-thirds of all farmers were small, that is in ownership or occupation of 20–100 acres (mainly within Lavrovsky's middle-peasant-size group), in which case there were 220,000 of them (presumably in the same ratio of freeholders to tenants, or 100,000 tenants of this group). Late nineteenth-century evidence suggests a decline of one-third of farmers, whether owners or tenants, since King's day. Small farmers probably numbered 130–140,000, giving a decline from a conjectural 220,000 small farmers in King's day of 40 per cent. But this ignores the more important feature that small farmers were still numerous at the end of the nineteenth century and outnumbered farmers of more than 100 acres [85: *14*]. Furthermore, Mingay claims that when the tenants are separated from the owner-occupiers the decline in the former was limited, while the decline of the latter was more dramatic [ibid.: *14*]. Though the trend of the two centuries before the late nineteenth favoured large units there is no evidence to show that the decline of small farms was either rapid or general [ibid.: *15–16*]. Finally, the probable timing of the major decline was put not during the period of parliamentary enclosure but rather in the seventeenth and early eighteenth centuries [ibid.: *26–32*]; which certainly takes the focus away from parliamentary enclosure but places it firmly in the narrower period of change before the mid-eighteenth century, a period perhaps not of such gradual change as supposed but rather of dramatic pruning of the small owner-occupier and some decline of the tenants.

There is some supporting evidence from eighteenth-century Scotland where, regardless of enclosure, there was a 'general movement in every part of Lowland Scotland to lay down larger farms and nearly always larger farms meant fewer tenants; dispossession and eviction became a common experience', and such changes 'had become a common folk memory in the 1790s [131: *135*]. In this case it was the eviction of tenants that occurred rather than the elimination, by whatever means, of owners and owner-occupiers as in England. In Scotland the term peasant refers to a tenant farming on a small scale or primarily for subsistence, as we have already indicated. In Roxburghshire and Berwickshire, which with the Lothians were pioneer agrarian areas, there were considerable reductions in tenant numbers in the eighteenth century. This resulted from the removal of runrig, and although there is ample evidence of enclosure and adjustments in farm layout, it was not necessarily or indeed primarily connected with the rationalisation of the tenantry and removal of runrig [126: *121–7*]. In Aberdeenshire in the late seventeenth century the differentiation of rural society was extreme and the stratification of the peasantry, regardless of enclosure, was almost complete when compared with England [125: *14–19*]. Here, enclosures were not linked with social evils, save some early eighteenth-century activity against the fencing of land, the loss of common pasturage, and the eviction of tenants associated with an increase in the cattle trade with England after the Union [130; 144: *116*]. Enclosure aided and abetted the process of structural change but itself was not the only nor necessarily the dominant factor in the move to capitalist agriculture which, after a hesitant start, flourished after 1780 in Scotland. In particular rich 'peasants' became 'capitalist farmers' during the profit inflation of the Napoleonic wars. Even later, however, there remained in areas like Aberdeenshire very large numbers of small tenants cultivating the edge of the moor and supplying labour to the larger ones [125: *20–1*].

(iv) THE RECENT DEBATES

Further research built upon Chambers' findings and questioned them. The outcome was a revolution in thinking concerning the economic costs and social consequences of enclosure. The debates are still alive and can be readily summarised [based mainly on 77; 78; 80; 104; 105; 107; 108; 111; 155]. The cost of enclosure was far in excess of what was ever imagined. This was partly because little regard had been given in the literature to fencing costs and other costs of improvement over and above what were often relatively small size costs of administration. Costs could not be deferred over any considerable time, certainly rarely as long as a full harvest cycle. Payment of costs was made in a number of ways and though if land was sold off it eased the social consequences, this practice was relatively narrowly confined to common and waste enclosures and nineteenth-century enclosures [39; 47; 108: *240–2*]. Where it did apply to the enclosure of open fields it reduced the size of individual allotments, which in some cases, with other reductions for tithe commutation and the appeasement of manorial rights, were reduced to uneconomic units. As a result many landowners, especially small ones, sold off their estates. On top of these problems and aggravations, unit costs were disproportionately larger for small estates [78; 152: *202–6*].

High costs could mean an inability to raise finances sufficient to meet them. The sale of land was sometimes necessary, sometimes inevitable, further reducing small-owner proprietorship. Improved incomes through improved productivity were insufficient in one year to cover expenses, and the raising of mortgages, though permitted, was set at a level which did not reasonably cover the full cost of an enclosure [108: *242–5*]. Mortgages therefore were often not taken up; similarly the diversion of income from one estate to pay for enclosing another was the privilege of a limited number of wealthier interested parties [ibid.: *245–7*].

It can be suggested (from evidence from the clayland counties of the Midlands) that these last points resulted in the hasty sale of many estates either upon or shortly after enclosure. This 'turnover' of land and landowners was particularly evident with small landowners and small estates [105; 80; 155: *208–33, 412–31*]. Chambers had discovered that far from small landowners disappearing because of enclosure, their numbers actually increased during the Napoleonic wars when enclosure was at its most intense. A head count from the land tax showed an increase in the proportion of owner-occupiers during the course of the war. The owner-occupiers in question epitomised peasant ownership in the guise of (relatively) self-sufficient man. But the head count, while a valuable exercise in the argument against the disappearance of the peasantry, disguised a much more important feature of the countryside. The heads in question changed faces in large numbers and with remarkable coincidence with enclosure. The rate of turnover within two or three years of enclosure in Buckinghamshire was over 30 per cent of the original owners, with 40 and 50 per cent as the norm and 60 per cent as not unusual [105: *568*]. In Warwickshire not only was this turnover coincident with enclosure, but also there was an absolute decline in the number of heads in the rural social structure in certain landowning groups, in particular of small landowners who declined 'as a class by perhaps 25 per cent within a decade of enclosure' [80: *343*]. The same absolute decline did not generally occur in Buckinghamshire. The only way the head count grew was in the sense identified by Chambers, through the recognition at enclosure of what was one form or other of common right. A failure to appreciate this point fully surely distorted Chambers' overall appraisal of enclosure.

If the changes took place, who were the new personnel? At the moment, on insecure or limited data, we might suggest that in many cases there was an influx of people quite unconnected with the parishes in question, merchants and other townspeople wishing to gain a social foothold in the countryside, widows and spinsters investing idle funds, and a move towards absentee landlordism in general, as well as local manoeuvring on the lower rungs of the agricultural and social ladder. The composite 'turnover' of farmers (in this case meant to mean owner-occupiers as well as tenants) is yet in an early state of investigation, but Walton offers the following tentative conclusions from his Oxfordshire study. Enclosure was accompanied by an increase in the rate at which holdings of both owner-occupiers and tenant farmers changed hands; this also provided the opportunity for completely new occupiers and tenants to enter the county as well as a redistribution of existing ones. However, the social consequences of this residential mobility did not necessarily result in the dispossession of small owner-occupiers or the extinction of small tenancies [111: esp. *251*]. Perhaps this identifies the opportunity to renegotiate leases afforded by the provisions of the acts of enclosure.

The observation of all these changes taking place must surely have aroused suspicion and hostility in places yet to be enclosed. There is growing interest in the opposition to enclosure, not only opposition to the enclosure of commons like Otmoor so popularised by the

Hammonds and others, but also opposition to open field enclosures by sitting tenants, owners, and those who possessed only common rights. While the nature of opposition is still little understood, it is evident below the surface both in the parliamentary record and in local history [95; 155; 79; esp. *107–8*; 157: *ch.6*].

Whether or not these fresh approaches give comfort to Marxist interpretations is questionable, since revised Marxist views now suggest that parliamentary enclosure was a mopping-up process, the final straw in a long-drawn-out saga of peasant appropriation by the march of capitalism (note the change of nomenclature, however, appropriation meaning buying out rather than expropriation, which means dispossession by force or conspiracy) [103: *ch.2*]. The evidence now seems to show both a history of peasant survival, to a greater or less degree, well into the nineteenth century, and peasants appropriating peasants as much as peasants being appropriated by the social and economic classes from above. Perhaps the time is ripe to review Rae's long-lost suggestion that the crisis for the peasantry (he used the term yeomanry) came in the post-Napoleonic wars crisis of depressed agricultural incomes [26; see also 36]. Perhaps the decades of enclosure can be viewed as ones in which capitalism emerged and built upon earlier movements towards commercial farming but was not confined to or synonymous with the misleading metaphor of 'bigness'. The peasant survival into the nineteenth century and the peasant turnover studies itemised earlier therefore might be regarded as commercialisation by small owner-occupiers, even of those who did not employ non-family labour, and therefore the disappearance of subsistence farming. Though commercialisation was not constrained by small size, yet it was also not a once and for all process everywhere at the same time. Thus we get the protracted survival of the peasantry which recent enclosure studies have identified.

(v) ENCLOSURE AND LABOUR SUPPLY

Was enclosure a crucial agent (not necessarily the only one) in the recruitment of an industrial labour force by which the expropriation of small owners and tenants swelled the ranks of the rural labourers, creating a surplus labour force in the countryside which, coupled with the more efficient use of labour in enclosed farms, marched to the towns seeking industrial work? Chambers addressed this important Marxist model of proletarianisation. In particular he attacked the idea that the enclosure commissioners were a capitalist pressgang. Maurice Dobb had suggested that any alternative implied that the emergence of a reserve army of labour arose from a growing population creating more hands than could be fed from the labour of the soil: 'If this were the true story, one might have reason to speak of a proletariat as a natural rather than an institutional creation and to treat accumulation of capital and the growth of a proletariat as autonomous and independent processes. But this idyllic picture fails to accord with the facts' [quoted in 45: *94*]. Chambers did not question the notion of an institutional origin of the proletariat but whether enclosure was the relevant institution. The growth of the proletariat was not separate from capital accumulation but the nature of their relationship was obscure [ibid.: *95*].

Chambers saw no general association between enclosure and population movements; he found that it was just as likely that the size of the population rose after enclosure without migrating, and that the population growth in mining, industrial and textile villages in Nottinghamshire was not significantly greater than growth in agricultural communities in the first three decades of the nineteenth century [ibid.: *101*]. His argument rested on demographic change rather than institutional change (or at least not on enclosure or the power of a landed ruling class as the institution). 'The only answer can be that at some unspecified time in the eighteenth century the movement of population had taken an upward turn in village and town alike and provided an entirely new supply of human material beside which the dislocations caused by enclosure were of a secondary importance' [ibid.: *120–2*]. So it was the unabsorbed surplus of rural population and not the main body which became the industrial workforce, and this surplus was the consequence of demographic change and not of institutional change, that is to say, not of enclosure [see also 30].

Chambers' exclusive use of Nottinghamshire as a study area has been criticised by Crafts as likely to produce a biased result. A larger study of the south and east Midlands in general found no evidence for an increase in population after enclosure, and therefore no evidence to advance Chambers' thesis of greater labour-using activity after enclosure. Moreover, there was a positive correlation between enclosure and out-migration [52: *176–7, 180–1*].

Crafts has further suggested that though the income elasticity of demand for food in the eighteenth century was high, a declining *share* of labour in agriculture was able to meet the extra food requirements of a growing population. Absolute numbers in agriculture actually rose, but proportionately slower than the growth of population in general. Output per man therefore rose substantially and the 'new farming' (not just enclosure) allowed the agricultural sector to raise this unit output per annum by the fuller employment of workers previously underemployed for much of the year. He concludes that though general labour opportunities rose, the increase in labour productivity and the declining share of the population engaged in agriculture in the face of a demographic revolution is the same as saying that in relative terms there was a release of labour [53: esp. *167*].

If enclosure did increase labour opportunities, for example for the construction and upkeep of fences, drains and roads, which was important to Chambers' argument, it opens up the intriguing prospect that enclosure, while it was efficient for agriculture, was inefficient in other ways; it absorbed and held back labour which otherwise may have become available for industry. Therefore for optimal resource allocation enclosure may have retained labour in agriculture which would have been better employed in industry [33: *408*]. We need to address the question of labour use and whether the general spirit of the agricultural revolution was labour-intensive or not.

In Lowland Scotland the tendency was towards the employment of fewer hands, and enclosure was not necessarily responsible for this. Even if the new husbandry improved unit labour productivity there was often a trade-off because of an extension of acreage under crops, at least until 1830 [131: *145–9*]. Even where the appearance and consolidation of larger than average farm units occurred by a process of joint tenancy, which inevitably led to the displacement of some tenants, there was not necessarily a flight from the land. In Aberdeenshire this process led to crofting on the improved fringes of the newly enclosed farms thus bringing much new land into cultivation [123: *74*]; and in some, not all, Highland areas agrarian changes created new settlements after 1750 and advanced cultivation into marginal lands. It was the post-Napoleonic wars collapse of prices which brought about displacement, eviction and clearance, and it continued up to and beyond the mid-nineteenth century [ibid.: *74*]. Besides, rural-urban or overseas migration just as easily demonstrates the pull effect from industry and the New World as it does the push effect from agriculture. In the Lothians there is evidence of this pull effect from industry, but equally, where a new labour-intensive activity like turnip cultivation was introduced it served to anchor labour to the village [142: esp. *xxviii–xxix*]. In yet other areas there was the breakdown of a dual economy, for example with the decline of handloom weaving in the mid-nineteenth century, which in turn led to the displacement of rural labour [131: *153, 156*].

Of vital importance is the issue of relative factor prices, in our case the relative movements of rent and wages. If land prices were rising relative to wages (as was the case from the limited empirical evidence) then increases in labour usage at enclosure may reflect a substitution effect of labour for land, offsetting what would have been a lower labour-land ratio caused by labour-saving techniques [33: *415*]. In other words, enclosure accommodated an increase in labour opportunities not out of labour intensity but because of movements in the relative prices of factors of production; the increased returns to land and the relatively decreased returns to labour. If this kept labour on the land it should also be seen in relation to the price of other labour uses, such as in industry. Wages in industry were higher than wages in agriculture. This could lead to an ultimate turnabout in the Marxist view of this history; enclosure anchoring the labour force on the land and industry trying to prise it off. Therefore if relative rural depopulation occurred, the institutional creation of a labour force was not enclosure nor agrarian capitalism, but industry itself. This is an important theoretical twist, and allows speculation on the role of enclosure in raising agricultural productivity so that a decreasing share of the labour force could provide a greater quantity of agricultural produce for an increasing non-agricultural labour force.

Finally, it has been argued that enclosure allocated resources more efficiently, the benefits of innovation exceeding the costs of introducing them, both the transactions costs and those costs required to differentiate property rights and create exclusive as distinct from communal ownership [for example, there may be costs involved in buying out opposition to enclosure, for which see 74: *134–8*; see also 32; 54]. The benefits can be measured as per capita productivity gains which ultimately shifted a growing proportion of the labour force to non-agricultural employment [33: *418*]. This is the same as saying that enclosure created, through efficiency gains, a surplus of labour which was eventually funnelled to industry, and not, as Chambers and the most recent traditional view said, of increasing labour opportunities. It seems to me that the way forward now is to investigate this approach more fully and to point out that the enclosure of common and waste should have produced the largest increases in unit labour productivity and therefore the largest reductions in labour. Common rights were the most intangible, non-exclusive property rights available. They were, therefore, the least productive aspect of village life and therefore offered the greatest possible benefits from enclosure, even at the high costs of achieving exclusive ownership. The enclosure of commons and wastes therefore should have produced a great shake out of unproductive commonality enjoyed by landless labourers, squatters, commoners and even small owners, who would collectively emerge as the reserve army of labour destined for the factories and towns. If this was the case, and it has yet to be tested, then the argument which maintains that enclosure induced productivity gains is strengthened, but the debate over the social distress caused by enclosure turns full circle, because it was these same socio-economic groups who were, according to the Hammonds' tradition, the gravest casualties of enclosure.

6 Conclusions

THERE were significant variations in the pattern of parliamentary enclosure across space and through time. There were equally significant variations in the land types which were enclosed. Two major peaks of activity can be identified, one before 1780 and the other during the period of the French Revolutionary and Napoleonic wars. These two peaks must be considered as separate events, separate in time of course, but also distinguishable in terms of location and the underlying economic motivation for them. Early (i.e. pre-1750) enclosures on the clay soils, especially the heavy clays of the Midlands, took place often with an eye to changing land use from traditional open arable fields into pastures, to take advantage of the comparative advantage these soils had for growing grass in preference to crops during a time of improved living standards, when dietary demand switched partially to a reduced bread and increased meat and dairy products consumption. These early enclosures issued into a major period of enclosing which peaked in the late 1760s and 1770s. The second peak of activity, after 1790 and reaching its height in the first decade of the nineteenth century, brought about the improvement of lighter soils, this time, on the whole, for maintaining and improving arable output, and also brought into cultivation much marginal land, the commons and wastes of the uplands, fenlands, heaths and moors, as well as residual wastes in lowland areas.

A number of economic factors can be identified which we may, by intuition and observation, suppose determined the timing and extent of the two enclosure movements of our period. These factors included inputs like changing prices, availability of money, changing population and other market forces; and outputs in terms of additions to incomes, such as improved rents, and efficiency gains through improved yields and larger output which raised incomes for farmers and landlords alike. The identification of these economic factors also helps to explain why the open fields and unproductive wastes persisted as long as they did. The retarding influence of the open fields on the improvement of British agriculture is subject to some debate, but then so also is the supposed and measured efficiency gain of enclosed fields over open ones. In general the open fields could be adjusted to a certain extent to meet changing economic circumstances but they were not completely adjustable. But overall there was an efficiency gain to be derived from farming in severalty. In the past we may have overestimated the aggregate additions to income, so we certainly must consider the possibility of a redistribution of income away from the small owners and farmers, whose inefficiency was measured by their lack of capital to finance agricultural improvement, to the larger landowners. This leads rather conveniently to a summary of the social consequences of parliamentary enclosure.

The social consequences are now subject to significant revisions. This is based on the economic cost of enclosures and the ability, or lack of ability, of landowners to finance them. In general the cost of enclosure was higher than previously thought. Early assessments failed to take into full account the costs of fencing and other physical costs of improvement over and above the sometimes small-scale costs of administration. A realisation that costs were larger than previously assessed has inspired a fresh approach to the possible social repercussions of enclosure. In general, and admittedly based mainly on evidence from the arable heartland of the Midland counties, it looks as though there was a considerable turnover in landowning personnel. Even if there was not a decrease in the numbers of landowners, and in particular in the numbers of the smaller owner-occupiers, the epitome of the independent peasant class, nevertheless many of these owners sold up at or shortly after enclosure. They were replaced by what appear to be people from their own agricultural and social class, though there is considerable scope for solid research on this issue. In addition, evidence showing that the number of owner-occupiers actually increased in some areas at certain times should not disguise this other consequence of enclosure, the faces and names attached to those numbers often did change dramatically. Besides, the recorded increase in owner-occupiers may be an illusion because owners of common rights only were recorded for the first time as landowners when their rights were transformed from a customary property right into a physical one. Often, these cottagers and other common right owners were the first to sell up their allotments. These newly acquired lands were often very small in size, incapable of supplementing their incomes in the way the commons and wastes had done, for example by providing pasturage for their few animals. They were also disproportionately more costly to enclose and fence than larger allotments. Small owners also had difficulty in meeting enclosure expenses and often sold up at enclosure. In addition there is evidence of a rationalisation of tenancies, though this aspect is still little understood and underresearched.

Thus, if there was an increasing turnover in the land market, and if there was a rationalisation of ownership and tenancy at the poorer end of the scale, including small owners and tenant farmers, cottagers, squatters and the landless, it brings into fresh focus the appearance of a landless labour force to fuel the fire of industrialisation, especially if enclosure improved labour productivity rather than extended labour opportunities. This is certainly the message from the most recent researches. Notwithstanding the demographic revolution which was in train and creating more hands than could be gainfully employed in an improved agricultural industry, enclosure is again under scrutiny as a possible contributor to the industrial labour force.

Bibliography

ABBREVIATIONS

AHR	*Agricultural History Review*
EcHR	*Economic History Review*, second series unless stated otherwise
EEH	*Explorations in Economic History*
JEEH	*Journal of European Economic History*
SGM	*Scottish Geographical Magazine*
TrIBG	*Transactions and Papers of the Institute of British Geographers*

(a) REVIEW AND BIBLIOGRAPHY

[1] J. Blum, 'Review Article. English Parliamentary Enclosure', *Journal of Modern History*, 103 (1981).
[2] J. G. Brewer, *Enclosures and the Open Fields: A Bibliography* (1972).
[3] R. Morgan, *Dissertations on British Agrarian History* (1981).
[4] M. E. Turner, 'Recent Progress in the Study of Parliamentary Enclosure', *The Local Historian*, 12 (Feb. 1976).

(b) SOURCES

[5] I. H. Adams, *Directory of Former Scottish Commonties* (Scottish Record Society, 2, 1971).
[6] I. Bowen, *The Great Inclosures of Common Lands in Wales* (1914).
[7] T. I. J. Jones, *Acts of Parliament Concerning Wales 1714–1901* (1959).
[8] Return, 'Return of Commons (Inclosure Awards)', *Parliamentary Papers – House of Commons*, 50 (1904).
[9] Return, 'Return of Inclosure Acts', *Parliamentary Papers – House of Commons*, 399 (1914).
[10] W. E. Tate, *A Domesday of English Enclosure Acts and Awards* (1978).

(c) CONTEMPORARY

[11] Board of Agriculture, *General Report on Enclosures* (1808).
[12] T. Davis, *General View of the Agriculture of Wiltshire* (1811).
[13] H. Homer, *An Essay on the Nature and Method of Ascertaining the Specific Shares of Proprietors upon the Inclosure of Common Fields* (1766).
[14] Reports, 'Three Reports from the Select Committee Appointed to take into Consideration the Means of Promoting the Cultivation and Improvement of the Waste, Uninclosed and Unproductive Lands in the Kingdom', *Parliamentary Papers, House of Commons Select Committee Reports*, 9 (1795–1801).
[15] T. Stone, *Suggestions for Rendering the Inclosure of Common Fields and Waste Lands a Source of Population and Riches* (1787).
[16] A. Young, *The Farmer's Tour through the East of England* (1771).
[17] ——, *General View of the Agriculture of Oxfordshire* (1813).

(d) BOOKS AND ARTICLES PRE-1940 (ENGLAND AND WALES)

[18] W. H. R. Curtler, *The Enclosure and Redistribution of our Land* (1920).
[19] E. Davies, 'The Small Landowner 1780–1832, in the Light of the Land Tax Assessments', *EcHR*, 1st Ser., 1 (1927).
[20] E. C. K. Gonner, *Common Land and Inclosure* (1912).
[21] H. L. Gray, 'Yeoman Farming in Oxfordshire from the Sixteenth Century to the Nineteenth', *Quarterly Journal of Economics*, 24 (1910).
[22] J. L. and B. Hammond, *The Village Labourer* (1911).
[23] A. H. Johnson, *The Disappearance of the Small Landowner* (1909).
[24] V. M. Lavrovsky, 'Tithe Commutation as a Factor in the Gradual Decrease of Landownership by the English Peasantry', *EcHR*, 1st Ser., 4 (1932–4).
[25] ——, 'Parliamentary Enclosures in the County of Suffolk, (1797–1814)', *EcHR*, 1st Ser., 7 (1937).
[26] J. Rae, 'Why have the Yeomanry Perished?', *Contemporary Review*, 44 (1883).
[27] G. Slater, *The English Peasantry and the Enclosure of Common Fields* (1907).
[28] T. H. Swales, 'The Parliamentary Enclosures of Lindsey', *Reports and Papers of the Architectural and Archaeological Societies of*

Lincolnshire and Northamptonshire, in two parts, old series 42 (1937), new series 2 (1938).

(e) BOOKS AND ARTICLES 1940 AND LATER (ENGLAND AND WALES)

[29] R. C. Allen, 'The Efficiency and Distributional Consequences of Eighteenth Century Enclosures', *Economic Journal*, 92 (1982).
[30] W. G. Armstrong, 'The Influence of Demographic Factors on the Position of the Agricultural Labourer in England and Wales, c.1750–1914', *AHR*, 29 (1981).
[31] T. S. Ashton, *An Economic History of England: the Eighteenth Century* (1955).
[32] B. D. Baack, 'The Development of Exclusive Property Rights to Land in England: An Exploratory Essay', *Economy and History*, 22 (1979).
[33] B. D. Baack and R. P. Thomas, 'The Enclosure Movement and the Supply of Labour during the Industrial Revolution', *JEEH*, 3 (1974).
[34] T. W. Beastall, *A North Country Estate: The Lumleys and Saundersons as Landowners 1600–1900* (1975).
[35] J. V. Beckett, 'Regional Variation and the Agricultural Depression', *EcHR*, 35 (1982).
[36] ——, 'The Decline of the Small Landowner in Eighteenth and Nineteenth-Century England: Some Regional Considerations', *AHR*, 30 (1982).
[37] M. W. Beresford, 'The Commissioners of Enclosure', *EcHR*, 1st Ser., 16 (1946).
[38] ——, 'The Decree Rolls of Chancery as a Source for Economic History, 1547–c.1700', *EcHR*, 32 (1979).
[39] B. J. Buchanan, 'The Financing of Parliamentary Waste Land Enclosure: Some Evidence from North Somerset, 1770–1830', *AHR*, 30 (1982).
[40] R. A. Butlin, 'Enclosure and Improvement in Northumberland in the Sixteenth Century', *Archaeologia Aeliana*, 45 (1967).
[41] ——, 'Field Systems of Northumberland and Durham', in A. R. H. Baker and R. A. Butlin (eds), *Studies of Field Systems in the British Isles* (1973).
[42] ——, 'The Enclosure of Open Fields and Extinction of Common Rights in England, c.1600–1750: A Review', in H. S. A. Fox and

R. A. Butlin (eds), *Change in the Countryside: Essays on Rural England, 1500–1900* (1979).
[43] J. D. Chambers, 'Enclosure and the Small Landowner', *EcHR*, 1st Ser., 10 (1940).
[44] ——, 'Enclosure and the Small Landowner in Lindsey', *The Lincolnshire Historian*, 1 (1947).
[45] ——, 'Enclosure and Labour Supply in the Industrial Revolution', *EcHR*, 5 (1953), and reprinted in E. L. Jones (ed.), *Agriculture and Economic Growth in England, 1650–1815* (1967).
[46] J. D. Chambers and G. E. Mingay, *The Agricultural Revolution, 1750–1880* (1966).
[47] J. Chapman, 'Land Purchases at Enclosure: Evidence from West Sussex', *The Local Historian*, 12 (1977).
[48] ——, 'Some Problems in the Interpretation of Enclosure Awards', *AHR*, 26 (1978).
[49] ——, 'The Parliamentary Enclosures of West Sussex', *Southern History*, 2 (1980).
[50] J. Chapman and T. M. Harris, 'The Accuracy of Enclosure Estimates: Some Evidence from Northern England', *Journal of Historical Geography*, 8 (1982).
[51] N. F. R. Crafts, 'Determinants of the Rate of Parliamentary Enclosure', *EEH*, 14 (1977).
[52] ——, 'Enclosure and Labour Supply Revisited', *EEH*, 15 (1978).
[53] ——, 'Income Elasticities of Demand and the Release of Labour by Agriculture During the British Industrial Revolution', *JEEH*, 9 (1980).
[54] C. Dahlman, *The Open Field System and Beyond: A Property Rights Analysis of an Economic Institution* (1980).
[55] H. C. Darby, 'The Age of the Improver: 1600–1800', in H. C. Darby (ed.), *A New Historical Geography of England* (1973).
[56] S. R. Eyre, 'The Upward Limit of Enclosure on the East Moor of North Derbyshire', *TrIBG*, 23 (1957).
[57] R. T. Fieldhouse, 'Agriculture in Wensleydale from 1600 to the Present Day', *Northern History*, 16 (1980).
[58] D. V. Fowkes, 'Mapleton an Eighteenth Century Private Enclosure', *Derbyshire Miscellany*, 6 (1972).
[59] D. B. Grigg, 'Small and Large Farms in England and Wales', *Geography, 48 (1963)*.
[60] ——, 'The Land Tax Returns', *AHR*, 11 (1963).
[61] ——, *The Agricultural Revolution in South Lincolnshire* (1966).

[62] M. Havinden, 'Agricultural Progress in Open Field Oxfordshire', *AHR*, 9 (1961).
[63] R. I. Hodgson, 'The Progress of Enclosure in County Durham, 1550–1870', in H. S. A. Fox and R. A. Butlin (eds), *Change in the Countryside: Essays on Rural England, 1500–1900* (1979).
[64] B. A. Holderness, 'Capital Formation in Agriculture, 1750–1850', in J. P. P. Higgins and S. Pollard (eds), *Aspects of Capital Investment in Great Britain 1750–1850* (1971).
[65] W. G. Hoskins, 'The Reclamation of the Waste in Devon, 1550–1800', *EcHR*, 1st Ser., 13 (1943).
[66] H. G. Hunt, 'The Chronology of Parliamentary Enclosure in Leicestershire', *EcHR*, 10 (1957).
[67] ——, 'Landownership and Enclosure, 1750–1830', *EcHR*, 11 (1958–9).
[68] S. A. Johnson, 'Some Aspects of Enclosure and Changing Agricultural Landscapes in Lindsey from the Sixteenth to the Nineteenth Century', *Reports and Papers of the Lincolnshire Architectural and Archaeological Society*, 9 (1962).
[69] E. Kerridge, *The Agricultural Revolution* (1967).
[70] V. M. Lavrovsky, *Parliamentary Enclosure of the Common Fields in England at the end of the eighteenth century and beginning of the nineteenth* (1940); this is an English translation of the title only. The book has never been translated but see the review by C. Hill, *EcHR*, 1st Ser., 12 (1942).
[71] ——, 'The Expropriation of the English Peasantry in the Eighteenth Century', *EcHR*, 9 (1956–7).
[72] D. N. McCloskey, 'The Enclosure of Open Fields: Preface to a study of its Impact on the Efficiency of English Agriculture in the Eighteenth Century', *Journal of Economic History*, 32 (1972).
[73] ——, 'The Persistence of English Common Fields', in W. N. Parker and E. L. Jones (eds), *European Peasants and their Markets: Essays in Agrarian History* (1975).
[74] ——, 'The Economics of Enclosure: A Market Analysis', in W. N. Parker and E. L. Jones (eds), *European Peasants and their Markets: Essays in Agrarian History* (1975).
[75] ——, 'English Open Fields as Behaviour Towards Risk', *Research in Economic History*, 1 (1976).
[76] J. M. Martin, 'Landownership and the Land Tax Returns', *AHR*, 14 (1966).

[77] ——, 'The Parliamentary Enclosure Movement and Rural Society in Warwickshire', *AHR*, 15 (1967).
[78] ——, 'The Cost of Parliamentary Enclosure in Warwickshire', in E. L. Jones (ed.), *Agriculture and Economic Growth in England 1650–1815* (1967).
[79] ——, 'Members of Parliament and Enclosure: A Reconsideration', *AHR*, 27 (1979).
[80] ——, 'The Small Landowner and Parliamentary Enclosure in Warwickshire', *EcHR*, 32 (1979).
[81] John Martin, 'Enclosure and the Inquisitions of 1607: An Examination of Dr Kerridge's Article, "The Returns of the Inquisitions of Depopulation"', *AHR*, 30 (1982).
[82] D. R. Mills, 'Enclosure in Kesteven', *AHR*, 7 (1959).
[83] G. E. Mingay, 'The Size of Farms in the Eighteenth Century', *EcHR*, 14 (1962).
[84] ——, 'The Land Tax Assessments and the Small Landowner', *EcHR*, 17 (1964).
[85] ——, *Enclosure and the Small Farmer in the Age of the Industrial Revolution* (1968).
[86] ——, (ed.), *Arthur Young and His Times* (1975).
[87] J. L. Purdum, 'Profitability and Timing of Parliamentary Land Enclosures', *EEH*, 15 (1978).
[88] B. K. Roberts, 'Field Systems in the West Midlands', in A. R. H. Baker and R. A. Butlin (eds), *Studies of Field Systems in the British Isles* (1973).
[89] E. and R. Russell, *Landscape Changes in South Humberside: The Enclosures of Thirty-Seven Parishes* (1982).
[90] R. E. Sandell, *Abstracts of Wiltshire Inclosure Awards and Agreements* (Wiltshire Record Society, 25 for 1969 published 1971).
[91] J. Saville, 'Primitive Accumulation and Early Industrialisation in Britain', *The Socialist Register*, 6 (1969).
[92] L. D. Stamp and W. G. Hoskins, *The Common Lands of England and Wales* (1963).
[93] W. E. Tate, 'Members of Parliament and the Proceedings upon Enclosure Bills', *EcHR*, 1st Ser., 12 (1942).
[94] ——, 'Parliamentary Counter-Petitions During the Enclosures of the Eighteenth and Nineteenth Centuries', *English Historical Review*, 59 (1944).
[95] ——, 'Opposition to Parliamentary Enclosure in Eighteenth Century England', *Agricultural History*, 19 (1945).

[96] ——, 'Members of Parliament and Their Personal Relations to Enclosure', *Agricultural History*, 23 (1949).
[97] ——, 'The Cost of Parliamentary Enclosure in England', *EcHR*, 5 (1952).
[98] ——, *The English Village Community and the Enclosure Movement* (1967).
[99] D. Thomas, *Agriculture in Wales During the Napoleonic Wars* (1963).
[100] J. G. Thomas, 'The Distribution of the Commons in part of Arwystli at the Time of Enclosure', *Montgomeryshire Collections*, 54 (1955).
[101] ——, 'Some Enclosure Patterns in Central Wales', *Geography*, 42 (1957).
[102] E. P. Thompson, *The Making of the English Working Class* (1963).
[103] K. Tribe, *Genealogies of Capitalism* (1981).
[104] M. E. Turner, 'The Cost of Parliamentary Enclosure in Buckinghamshire', *AHR*, 21 (1973).
[105] ——, 'Parliamentary Enclosure and Landownership Change in Buckinghamshire', *EcHR*, 28 (1975).
[106] ——, 'Enclosure Commissioners and Buckinghamshire Parliamentary Enclosure', *AHR*, 25 (1977).
[107] ——, *English Parliamentary Enclosure* (1980).
[108] ——, 'Cost, Finance, and Parliamentary Enclosure', *EcHR*, 34 (1981).
[109] ——, 'Agricultural Productivity in England in the Eighteenth Century: Evidence from Crop Yields', *EcHR*, 35 (1982).
[110] ——, (ed.), *Home Office Acreage Returns* (HO67), (List and Index Society in four volumes, 189–90, 1982, and 195–6, 1983).
[111] J. Walton, 'The Residential Mobility of Farmers and its Relationship to the Parliamentary Enclosure Movement in Oxfordshire', in A. D. M. Phillips and B. J. Turton (eds), *Environment, Man and Economic Change* (1975).
[112] M. Williams, 'The Enclosure and Reclamation of Wasteland in England and Wales in the Eighteenth and Nineteenth Centuries', *TrIBG*, 51 (1970).
[113] ——, 'The Enclosure and Reclamation of the Mendip Hills', *AHR*, 19 (1971).
[114] ——, 'The Enclosure of Wasteland in Somerset', *TrIBG*, 57 (1972).
[115] E. M. Yates, 'Enclosure and the Rise of Grassland Farming in

Staffordshire', *North Staffordshire Journal of Field Studies*, 14 (1974).
[116] J. A. Yelling, 'Common Land and Enclosure in East Worcestershire, 1540–1870', *TrIBG*, 45 (1968).
[117] ——, 'Changes in Crop Production in East Worcestershire, 1540–1867', *AHR* 21 (1973).
[118] ——, *Common Field and Enclosure in England 1450–1850* (1977).

(f) SCOTLAND

[119] I. H. Adams, 'The Land Surveyor and His Influence on the Scottish Rural Landscape', *SGM*, 84 (1968).
[120] ——, 'Economic Process and the Scottish Land Surveyor', *Imago Mundi*, 27 (1975).
[121] ——, 'The Agricultural Revolution in Scotland: Contributions to The Debate', *Area*, 10 (1978).
[122] ——, 'The Agents of Agricultural Change', in M. L. Parry and T. R. Slater (eds) ([*140*] *below*).
[123] J. B. Caird, 'The Making of the Scottish Rural Landscape', *SGM*, 80 (1964).
[124] ——, 'The Reshaped Agricultural Landscape', in M. L. Parry and T. R. Slater (eds) ([*140*] *below*).
[125] I. Carter, *Farmlife in Northeast Scotland 1840–1914* (1979).
[126] R. A. Dodgshon, 'The Removal of Runrig in Roxburghshire and Berwickshire 1680–1766', *Scottish Studies*, 16 (1972).
[127] ——, 'Towards an Understanding and Definition of Runrig: the Evidence for Roxburghshire and Berwickshire', *TrIBG*, 64 (1975).
[128] ——, 'The Origins of Traditional Field Systems', in M. L. Parry and T. R. Slater (eds) ([*140*] *below*).
[129] R. A. Gailey, 'Agrarian Improvement and the Development of Enclosure in the South-West Highlands of Scotland', *Scottish Historical Review*, 42 (1963).
[130] I. F. Grant, 'The Social Effects of the Agricultural Reforms and Enclosure Movement in Aberdeenshire', *Economic History*, 1 (1926–9).
[131] M. Gray, 'Scottish Emigration: The Social Impact of Agrarian Change in the Rural Lowlands, 1775–1875', *Perspectives in American History*, 7 (1973).

[132] H. Hamilton, *An Economic History of Scotland in the Eighteenth Century* (1963).
[133] J. E. Handley, *Scottish Farming in the Eighteenth Century* (1953).
[134] ——, *The Agricultural Revolution in Scotland* (1963).
[135] J. H. G. Lebon, 'The Process of Enclosure in the Western Lowlands', *SGM*, 62 (1946).
[136] D. R. Mills, 'A Scottish Agricultural Revolution?', *Area*, 8 (1976).
[137] A. C. O'Dell, 'A View of Scotland in the Middle of the Eighteenth Century', *SGM*, 69 (1953).
[138] M. L. Parry, 'A Scottish Agricultural Revolution?', *Area*, 8 (1976).
[139] ——, 'Changes in the Extent of Improved Farmland', in M. L. Parry and T. R. Slater (eds) ([*140*] *below*).
[140] M. L. Parry and T. R. Slater (eds), *The Making of the Scottish Countryside* (1980).
[141] T. C. Smout, *A History of the Scottish People 1560–1830* (1969).
[142] ——, Introduction to Sir John Sinclair (ed.), *The Statistical Account of Scotland 1791–99*, Vol. II, *The Lothians* (1975).
[143] T. C. Smout and A. Fenton, 'Scottish Agriculture before the Improvers: An Exploration', *AHR*, 13 (1965).
[144] J. A. Symon, *Scottish Farming Past and Present* (1959).
[145] B. M. W. Third, 'Changing Landscape and Social Structure in Scottish Lowlands as Revealed by Eighteenth Century Estate Plans', *SGM*, 71 (1955).
[146] G. Whittington, 'The Problem of Runrig', *SGM*, 86 (1970).
[147] ——, 'Was there a Scottish Agricultural Revolution?', *Area*, 7 (1975).
[148] ——, 'Field Systems of Scotland', in A. R. H. Baker and R. A. Butlin (eds), *Studies of Field Systems in the British Isles* (1973).
[149] I. D. Whyte, 'The Agricultural Revolution in Scotland: Contributions to the Debate', *Area*, 10 (1978).
[150] ——, *Agriculture and Society in Seventeenth Century Scotland* (1979).
[151] ——, 'The Emergence of the New Estate Structure', in M. L. Parry and T. R. Slater (eds) ([*140*] *above*).

(g) THESES (see also [3] above, pp. 69–73)

[152] J. R. Ellis, *Parliamentary Enclosure in Wiltshire* (PhD, University of Bristol, 1971).

[153] H. G. Hunt, *The Parliamentary Enclosure Movement in Leicestershire, 1730–1842* (PhD, University of London, 1956).

[154] J. M. Martin, *Warwickshire and the Parliamentary Enclosure Movement* (PhD, University of Birmingham, 1965).

[155] J. M. Neesom, *Common Right and Enclosure in Eighteenth Century Northamptonshire* (PhD, University of Warwick, 1977).

[156] W. S. Rodgers, *The Distribution of Parliamentary Enclosures in the West Riding of Yorkshire, 1729–1850* (MComm, University of Leeds, 1953).

[157] M. E. Turner, *Some Social and Economic Considerations of Parliamentary Enclosure in Buckinghamshire, 1738–1865* (PhD, University of Sheffield, 1973).

[158] J. R. Walton, *Aspects of Agrarian Change in Oxfordshire, 1750–1880* (DPhil, University of Oxford, 1976).

Index

Aachen, 160, 161
Aberdeenshire, 234, 275, 280
Aberford, 167
absentee ownership, 270, 272, 277; *see also* landlords
accounts and accounting, 90
Acts and Bills: England and Wales, 214, 218–19, 228–9, 231, 235, 242, 245, 247, 255–6, 261–4, 266; Scotland, 232–4
Adams, I. H., 230
advertising, 98
Africa, 7, 23
agrarian communities, 155, 164, 186, 188, 192
'agriculturalisation', 180
agriculture: cereal production, 156, 157, 162, 163, 180, 186, 195; commercial, 158, 168, 171, 172, 175–6, 187, 193; pastoral, 156, 157, 162, 163, 180, 186–7, 195; regional specialisation, 155–6, 167, 175–6, 179, 180
Aldcroft, D. H., 87, 102, 103, 104, 122
Alexander, David, 121
Alford, B. W. E., 119
Allen, R. C., 111, 113, 123, 245–6
Almquist, E. L., 187
amateurism of British enterprise, 102, 108
America, 161, 167
animal husbandry, 229, 240–1, 252–3, 284–5
Anson, Sir Wilfrid, 77
Anstey, Rev. M., 83
anvils, 158

apprenticeships, 39, 120
arable, 220–2, 225, 226, 228, 238, 240, 241, 245, 248, 252–3, 283
Arden Forest, Warwickshire, 228
Argyllshire, 233
aristocracy, 25
Arkwright, (Sir) Richard, 7, 9–11, 12–14, 23, 37, 39–40, 49–50, 57, 60, 73, 90
Arkwright-type mills, 19, 39, 50, 56
Armagh, city, 167
Armagh, county, 163, 195
Ashton, T. S., 79, 153, 244, 253
Ashworth Bros., 40, 51, 60, 93
Associated Portland Cement Manufacturers Ltd, 76–7
Austins, E. E. and A., 91
Avon Valley, Warwickshire, 228
Ayrshire, 230–1

Bairds of Gartsherrie, 120
bakers, 157
Barnett, Correlli, 113
Barton upon Humber, Lincolnshire, 242
banks, 26, 58
Beard, C., 153
Bedale, 167
Belfast, 167, 176, 177
Belgium, 172, 173, 175, 176–7
Benson, Rev. Dr., 174
Bentley, Thomas, 73
Benyons of Leeds, 93
Berwickshire, 233, 275
Birmingham, 161
Bishopstone, Buckinghamshire, 247–8

297

Blackwell Hall, 3–4
bleaching, 15, 48
Board of Agriculture, 225
Bolton Report (1971), 123
Bosbury, Herefordshire, 243
Boswell, Jonathan, 124
Bottesford, 186–7, 195
Boulton, M., 175
Boulton and Watt, 73, 89, 90–1
Bowen, I., 228
Boyce, Gordon, 123
Bramah, Joseph, 91
branding, 98, 121
brass industry, 74
Braun, R., 155, 190
brewing industry, 76, 91, 196
Briggs, Asa, 114
Brittany, 92
Brown, John, of Sheffield, 96
Brown, William, 89
Bubble Act (1720), 72, 74
Buckinghamshire, 240, 243, 247–8, 259–60, 263–4, 267–8, 272, 277
Buddenbrook syndrome, 82–3, 120
building crafts, 157, 196
Burn, Duncan, 103
Burnham, T. H. and Hoskins, G. O., 67, 113
business archives, 68, 80, 87–8, 91, 104, 107, 120–1, 123
butchers, 157
Butt, John, 82
Byatt, I. C. R., 122
Byres, T. J., 120

Caird, J. B., 230
Calico Printers' Association, 71, 77
calico printing, 4, 9, 20, 26, 48, 52–3, 58, 60
Cambridgeshire, 213, 219, 226
Cannadine, David, 88
capital, 4, 18–26, 57–8, 70, 73, 74, 124, 238, 243–4, 247, 253–4, 258, 261–2, 271, 284; accumulation, 172; agrarian, 167, 188, 216, 266, 268, 273, 275, 278, 281; fixed, 151, 157, 170–1, 173, 174; sources of, 170–1, 172, 173–4, 175, 178; working, 173, 174
capitalism, 151, 153, 154, 155, 171, 184, 192
capitalists, *see* merchant-capitalists
carpenters, *see* building crafts
Cartwright, Major John, 11, 16, 91
Casson, Mark, 119
cattle trade in Scotland, 232, 275
cement industry, 76
centralized workshops, 170, 176–7, 196; *see also* cottage workshops; factory industry
Chambers, Thomas, 88
Chapman, Stanley D., 84
Chapman, S. J. and Marquis, F. J., 85
Checkland, S. G., 117, 124
chemical industry, 15, 50, 83, 91, 106
chintz, 7
church, 214, 246, 267–9; *see also* tithes
Church, R. A., 85, 120, 121
Clapham, J. H., 76, 153, 177
Clark, C. and J., of Street, 110
clerks, 214, 255–6, 263–5
cloth, *see* cotton; linen; new draperies; silk; textile industry; woollen industry; worsteds
clothiers, 165, 166
clothing industry, 83, 151, 157, 196
coal industry, 85, 95, 105, 153, 177, 179
Coalbrookdale Co., 95
Coats, J. & P., 110
Coleman, D. C., 69, 82, 108, 114, 124, 156; and MacLeod, 124
Coleman, J. E., 96
Collins, B., 189
Cologne, 160
commercial travellers, 67, 98, 99, 109, 123
commission agents, 98, 99, 109, 121

298

commissioners, 213, 214, 247, 255–7, 260–2, 263–4
common grazing, 229
common rights, 213, 216, 244–5, 267, 277–8, 282, 284
Commons Registration Act (1965), 215
communal ownership, 213, 214, 233, 257, 259, 281–2
company directors, 71, 75, 77, 85
company law, 70, 72, 73, 74, 91
consols, yield on, 247, 251–4
consular reports, 102, 109, 110, 122
consultants, 71, 110
contraception, 189
copper industry, 74
corporate economy, 75, 78, 85
cost of enclosure, 214, 247–9, 252, 255–65, 267, 272, 275–6, 281–2, 284–5
costs: of cotton yarns, 29, 45; of power, 17
Cotswolds, 158
cottage industries, 152, 155, 157, 158, 170, 171, 174, 176, 191, 193, 194, 195, 196, 198; workshops, 151, 168, 173, 196, 197; *see also* centralized workshops; dual occupations; farmer-manufacturers; peasant-manufacturers; putting-out; rural industries
cottagers, 267, 270–1, 284–5
cotton industry, 73, 74, 76, 80, 82, 83, 84, 88, 89, 90, 91, 93–4, 95, 103, 105–6, 114, 120, 158, 160, 161, 163, 193, 196, 197–8
cotton mills: building of, 50, 57; cost of, 19; number of, 19–21, 52, 56–7; organisation of, 9, 12, 14, 39–41; size of, 16–17, 19, 52, 57
cotton mules, 173
Court of Sessions, Scotland, 234
Courtaulds, 94, 124
Cowling, K., Stoneman, P. *et al.*, 124

Crafts, N. F. R., 88, 280–1
Crawshay & Co., 90, 95
credit, 4, 20, 24–6
crises, commercial, 26, 34
Crompton, Samuel, 9, 12–13, 57, 59
Crouzet, François, 79–80, 106
Cumbria, 221
Cunningham, W., 156
Curtler, W. H. R., 216, 265
cutlery industry, 76; *see also* metal-working industries
cycle industry, 104

Dale, David (& Co.), 20, 22, 39, 73
damask, 188
Darby, H. C., 236
Darwin, John, 95
Davenport-Hines, R. P. T., 114
Davies, E., 267, 269–70
Davis, Ralph, 123
Davis, R. B., 123
Davis, T., 240
debentures, 75
d'Eichthal, G., 120
deindustrialisation, 152, 169, 176–80, 187, 197
Dent, 167
demand, 238, 279–80, 283; *see also* exports, home market
depopulation, 236, 241, 279–81
depressions, economic and agricultural, 225, 238, 240–1, 249, 252, 270–1, 278, 280
Derbyshire, 240, 269
Devon, 226
Dictionary of Business Biography, 83, 86, 114, 117
Dictionary of Scottish Business Biography, 83, 117
diffusion of enclosure, 252–3
discipline in factories, 6, 39–40
diversification, 76
Dobb, M., 154, 279
Docker, Dudley, 114
domestic system, 5, 10, 42–4, 49–50

299

Dorset, 218
Douglas, William (& Co.), 13, 20, 22
Downs, of Sussex, 226
drainage and underdrainage, 213, 223, 262
dressmakers, *see* clothing industry
dual occupations, 161, 180, 195; *see also* cottage industries; farmer-manufacturers; peasant-manufacturers; putting-out; rural industries
Dublin, 167
DuBois, A. B., 74
Dugdale, John, 94
Dunbartonshire, 233
Dundonald, Lord, 91
Durham, 225, 226, 228, 237, 240, 241
Dutch engine loom, 4, 45
dyeing, 158

East Anglia, 158, 174, 175, 176, 179, 219, 221
East India Co., 4, 7, 28
Easton, Richard, 96
economic development, 153, 154, 156, 179, 198–9
educational system, 84, 108, 113
efficiency gains, 243–4, 255, 262, 281–2, 283–4
Elbaum, Bernard, 112, 124
Elmstone Hardwicke, Gloucestershire, 215
embroidering, 183, 198
emigration, 189
enclosure: definition of, 213; new employment and labour productivity of, 266, 279–82, 285; non-parliamentary, 214, 218, 235–7; Tudor, 245
engineering industry, 76, 83, 84, 90–1, 103, 104, 106–7
England, 153, 159, 166, 168, 171, 172, 173, 174, 176, 177, 178, 179, 184, 185, 188, 194, 195, 196

English Sewing Cotton Ltd., 76
entrepreneurs: function of, 69–71, 73, 111, 112; independence of, 111, 123; motivation of, 81, 124; origins of, 79–80, 83–5; religious persuasion of, 80; reputation of, 67–9, 87–90, 116
entrepreneurship: definition of, 69–71; dynamic nature of, 70, 71, 93; methods of measuring quality of, 95, 97, 103, 104–5, 106–7, 112, 122; quality of British, 67, 68, 71, 87–115
Epping Forest, Essex, 225
Erickson, Charlotte, 80, 84, 117
Ernle, Lord, 235
Essex, 188, 225
European market, 33
Evans, G. H., 69
exports, 34–6, 52–3, 61–2

factor prices, 248–54, 281–82
factory colonies, 39–40, 50, 60–1
factory system, 9, 12–13, 16–17, 50, 152, 154, 156, 157, 161, 169, 170, 171, 172, 173, 174–5, 176, 177–8, 179, 180, 193, 194, 196; *see also* centralized workshops
Fairbairn, William, 16–17
fallows, 222, 240, 242–3, 245
family: formation of, 155, 181–2, 184–5, 189–90; labour, 165, 177, 180, 189–90; life-cycle, 182–3; size, 183, 189, 197–8; structure, 186, 189–90; *see also* household
family businesses, 71, 73, 74, 76, 80, 83, 97, 98, 100–1
'family strategies', 190
farmer-manufacturers, 152, 164, 165, 189; *see also* cottage industries; dual occupations; peasant-manufacturers; putting-out; rural industries
farmers, *see* tenants,

300

owner-occupiers
farmer-weavers, *see*
    farmer-manufacturers
Farnie, D. A., 120
fashion, 8, 32, 52–3, 62
fences and fencing costs, 255–7,
    261, 262, 263–5, 276, 280,
    284–5
Fenner, J. H. & Co., 123
fens, 213, 225, 226, 283
fertility, 182, 186, 187, 188, 189
feudalism, 154, 155, 178–9, 182
Fife, 234
financing of enclosure, 255, 257–8,
    260–1, 276, 284
Finchley Common, Middlesex, 225
Finlay, James and Kirkman, 73
firm, structure of, 70, 72–8; age
    structure of, 82–3, 92–3
Fitzwilliam estates, 243
Flanders, 158, 160, 164, 168
flax-spinners, 82, 90, 93
Flinn, M. W., 70, 80
Floud, R., 103, 106
footwear industry, 83, 104, 110; *see
    also* leather industries
Forth-Clyde region, 233
framework knitting, 5–6, 15–16,
    43, 50, 157, 164, 168, 186–7,
    188, 189, 191, 195; *see also*
    hosiery
France, 158, 176, 179, 185
fraudulent practices, 89
freeholders, 214, 268–70, 272, 274
fustian, 3–5

Garbett, Samuel, 91
Gardom, Pares & Co., 25
Gatrell, V. A. C., 73, 120
Germany, 158, 160
Ghent, 168
Girouard, Mark, 120
Glasgow, 13, 15, 31, 37, 43
Gloucestershire, 159, 162, 179,
    215, 226, 242–3
Gonner, E. C. K., 215
Gott, Benjamin, 88, 90

Gourvish, T. R., 85
grain yields, 242, 246, 283
Gray, Herbert and Turner,
    Samuel, 113, 122
Gray, M., 231
Great Exhibition (1851), 98
Green, Edwin and Moss, Michael,
    114
Greenwood & Batley, 106, 111
Greg, Edward Hyde, 119
Greg, Samuel (& Co.), 37–9, 60
Grigg, D. B., 69–71
Guests of Dowlais, 95
guilds, 161, 162

Habakkuk, H. J., 102
Hagan, E. E., 80
Halifax, 168
Hammonds, J. L. and B., 216,
    266–7, 277–8, 282
handloom weavers, 5, 14–16,
    42–4, 48, 63
Hargreaves, James, 9, 13, 19, 56
Harley, C. K., 113
Harmsworth, Alfred, 103
Harris, Frank, 120
Harrison, A. E., 104
Hartwell, Buckinghamshire, 247
Harvey, Charles E., 112
Haut Huntre, Lincolnshire, 267
Havinden, M., 239
Hay, Donald A. and Morris,
    Derek J., 124
heaths, 213, 225, 283
Herefordshire, 243
Hessle, East Yorkshire, 247
Highlands, of Scotland, 231, 233,
    280
historical economists, 154, 156
Hobsbawm, E. J., 101, 107, 109,
    111
Hodge, P. R., 96
Hodgson, R. I., 237
Hoffman, R. J. S., 122, 123
Holderness, B. A., 261–2
Holdsworth, W. B. & Co., 93
home market, 7–9, 45, 52–3

301

Homer, Henry, 258, 262
Honeyman, Katrina, 80
hosiery industry, 74, 80, 83, 163, 177, 195; *see also* framework knitting
Hounslow-Heath, Middlesex, 225
household formation, 152; functions, 152, 181–2; size, 152, 184–5, 190, 197–8; structure, 152, 181, 184–5, 190, 197–8; *see also* family
housing, 50
Howe, A., 84
Huddersfield, 168
Hudson, Patricia, 90, 119
Hunt, H. G., 249, 271, 272
Huntley & Palmers, 111
Hyde, Francis E., 122

immiseration, 152, 184,191–2, 198
Imperial Tobacco Company, 77
imports of raw cotton, 30–1
Indian textile industry, 4, 7, 12
industrial development, 153, 155, 193, 194
Industrial Revolution, 70, 78, 81, 82, 87–91, 95, 114, 115, 151,153, 154, 155, 171
industrialisation, 152, 155, 196–7, 262, 272, 273, 280, 281–2, 285
inefficiencies of the open fields, 239–41, 283–4
infield-outfield, 231
inheritance customs, 181, 185, 186, 187
innovation, 69, 71, 95–8, 114
insurance industry, 74
interest rates, 244, 247, 249–54, 271
Ireland, 159, 167, 176, 177–8, 180, 187, 189, 195, 197
iron and steel industry, 46, 50–1, 67, 74, 80, 83, 84, 91, 94–5, 103, 105, 110, 111, 112, 120, 157, 196; *see also* metal-smelting industries

iron mongers, 167

Jefferys, J. B., 121
jenny spinning, 9, 13, 19, 56
Jeremy, David, 83
Johnson, A. H., 215
joint-stock companies, 70, 72, 74, 75, 81, 83, 97, 116
Jones, E. L., 155
Jones, Haydn, 120
Jones, T. I. J., 228

Kay, John, 45
Keir, James, 91
Kennedy, W. P., 119, 124
Kent, 260
Kerridge, E., 235–6, 239
Kesteven, division of Lincolnshire, 240, 248, 268
Kincardinshire, 233
Kindleberger, C. P., 108, 109
King, Gregory, 274
King's Sedgemoor, Somerset, 267

labour: cost of, 157,161–2, 170, 172, 173, 176–7, 181, 194, 195, 196–8; demand for, 170, 172, 183; family, 165, 177, 182, 197–8; markets, 156, 173; productivity of, 160, 177, 178; rural, 159, 160; supply of, 37–8, 262, 266, 271, 275, 278–82, 285; *see also* family labour
labour force, 94, 113–14
lace industry, 76
Lake District, 221, 225
Lancashire, 175
land tax, 216, 270, 276
Landes, David, 68, 102, 103, 104, 108
landless and landlessness, 267, 270–1, 272, 282, 285
landlords, 80–1, 94–5, 102, 241–2, 243–5, 248, 253–5, 268–9, 277, 283

Languedoc, 158
Latton, Wiltshire, 243
Lavrovsky, V. M., 267–9, 272, 274
Lazonick, William, 111, 112, 114, 119
lead mining industry, 80
leases, 245, 277
leather industry, 104, 151, 152, 157, 167, 196
Lebon, J. H. G., 230
Lee, C. H., 89, 114, 124
Lee, George, 90
Lee, Sir William, 247–8
Leeds, 168
Leicestershire, 164, 168, 186, 189, 195, 219, 236, 241, 249, 259, 269, 271, 272
Levine, A. L., 102, 109
Levine, D., 188, 189
Levy, H., 271
Lewchuk, W., 113
Liège Basin, 161
limited liability, 70, 74, 75
Lindert, P. H. and Trace, K., 106
linen industry, 37, 50, 76, 89, 158, 159, 160–1, 163–8, 176–8, 187, 189–90, 191, 195, 196
Lisburn, 167, 168
Lithgow, William Todd, 86
Lloyd, Charles, 90
Lloyd, Foster & Co., 95
Lloyd-Jones, R. and Le Roux, A. A., 120
Liverpool, 30–1
Livesay, Hargreaves & Co., 15, 26
Locke, R. R., 106, 113, 116
Lombe, Thomas and John, 6
London, 3–4, 6, 8, 30–3, 39, 163, 166, 167, 186
Londonderry, 167
looms, 158, 177, 183
Lothians, the, 233, 275, 281
Low Countries, 158, 172, 173, 175
Lowlands, of Scotland, 231, 233, 238, 275, 280
Lupton, William, 91

Lurgan, 167

MacFarlane, A., 184
machine builders, 38, 171, 175
machinery, 157–8, 172–4, 176–7, 179
Macintosh, Charles, 191
MacLeod, Christine, 114
McCloskey, D. N., 103–6; and Sandberg, L. G., 68, 121–2, 235–6, 239, 244, 247, 252
McConnel & Kennedy, 13, 22, 24, 31, 51, 61, 89, 90
McKendrick, Neil, 124
McLelland, D. C., 80
Maine, 158
management, 69, 70–2, 75, 77, 85, 91–5, 116
managerial capitalism, 77–8
Manchester, 4, 15, 30–3, 37, 59
Mann, Thomas, 82
Mapleton, Derbyshire, 240
marginal land, 219, 221, 226, 249, 281, 283
marketing strategy, 98–100, 102, 109–11, 122
markets for British cottons, 7–9, 33–6, 45, 52–3
marriage, 181–3, 184, 186–9, 190, 192, 197–8
Marshall, Alfred, 72, 92, 122
Marshall, John, of Leeds, 82, 90, 93
marshes, 229, 241
Martin, J. M., 238, 258, 261, 270
Marxist historical writings, 154, 155, 166, 171, 216, 269, 278–9, 282
Maudslay, Henry, 91
Medick, H., 181, 182, 184, 189, 191
Mendels, F., 151, 154–7, 160, 170, 171, 173, 175, 191
merchants, 6, 25–6, 30–4, 61–2, 152, 158, 164–8, 171, 183, 188, 193
mergers, 76, 110, 112, 117

303

metal-smelting, 151, 157, 196–7; see also iron smelting
metal-working industries, 151, 157, 160, 161, 165–6, 171, 191, 196
Middlesex, 221, 225, 260–1
Midlands, of England, 213, 219, 226, 231, 236, 241, 243, 249, 267, 269, 276, 279, 283, 284
Military Survey in Scotland, 233
mills, 157, 174, 175, 196
Millward, R., 166
millwrights, 38
Minchinton, W., 119
Mingay, G. E., 235, 249, 270, 273, 274
mining, 151, 153, 196
Minton, T., 91
models in history, 151, 152, 155, 193, 198–9
Mokyr, Joel, 121, 171, 172, 175, 178
money supply, 238, 253–4, 283
Montgomery Act of 1770, 233
moors, 213, 225, 229, 230, 283
Morfitt, John, 93
Morley, I. & R., 32
mortality, 184, 188, 191
mortgages, 247, 265, 276
mule spinning, 13–14, 16–17, 41–2, 56, 63
Muslims, 13

Napoleonic Wars, 219, 225, 226–8, 231, 233, 238, 245, 249, 252, 254, 260, 262, 268, 269, 270, 271, 275, 276, 278, 280, 283
Needham family, of Litton, 91
Nef, John U., 153
Netherlands, 172–4, 184
Nevitt, T. R., 114
new draperies, 3, 156
Newnes, George, 103
Newry, 166
Newton, George, 88
Nicholas, S. J., 106, 121, 122

Norfolk, 179, 213, 226
Normandy, 163, 195
Northamptonshire, 219, 228, 236, 242
Northumberland, 226, 228
Norwich, 148
Nottingham, 15, 31–2, 37
Nottinghamshire, 243, 269, 279

O'Dell, A. C., 233
Oldham 'limited', 76, 85
Oldknow, Samuel, 13, 23–4, 26, 32, 61, 90
Olsen, Mancur, 112, 124
O'Malley, E., 178
opportunity costs, 157, 163, 170, 175, 243, 246–7, 253–4
opposition to enclosure, 236, 255, 266, 267, 272, 277–8, 281
Otmoor, Oxfordshire, 267, 277–8
owner-occupiers, 254–5, 269–71, 273, 274–5, 276, 277, 284
Oxfordshire, 219, 242, 243, 259–61, 267, 277–8

paper-making, 157, 196
parishes, 164; open and close, 268–9
partnerships, 70, 72–4, 75, 80, 81, 83, 92
pasture and pastoralism, 221, 222, 225–6, 229, 230, 238, 240, 241, 245, 252–3, 283, 284–5
patents, 91, 95–7, 98
Pays de Caux, 163, 164, 185
peasant-manufacturers, 157, 161, 165, 166, 182–3, 190, 191, 192, 193, 195, 197–8, 216, 268–70, 273–4, 276–8, 284; see also cottage industries; dual occupations; farmer-manufacturers; putting-out; rural industries
Pease, Joseph Whitwell, 119
Peek, Sir H. W., 81
Peel, Robert (& Co.), 11, 13–14, 73, 90

Pennines and Pennine counties, 213, 221, 225, 226, 228
Perkin, H., 81, 84
Perthshire, 233
Phillipi, O. E., 110
Picardy, 158
plantations, 7, 28
Platt, D. C. M., 117, 121, 122, 123
Playfair, Lyon, 94
Pollard, S., 88, 90; and Robertson, R., 124
population, 152, 155, 158–9, 162, 170, 172, 181, 183, 185, 186–7, 188–9, 191, 225, 226, 238, 279–81, 283, 285
potatoes, 163, 186, 191
pottery industry, 76, 91
power looms, 13, 16, 50
preference shares, 75
prices, 17, 28–9, 31, 37, 225, 238, 246, 249–54, 260, 271, 280, 283
private companies, 75, 93, 110, 116
productivity, 12, 51, 57, 239, 241–6, 262, 276, 281–3, 285
profits, 23–4, 51–3
proletarianisation, 152, 216, 266, 272, 273–4, 279; *see also* wage-earners
property rights, 216, 239, 244–5, 281, 284
proto-factory, 9, 49
Prussia, 178
Purdhum, J. L., 243–4, 246–7
putting-out, 155, 166; *see also* cottage industries; dual-occupations; farmer-manufacturers; peasant-manufacturers

quasi-rents, 173

Radcliffe, William, 5, 14, 16, 42
Radipole, Dorset, 218
Rae, J., 278
railways, 50, 85, 92, 95–6
Ramsay, G. D., 165, 166

Rathbone Bros & Cp., 82, 121
Reader, W. J., 75, 114
reafforestation, 232
recruitment of labour, 37–9
Redford, Arthur, 121
redistribution of income, 245–6, 268, 284
Redlich, Fritz, 69
regulation of open fields, 239–41
Renfrewshire, 230–1
rent, 241–2, 243–6, 247, 249, 253–5, 271, 281–2, 283
Reynolds, Richard, 90
Rhineland, 160–1
Richardson, H. W., 107
Richmond, Lesley and Stockford, Bridget, 121
riots, 14
roads, 213, 255–6, 261–2, 263–5, 279
Roberts, Richard, 16–17, 50
Robinson & Co., 20, 23–4
Roebuck, John, 15, 90
Rose, Mary, 119
Rostow, W. W., 46, 51, 64, 154
Rouen, 164
Roxburghshire, 275
Roy's map, 233
Rubinstein, W. D., 85–6, 114
runrig, 231–3, 275
rural industries, 151, 152, 155, 156, 158, 160, 161, 163, 166, 168, 172, 181, 185, 186–8, 193–5, 197–8; *see also* cottage industries; dual occupations; farmer-manufacturers; peasant-manufacturers; putting-out

St. Monday, 171
Salford Twist Mill, 89
Salt, Sir Titus, 81
Sandberg, L. G., 103–6
Sanderson, Michael, 109
Sandlands, 225
Saul, S. B., 97, 102, 103, 124
Saville, J., 273–4

Saxony, 158
Schofield, R. S., 172, 188
Schumpeter, Joseph, 69, 111
Scotland, 167, 213, 218, 226, 230–4, 273–5, 280–1
Sedrup, Buckinghamshire, 247
Select Committee of 1800, 261–3
services, 85, 114–15, 124
severalty, 213, 234, 240, 242, 258, 284
Shadwell, Arthur, 119
Shaw, Christine, 83
Sheffield, 161
Shepshed, 168, 186–9, 190
shipbuilding industry, 76, 110, 122, 123
shipping industry, 74, 122, 123
Sigsworth, Eric M., 103, 104
Silesia, 158, 164, 166, 176, 178–9
silk industry, 4, 6–7, 20, 50, 76, 80, 94, 158, 160, 161, 179
Sinclair, Sir John, 225
Singer Manufacturing Co., 123
Skipton, 167
Slater, G., 215, 235
small owners, 256–8, 268–72, 273–4, 276–8, 282, 284–5
Smiles, Samuel, 18, 84, 92
Smith, Adam, 91, 195
Smith, Roland, 120
social mobility, 18, 19
solicitors, 256, 262–5
Solway Firth, 233
Somerset, 162, 179, 213, 225, 238, 249, 257, 261, 267
Spain, 160
specialisation, 100, 101
Spencer, George & Co., 96
spinners, spinning, 160, 165, 166, 168, 173, 177, 183, 187, 190, 195, 198
spinning jennies, 173
spinning wheels, 148
Spode, Josiah, 91
squatters, 267, 270–1, 282, 285
Staffordshire, 228
Standish, Gloucestershire, 242–3

steam power, 10–11, 16–17, 57
stinting, 213, 240
stocking frame, 5–6, 45
Stockport, 7, 16, 37
Stone, T., 248
Strutt, Edward, 81
Strutt, Jedediah (& Co.), 7, 13, 31, 39, 50, 60, 90, 174
Stuart, J., 165
Stubs, Peter, 95
Suffolk, 162, 195, 226, 268
Surrey, 221
surveyors, 214, 247, 256–7, 262–5
Sussex, 176, 219, 226, 261
Swiss industry, 13, 155, 187–8

Tann, Jennifer, 89
Tate, W. E., 216, 221–2, 258, 265, 267
Tees and Tyne valleys, 226
tenants and tenant farming, 233, 241–2, 245–6, 249, 254, 272, 273–4, 277–8, 280, 283–5
Tennant, Charles, 15, 91
tariffs, 178, 179
Terling, 188
textile industry, 151, 152, 155, 158–63, 168, 174, 177, 179, 187, 195, 197; *see also* cloth; cotton; linen; new draperies; silk; woollen industry
Thirsk, J., 155, 162, 163, 185
Thomas, J. G., 229
Thomas, W. A., 120
Thompson, E. P., 266
Thompson, James, 94
Thrale, Henry, 91
Tilly, C., 153
Tilly, L., 190
Tilly, R., 153
tinplate industry, 99, 123
tithes and tithe fencing, 214, 241, 246, 247, 255–6, 261–2, 263–4, 267–8, 276
tobacco industry, 76, 77
towns: as commercial centres, 151, 158, 167–8, 173, 175;

industry in, 157, 168, 193, 195–6
Toynbee, A., 153
trade: international, 151, 152, 155, 156, 157, 159, 168, 176, 178, 179, 182, 183–4, 193, 194, 196; local, 157, 169, 196
trade associations, 76, 110
trademarks, 99–100, 121
Trebilcock, Clive, 114, 124
Truman, Sir Benjamin, 91
Turner, M. E., 242, 261
turnover of land, 276–8, 284–5
Twente, 158
Tyson, R. E., 120

Ulster, 158–60, 163, 164, 165, 167, 168, 176–8, 189–90, 191, 195
underemployment, 157, 162, 170, 181
United States: as a supplier of cotton, 28–9, 47; as a market, 33
United Turkey Red Co., 111
Unwin, G., 156
usury, 244, 247

Vale of Aylesbury, Buckinghamshire, 241
Vickers, Thomas, 75

wage-earners, 154, 165, 166, 168, 183, 192, 198
wages, 16, 37–41, 51, 172, 173, 181, 183, 191, 192, 281–3
Wakefield, 168
Walker, Joshua & Co., 90, 94–5
Wales, 218, 219, 223, 225, 226, 228–9, 231, 273
wallpaper industry, 76
Walsall, 161
Walton, J. R., 277
wars, 253; French, 20, 24, 26, 29–30, 33–4; *see also* Napoleonic Wars

Warwickshire, 219, 228, 234, 236, 238, 241, 242, 243, 259–60, 263–5, 267, 268, 272, 277
water power, 10–11, 16, 19, 37–8
Watt, J., 175
Weald, the, 143, 176, 226
weavers, weaving, 157, 160, 165, 166, 168, 177, 178–9, 183, 187, 190, 191, 194
Wedgwood, Josiah, 73, 90, 91, 98
West of England, 174, 176, 179
West Indies, 7, 28
West Midlands, 161, 165–6, 171, 191
West Riding, 158, 159, 163, 165, 167, 179
Westmorland, 163
Westphalia, 158
wheelwrights, 175
Whitbread family, brewers, 91
Whitney's gin, 28
Whittington, G., 230
wholesalers, 99–100
Whyte, I. D., 231
Wiener, Martin, J., 112, 124
Wilkinson family, ironmasters, 90
Wilkinson, John, 93
Williams, M., 249
Wilson, Charles, 73, 103, 104, 114, 116, 124
Wilson, Richard, 119
Wilsons of Wilsontown Ironworks, 91
Wiltshire, 159, 162, 167, 179, 195, 221–2, 243, 259, 261, 263, 269
Winter, J. M., 124
woollen industry, 4, 20, 29–30, 50, 76, 82–3, 90, 100, 104, 120, 158–61, 165, 166, 173–4, 176, 177, 179, 194, 195–6; *see also* new draperies; textile industry; worsteds
worsteds, 49–50, 163, 165, 166, 179
Wrigley, E. A., 172, 188
Wupper valley, 160

Yelling, J. A., 242, 245, 246, 249
yeomanry, 278
Yorkshire, 159, 163, 167, 174, 179, 191, 221, 226, 228, 247

Young, Arthur, 163, 191, 241–2, 246

Zurich, 187–8, 190